July 1991, At the Coup 裴炯逸.

Between Past and Present

Neil Asher Silberman

BETWEEN PAST
AND
PRESENT

*Archaeology, Ideology, and Nationalism
in the Modern Middle East*

ANCHOR BOOKS
DOUBLEDAY
NEW YORK   LONDON   TORONTO   SYDNEY   AUCKLAND

AN ANCHOR BOOK

PUBLISHED BY DOUBLEDAY

a division of Bantam Doubleday Dell Publishing Group, Inc.
666 Fifth Avenue, New York, New York 10103

ANCHOR BOOKS, DOUBLEDAY, and the portrayal of an anchor
are trademarks of Doubleday, a division of Bantam Doubleday
Dell Publishing Group, Inc.

Between Past and Present was originally published
in hardcover by Henry Holt and Company, Inc. in 1989.
The Anchor Books edition is published by arrangement
with Henry Holt and Company, Inc.

Library of Congress Cataloging-in-Publication Data
Silberman, Neil Asher, 1950–
   Between past and present: archaeology, ideology, and
   nationalism in the modern Middle East / Neil Asher
   Silberman.—1st Anchor Books ed.
      p.   cm.
   Includes bibliographical references.
   1. Archaeology—Political aspects—Middle East.
   2. Archaeology—Middle East—History—20th century.
   3. Middle East—Politics and government.
   4. Nationalism—Middle East—History—20th century.
   I. Title.
   [CC101.M628S57   1990]   90-34991
   930.1—dc20   CIP
   ISBN 0-385-41610-5

For Ellen and Maya

Contents

Map follows page xii

Acknowledgments

◫ This book is the product of a two-and-a-half-year research fellowship in the Middle East and the eastern Mediterranean, during which I had the opportunity to visit ongoing archaeological projects in seven countries in the region and to assess their political and social impact. As an observer rather than a direct participant in the archaeological scene, I was able to view the past from many perspectives; in this book I have attempted to describe the unique background of each excavation I visited as well as its relevance to the problems and challenges shared by all archaeologists in the region. The chapters that follow are not meant to describe the discovery of a single, objective past. They are meant, rather, to explain how historical perceptions are constantly changing—and how those changing perceptions play a powerful role in the modern societies of the Middle East.

My travel and research in that region was made possible by a grant from the Institute of Current World Affairs (ICWA), in whose monthly newsletters much of this material originally appeared. My special thanks go to the trustees of the institute, and especially to Peter Bird Martin, executive director of the ICWA and founder of the South-North News Service, whose advice, encouragement, and editorial suggestions were always welcome—and benefited me greatly at a time when my archaeological observations were still rough journal entries. I'm also grateful to Louise Cunningham, the program administrator of the ICWA, for her help and support throughout my fellowship.

The development of my ideas about the role of the past in the present was deeply influenced by a number of scholars whose own archaeological work is not directly described in this book. As in the past, Professors Moshe and Trude Dothan of the University of Haifa and the Hebrew University of Jerusalem were a source of inspiration, friendship, and archaeological expertise. They provided me with a constant sounding board for my theories—with which they did not always agree—and offered me valuable assistance in all phases of my work.

I also benefited from long conversations about the implications of archaeology, politics, and society in the Middle East with Dr. Aharon Kempinski of Tel Aviv University, Dr. Magen Broshi of the Shrine of the Book at the Israel Museum, Meron Benvenisti of the West Bank Data Project, and Amos Elon. Dr. Thomas Levy of the Nelson Glueck School of Biblical Archaeology in Jerusalem and his wife, Alina; Drs. Steve and Arlene Rosen of the Israel Department of Antiquities and the Geological Survey of Israel; and Ann Killebrew of the Hebrew University offered their continual friendship and valuable archaeological perspectives. I also want to express my appreciation to Dr. Albert Glock and Ghada Ziadeh of Bir Zeit University for our often intense, always enlightening, discussions about the potential power of Palestinian archaeology.

During the academic years 1985–86 and 1986–87, my work was made easier by having the use of an office and research facilities at the Institute of Archaeology of the Hebrew University of Jerusalem. I would especially like to thank the institute's academic administrator, Ora Sinai; the institute's chief librarian, Nira Naveh; and former administrator Aviva Rosen. Among the faculty, Professors Amihai Mazar, Gideon Foerster, Ephraim Stern, Benjamin Mazar, and the late Yigael Shiloh were helpful to me in our discussions of the history and future of Near Eastern archaeology.

In my travels through the other countries of the eastern Mediterranean and the Middle East, I was helped by many people, of whom I'd like to single out a few. At Pylos in Greece, Aphrodite Hassiakou of the University of Athens provided welcome archaeological expertise and familiarity with the region; in Turkey, Paul and Mengü Rahe assisted me in getting my bearings in Istanbul and planning a trip to Troy; in Cyprus, Demetrios and Sarah Michaelides offered their generosity and friendship; and in Egypt, Kenneth Cline introduced me to the sometimes confusing urban geography of Cairo. I'd also like to thank Gamil Hefny Abdel Malik, director of the government tourist office in Luxor; Alfi Henry, director of the Elephantine Island Museum; and his assistant, Mahmud Yusuf Ali.

My trip to the Yemen Arab Republic was made possible by the trustees and friends of the American Schools of Oriental Research—particularly Joy Ungerleider-Mayerson and Professor Philip Mayerson—who invited me to join their annual tour. My special thanks also go to Merilyn Phillips Hodgson, president of the American Foundation for the Study of Man (AFSM), and to Dr. Jeffrey Blakely, Project Director, and Dr. James Sauer, then serving as President of the American Schools of Oriental Research and chief archaeologist of the survey team in Wadi al-Jubah. In Jordan, I enjoyed the hospitality of Rabih and Muna Masri, and the archaeological and practical assistance of Dr. David McCreery, director of the American Center of Oriental Research in Amman, and Robin Brown of the State University of New York at Binghamton.

The staff of the Yale University Library was, as usual, efficient in helping me track down obscure bibliographic references. And I would especially like to thank Dr. Demetrios Michaelides, Professor Franz Georg Maier, Dr. Marie-Louise von Wartburg, Dr. Amos Kloner, Professor Manfred Bietak, Dr. Horst Jaritz, Professor Bezalel Porten, Dr. Jeffrey Blakely, Professor Ofer Bar-Yosef, and Dr. Thomas Levy for reading and commenting on drafts of the chapters concerning their work. I greatly appreciated their correction of factual errors and misinterpretations. Naturally, I am alone responsible for the ideas I have expressed about their work and its modern social, ideological, and political context.

My thanks also go to Deborah Harris and Beth Elon of Domino Press in Jerusalem and to my editors at Henry Holt, Rob Cowley and Channa Taub, for their faith, patience, and skill in getting this book into print.

Finally, on a more personal note, I'd like to thank Brooks Edwards, whose timely assistance on an earlier book has never been properly acknowledged. To my sister and brother-in-law, Ellen and Ron Lemoine, and to my parents, Barbara and Saul Silberman, I can only hope that this book will be reason enough to have suffered occasional worry and repeated bouts of jet lag to visit a new member of the family born so far from home.

And to my wife, Ellen, no simple thanks are possible for her love and constant support. It was she who encouraged me to leave a quiet and comfortable existence in Connecticut and set out on a long journey. This book is dedicated to her—and to Maya, who joined us on the way.

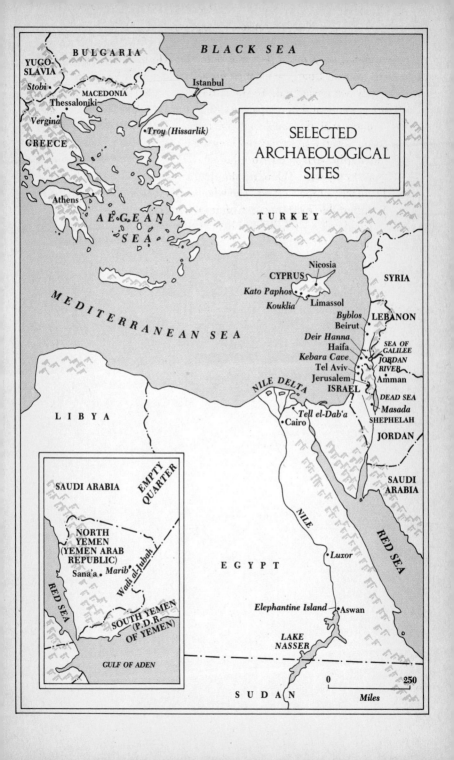

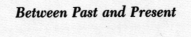

Between Past and Present

INTRODUCTION

The Power of the Past

▣ "To everyone who looks back on his past life," wrote the English antiquarian Benjamin Thorpe in 1851, "it presents itself rather through the beautifying glass of fancy, than in the faithful mirror of memory; and this is more particularly the case the further this retrospection penetrates into the past. . . .

"Among nations," Thorpe continued, "the same feeling prevails. They also draw a picture of their infancy in glittering colors. The fewer the traditions they have, the more they embellish them; the less trustworthy the traditions are, the more they sparkle in the brilliancy which fancy has lent them, the more the vain-glory of the people will continue to cherish, to ennoble and diffuse them from generation to generation, through succeeding ages. Man's ambition is two-fold: he will not only live in the minds of posterity; he will have also lived in ages long gone by. He looks not only forward but backwards also; and no people on earth is indifferent to the fancied honor of being able to trace its origins to the gods, and of being ruled by an ancient race."

By Thorpe's time, the search for the past had become a patriotic undertaking in virtually every western European nation. In his own country, the dramatic, dislocating changes brought about by the

Industrial Revolution had awakened among the English public a romantic fascination with long-dead ancestors and simpler times. Since at least the time of Henry VIII in the sixteenth century, British antiquarians had pored over the medieval records of their nation; collected folk traditions of ancient kings and battles; and mapped and measured the ancient barrows, hillforts, and mysterious stone circles that lay scattered across the countryside. But now, in an age of rapid modernization, the past was taking on a more focused, modern significance—as a source of political symbols and ideals. In the myths, chronicles, and surviving monuments of the ancient Britons and the later Anglo-Saxons, antiquarians and politicians found vivid illustrations of their people's unique "national character" that explained and justified Great Britain's unique position in the world.

The enigmatic ruins of Stonehenge and the huge standing stones of nearby Avebury evoked imaginative speculations on the exceptional scientific and spiritual gifts of the ancient Druids, whose achievements seemed to presage those of their distant British descendants of the nineteenth century. And the Anglo-Saxons provided even more vivid parallels to the present. In tracing ancient Saxon *witenagemot* councils, many British antiquarians—like Benjamin Thorpe himself—recognized the origins of their own parliamentary government; in the early Saxon church they saw a Christianity unsullied by later popish corruption; and in the chronicles of King Alfred and the rich tombs of Saxon kings and nobles, they saw early evidence for energetic, individual initiative and for the accumulation of personal wealth.

In Great Britain—as in France, Holland, Denmark, Switzerland, Sweden, and Germany—the national rediscovery of ancient relics and texts represented the retaking of a national birthright, a birthright in which the elements most highly prized in the present were accordingly stressed in the past. It didn't matter if the ancestors in question were the Britons or the Anglo-Saxons in the United Kingdom, the Celts in France, the Goths in Scandinavia, or the Teutons in Prussia and Germany. Pride in one's nation's ancestors was just another expression of pride in one's modern nation. "The Englishman has inherited the noblest portion of his being from the Anglo-Saxons," proudly wrote Benjamin Thorpe's longtime collaborator and fellow

Saxonist John Kemble, calling his readers' attention to the fact that despite invasion, conquest, reformation, and revolution, "we bear a marvelous resemblance to our forefathers."

There were, of course, other, more distant forefathers worth resembling, and the study of ancient texts and the search for ancient monuments was not restricted to the bogs, barrows, and rolling hills of northwestern Europe. The Bible and Greek and Roman literature—no less than the local myths and traditions—were seen as the spiritual inheritance of the people of Europe; for centuries, European pilgrims, traders, and scholars had been exploring the lands of the ancient Greeks and the lands of the Bible, paying homage to their spiritual forefathers in Athens and Jerusalem, and often bringing back relics of biblical and classical antiquity. By the middle of the nineteenth century, however, antiquarianism had ceased to be the pastime of adventurous individuals and had become a national quest. And the impressive monuments of classical and biblical civilization began to take on a far more public significance than the saints' relics of the Middle Ages or the gentlemen's "cabinets of curiosities" of the seventeenth and eighteenth centuries.

"The record of the Human Past is not all contained in printed books," noted Charles Newton of the British Museum in his essay "On the Study of Archaeology," published in 1851—the same year in which Benjamin Thorpe mused on the selective, romantic memory of nations: "Man's history has been graven on the rock of Egypt, stamped on the brick of Assyria, enshrined on the marble of the Parthenon." The fledgling science of archaeology had already begun to shed new light on some of the most ancient and momentous epochs in European prehistory, and now with the active encouragement of their governments, the archaeologists of the various European powers vied with one another to stake a national claim on the glories of classical and biblical antiquity—by shipping home the greatest quantity or finest examples of the precious Egyptian rock, Greek marble, and Assyrian brick.

The pace of the collection of classical and biblical antiquities had been building steadily for decades, eventually becoming an index of imperial prestige. By the middle of the nineteenth century, that prestige could be measured in sheer tonnage—at least in Germany,

England, and France. In addition to the ancient finds displayed in private collections in those countries, the Louvre, the British Museum, and the Berlin Museum had become truly *national* cabinets of curiosities. The Rosetta Stone, the Elgin Marbles, and the ancient Egyptian obelisk from Luxor erected by King Louis-Philippe in the Place de la Concorde in Paris were all prized national possessions through which those modern nations expressed their physical attachment to the biblical and classical past.

In an age of modern empires, the history of ancient empires was rewritten. In the year 1851, during which Charles Newton and Benjamin Thorpe wrote about the importance and danger of national retrospection, new archaeological discoveries attracted unprecedented public attention in Europe as symbols of its ancient cultural heritage. Under the steel-and-glass galleries of the great Crystal Palace Exhibition in London—amid the most modern industrial machinery and primitive curiosities from the wild lands of Asia, Africa, South America, and Polynesia—visitors gaped in amazement at the gigantic winged, human-headed cherubs that had recently been brought back from the long-buried palaces of Mesopotamia by Her Majesty's consul in Mosul, Austen Henry Layard.

Through these finds—and the finds of Layard's rival, the French consul in Mosul, Paul-Émile Botta—the ancient Assyrian Empire, known otherwise only from the indirect testimony of the Bible, had been resurrected in all its splendor, to take its place with the empires of the Romans, the Egyptians, and the Greeks. By the end of the nineteenth century, the Sumerians, the Hittites, the Mycenaeans, and the Minoans had been added to the cast of characters in a new, archaeologically-based framework of ancient history. And in the achievements of all those earlier civilizations, Europeans, not accidentally, recognized some of the qualities that they most admired in themselves.

Greece was the first of the nations of the ancient world to undergo a thorough transformation. Since the Renaissance, ancient Greek sculpture and vases had been avidly collected by aristocrats from all over Europe, and, beginning in the middle of the eighteenth century, a wave of less acquisitive travelers—attracted by the romantic, ruined landscape of the Greek mainland and the Aegean islands—began to sketch, map, and catalog the vast store of Greek antiquities. The famous cities of Athens, Sparta, Olympia, Halicarnassus, Delphi, Corinth, and Ephesus—so long depicted by European artists in purely imaginary landscapes—could at last be accurately pictured in their true topography.

The events of Greek history were gradually matched to the stages of Greek artistic development, proceeding from the naïve sculpture and vase-painting of the Geometric period at around 1000 B.C. to the last flicker of pagan Hellenistic culture at the end of the Roman period in the fourth century A.D. And the architectural legacy of the ancient Greeks was finally understood at least in its main outlines as British, Austrian, German, French, and American expeditions mounted large-scale excavations at the sites of ancient cities and temples on the Greek mainland, along the western coast of Asia Minor, and on the island of Cyprus as well.

This intense interest in Greek antiquities arose from a genuine feeling of kinship, for at the end of the eighteenth century, European linguists had postulated that the ancient Greeks and the later Europeans had both sprung from an original Indo-European linguistic stock—and presumably race—that was quite distinct from the linguistic and racial makeup of the Semitic peoples of the Middle East. In the epics of Homer, Europeans came to see an earlier reflection of their own northern ballads and legends, robust tales of adventure and horror, not moralizing allegories. The ancient Olympic Games were also seen as an embodiment of the true Aryan character, and Kaiser Wilhelm II personally underwrote the massive German excavations at Olympia in the 1870s—a successful, if highly romanticized, European resurrection of the ancient Greek spirit, followed by the even more romantic resumption of the Olympic Games in Athens in 1896. And with Heinrich Schliemann's discovery (1876–85) of the earlier Mycenaean civilization on the Greek mainland, and Arthur Evans's discovery (1900–1905) of the even earlier Minoan civilization of Crete, archaeology had been able to show that European roots in the prehistory of the ancient Mediterranean ran unexpectedly deep.

Along the Nile, at the temples and tombs of ancient Egypt, there was no direct blood connection, but European scholars nevertheless recognized their spiritual and political heritage. As in Greece, the relentless plunder of the antiquities collectors eventually gave way to more systematic study, and to a view of ancient Egypt that placed the modern nations of Europe—not the modern Egyptians—in the position of legitimate heirs. Until the 1820s, the history of ancient Egypt was known only from the vague reports of Greek and Roman authors and from the uniformly hostile references in the Old Testament. But with Jean-François Champollion's decipherment of hieroglyphics with the aid of the Rosetta Stone, the ancient Egyptians began to speak again—with the aid of trained European interpreters.

The tombs and monuments of Egypt were covered with square miles of hieroglyphic inscriptions and visual depictions of ancient Egyptian daily life, warfare, and ritual. By the end of the nineteenth century, European scholars had compiled a detailed chronology and had begun the serious study of the development of Egyptian administration and government from the time of the first political union of Upper and Lower Egypt around 3000 B.C. The basic institutions of kingship, public administration, and public engineering so highly esteemed in Europe were now seen as springing from the thick mud of the Nile. And at a time when modern freethinkers were beginning to question the theological authority of organized religion, the elaborate Egyptian philosophy of life-beyond-death entranced the general public in America and Europe and spawned the expensive gentleman's pastime of wintering in Egypt and supervising the excavation of some ancient Egyptian gentleman's tomb.

In the Holy Land and the neighboring lands of the Bible, the traditional veneration of sacred shrines and ancient sites was changed—at least superficially—with the spread of modern archaeology. The authenticity of many icon-laden shrines of biblical events and personalities was challenged by the findings of a new wave of skeptical scholars from Europe and America, who mapped and described the biblical landscape in modern archaeological terms. The adoption of excavation techniques pioneered in Greece and Egypt provided a means to uncover the Holy Land's biblical ruins, and as British, French, German, Austrian, and American archaeologists began to strip away the superimposed ruins of the sites of famous biblical cities, a new scripture of potsherds, cuneiform tablets, and architectural plans emerged.

Scholars succeeded in synchronizing the events of biblical history with the history and cultural development of ancient Egypt, Mesopotamia, and Greece. They revealed the extent and sophistication of the Canaanite culture that predated the biblical period by more than a thousand years. The discovery of prehistoric remains in the Galilee and the Jordan Valley extended the Holy Land's history even further—well back into the Stone Age. And the Bible itself now came to be seen as a reflection of ancient Near Eastern civilization in general, as just a part of the rich cultural heritage of the various ancient societies of the Middle East.

Linking all the regional discoveries was an overarching framework for ancient history that had originally been worked out in the bogs and barrows of Europe, by European archaeologists. With the general acceptance of the "three-age system" pioneered in Denmark—tracing the steady technological progress of man through ages of stone, bronze, and iron—archaeological cultures in all nations were synchronized in a universal framework in which the steady development of technology and political institutions were the principal concerns.

This past closely mirrored the dreams of the present; it was perfectly suited to an international, industrialized society. No longer divided among the versions of separate religious or cultural traditions, the past had become the technological and economic success story of the Western world. In the archaeological remains of the Middle East and the eastern Mediterranean, Europeans now saw evidence for the seemingly inevitable upward progress of Western man from hunter to herder to farmer to townsman to citizen of kingdoms and empires—all the way up to the eventual culmination of human progress in the modern nation-states of Europe of the late nineteenth and twentieth centuries.

Today, archaeological images not only are the basis for our understanding of the rise of Western civilization, they also have become the official national symbols of modern peoples. In the lands of the Middle East and the eastern Mediterranean, where the nineteenth-century European archaeologists were the most active, modern nation-states have arisen—nation-states determined to claim ancient glories for themselves. Throughout the region, national parades and celebrations, postage stamp and banknote symbols, even the rhetoric of newspaper articles and political slogans memorialize and romanticize various golden ages, finding historical validation in a nation's distant past for modern economic programs, foreign relations—and even boundaries.

Ancient ruins, once mute elements of the landscape, have been transformed into national shrines and popular tourist attractions. Departments of antiquities, university archaeology departments, and national museums have become respected institutions, crucial to the exercise of a nation's sovereignty over its own archaeological heritage. While foreign expeditions continue to arrive in the Middle East to excavate ancient tombs, temples, and cities, they now do so under the strict control and supervision of local archaeological authorities. And the local archaeologists, who are now taking an ever-greater role in the digging, have a quite different personal relationship to the antiquities they uncover. For them, the material remains of the ancient cultures of their countries represent not only great stages of development of Western civilization, but also cherished episodes of national history.

In each country of the region, the story is similar, differing only in the ethnic associations, the period of greatest interest, and the specifics of artifact types. Greece was the first of the countries of the region to experience a direct connection between archaeological discovery and national feeling; from the time of the Greek War of Independence against the Ottoman Empire in the 1820s, romantic visions of ancient Greek heroes and cultural achievements have defined and legitimated the authority of the modern political leadership. By the late twentieth century, the value of archaeology was one of the few things that virtually all Greeks could agree on—offering conservative politicians conservative ideals and offering socialists a patriotic, anti-imperialist issue in their culture minister's persistent demand that the British government return the Elgin Marbles to Greece.

Soon many more new nations began to recognize the political and ideological power of antiquity. The Republic of Turkey, in its attempts to deemphasize Muslim and Ottoman traditions, has lavished considerable pride and funding on the monuments of the Neolithic and Bronze Age peoples of Asia Minor, particularly the ancient

Hittites. And on the now-divided island of Cyprus, whose northern sector was invaded in 1974 and occupied by the Turkish army, the abundant archaeological evidence of the island's distinctively Greek culture from the Late Bronze Age onward has become the focus of considerable pride and national symbolism for the members of the Cypriot Greek community.

In Egypt, the national fascination with the pharaonic past has waxed and waned several times in the last century, in direct relation to the country's political position in the modern world. At times when the country has felt isolated and threatened, its leaders have been more likely to invoke glorious images from the Egyptian past. The first major outpouring of nationalist interest in ancient Egypt came in the 1920s, soon after the discovery of the tomb of Tutankhamun by the British archaeologist Howard Carter and his patron, the Earl of Carnarvon—and at a time when Egypt was moving toward independence from British colonial rule. And while this early interest died down during the pan-Islamic agitation of the 1930s, it was resurrected again in the 1950s in the adoption of ancient symbols by the government of Gamal Abdel Nasser, and again in the 1970s in the pharaonic romanticism of Anwar Sadat.

In the neighboring State of Israel, the influence of the past was never subject to the initiative of individual leaders; political Zionism, from its inception in the nineteenth century, drew its emotional power from a skillful evocation of images from antiquity. And in the early decades of the twentieth century, the growing Jewish community in Palestine began to take an active interest in excavation and exploration as a national rather than a religious quest. Each discovery of indentifiably Jewish or Israelite ruins was seen as a physical confirmation of the modern Jewish right to the land. And by the 1960s, participation in excavations had come to be a ritual for Israeli schoolchildren, soldiers, and foreign visitors. Nowhere else in the Middle East was the message of national rebirth conveyed so successfully—through excavated sites such as Hazor, Megiddo, and Masada, and through artifacts such as the Bar Kochba Letters and the Dead Sea Scrolls.

Throughout the entire region, an age of imperial domination had given way to an era of independent nation-states in conflict, and

Benjamin Thorpe's antiquarian musings of 1851 still seemed uncannily true. The ambition of each of the modern nations of the Middle East and the eastern Mediterranean *was* twofold. They were not content to exist only in the present but also sought to resurrect their greatness in the past. Each nation still drew a picture of its infancy in glittering colors. But, as I discovered, it was now archaeologists—not the traditional storytellers and mythmakers—who determined which colors each nation's poets, prophets, and politicians should use.

In the autumn of 1984, I began a two-and-a-half-year trip through the Middle East and the eastern Mediterranean—from Yugoslavia in the north to North Yemen in the south—to visit archaeological excavations and to speak with archaeologists all over the region about the social and political impact of their work. In the chapters that follow, I describe some of the most intriguing personalities and historical problems that I encountered—roughly following the geographical order of my travels—from the Aegean region, to Cyprus, across the eastern Mediterranean to Israel, then to Egypt and southern Arabia. In the final chapters, I return to Israel to describe some of the emerging trends in the archaeology of the region and suggest their possible impact on our understanding of the region's ancient history.

I wasn't a complete stranger to the Middle East or to the archaeological profession: In my early twenties I had lived in Jerusalem, and I had been trained as an archaeologist. In the course of my studies, I had become familiar with many of the artifacts and monuments of the region's ancient civilizations; I knew of the reputations of many of the region's most prominent scholars. And even after leaving Israel, I still read the archaeological journals to keep up on the latest scholarly developments and controversies.

But now, as I returned to the region, my concern lay more squarely in the present—in an attempt to discover how deeply modern archaeological interpretation and modern ideology were intertwined. From my own experience in Israel, I knew that the past possessed a powerful symbolic value. In writing a book on the politics of nineteenth-century Middle Eastern archaeology, I had learned how susceptible archaeological interpretations were to academic, nationalistic, and religious pressures that lay behind the scenes. I knew that the broken pottery, soil layers, crumbled buildings, and fragmentary inscriptions uncovered in archaeological excavations were often highly ambiguous evidence—pieces of a huge and complex mosaic that could be fitted together in a number of ways. And now I came back as an observer, rather than as a participant, to see how those fragments were being fitted together, to see how interpretations of the foreign and local archaeologists working in the region were influenced by—or themselves affected—contemporary politics and nationalism.

What follows, then, are some pages from a travel journal of a trip through the world of modern archaeology. Since the time of my trip, many new discoveries have been made and some scholarly opinions have shifted, but the basic social and political power of Middle Eastern archaeology remains the same. The personalities and historical questions that I describe in the following pages are glimpses of a past that is still under construction, a past that is different in every country of the eastern Mediterranean and the Middle East. Yet, as I discovered during my travels, there are similarities that transcend the specific details of ancient settlement patterns, architectural styles, and pottery types.

The modern archaeological exploration of the Middle East and the eastern Mediterranean may, like the "beautifying glass of fancy" described by Benjamin Thorpe in 1851, provide some surprising reflections of the deepest hopes and fears of the people of that region today.

1

Who Were the Macedonians?

Beyond the rich, rolling plains of southern Serbia, the mountains rose again. The main highway toward Greece led south along the gorge of the Vardar River, which slowly changed from a towering rocky canyon to a wide gravel bed deeply cut in its center by a narrow, rushing stream. The surrounding rugged landscape seemed as unfamiliar to me as the region's modern culture. Slavic names were printed in both Latin and Cyrillic characters on the storefronts and road signs. I knew that Yugoslavia possessed a rich archaeological record of Stone Age sites, sprawling Bronze Age towns, and Roman cities. Yet somehow Yugoslavia seemed difficult to fit into my mental image of the classical world. That world—where I was now headed to begin my archaeological journey—lay along the rim of the Mediterranean in Greece, Turkey, Egypt, and the Levant. And unlike the modern nations of that region, where ancient cultures were venerated as spiritual and ethical models for their modern populations, modern Yugoslavia seemed, at least officially, to discredit much of what had transpired here in antiquity.

Yugoslavia's borders, its name, its system of government, were all modern innovations. The structure and ideology of the modern state was seen as a revolutionary solution to the country's long historical nightmare of foreign domination, ethnic conflict, and rural poverty. This left the past as a concession for tourists, not a romantic national origin. In the seaside town of Split, a huge black-and-white poster portrait of Tito in the main square glowered down the main promenade toward the ruins of Diocletian's palace, disguised almost beyond recognition behind the laundry lines and wooden shutters of the apartments it now contained. And farther south, at the tourist haven of Dubrovnik—the immaculately restored medieval port of Ragusa, with its quaint scrubbed and recemented buildings and cobblestone streets—gave no sense of a venerated tradition. It seemed as if the elegant boutiques, outdoor cafés, and gift shops around the main piazza—with their framed pictures of Tito behind the cash registers—were built on a medieval plan as a clever merchandising gimmick by the local *Turisticki Ured*, or tourist board.

But now, in the southernmost region of the country, I had a clear historical objective, a place where vivid images of the classical world came easily to mind. Even if the main city of this region, Skopje, was a faceless modern sprawl of concrete apartment and office buildings, even if the "Yugoslav Socialist Republic of Macedonia" was a ponderous modern title, the name "Macedonia" embedded within evoked a coherent series of seductive images, a pole apart from the present Slavic and socialist reality. The historical images of Macedonia brought to mind the triumphant spread of Hellenism eastward, efficient and deadly phalanx formations, Hellenistic armor, gold vessels, and painted pottery. From Macedonia, Greek culture became "Western" culture at the end of the fourth century B.C. This land was, after all, the homeland of Philip of Macedon and his son, Alexander the Great.

The story was so commonplace, so familiar that it was hardly worth rereading in the guidebooks—of how in 359 B.C. an ambitious and ruthless Macedonian king named Philip, taking advantage of the decline of Athens and Sparta, began a campaign of conquest that would ultimately transform his remote northern kingdom into an international empire. Skillfully uniting the scattered peoples who lived in the mountains and plains of Macedonia, he began a process of military and cultural expansion that did not end until the death of his son Alexander in Babylon thirty-six years later—by which time the lands and peoples as far east as the Indus Valley had been brought under at least nominal Macedonian rule. At first thought, Southern Yugoslavia might not seem to be rich in classical associations, but few historians would question the role played by the ancient Macedonians, who wholeheartedly absorbed and spread Hellenic culture throughout the known world.

Yet the archaeology of Macedonia both concealed and reflected a serious political problem, in the Hellenistic period and in the twentieth century. In the fourth century B.C., the politicians and orators of Athens shuddered at the thought of Macedonian supremacy and expressed their outrage in clearly ethnic terms. At the time of Philip's rise to power, Isocrates voiced serious doubts about the "Greekness" of the Macedonians' racial background, and the great orator Demosthenes, in his "Philippics," condemned them for their barbarism, for their lack of elegance. Even with the far-flung conquests of Philip and Alexander, the Macedonians apparently were not considered true Hellenes, at least by the Hellenes farther south. For while the Macedonians wholeheartedly absorbed and spread Greek culture, their own local language and traditions were also influenced by the steady migration down the Vardar Valley of peoples, tribes, and trade goods from the cultures of central Europe.

In the sixth century A.D., when the Greco-Roman civilization was no longer as strong as it once had been, the trickle of northern migrants to Macedonia became a flood. Within the first fifty-eight years of the sixth century, Macedonia was invaded four times in quick succession—by Bulgars, Slavs, Huns, and Goths. The traditional texts describe these as violent, bloody invasions, but even if they were actually just intensified waves of migration—the mass movements of hungry families, not killers—the ethnic makeup and language of Macedonia was changed forever. The language still spoken there and written in Cyrillic characters—called "Macedonian"—is a south Slavic dialect, closely related to Bulgarian. And the Slavic invasions were not the last of the changes. After the Ottoman conquest of the country in 1364, a bitter Turkish icing was added to the already strange layer cake of Macedonian nationality.

The ancient empire of Philip and Alexander lay buried beneath all these changes, and a modern problem of boundaries inevitably arose. Toward the end of the nineteenth century, the people of Macedonia saw the possibility of independence from the Ottoman Empire; their local culture of church, language, and ancient legends eventually became the rallying point for a fervent, sometimes violent Balkan nationalism. The liberation of Macedonia from foreign domination was the goal of this movement, but Macedonia's erstwhile allies in the neighboring countries had other ideas. All of them quietly jockeyed for position to take Macedonia for themselves.

Early in this century, the issue of Macedonia was settled, at least temporarily. In 1912, the kingdoms of Serbia, Greece, and Bulgaria jointly wrested Macedonia from the dying Ottoman Empire, soon attacking one another like hungry scavengers and tearing apart their Macedonian prey. The result was not one but three Macedonias: Greece received the coastal plain around the Bay of Thessaloniki; Serbia, now Yugoslavia, got the highlands; and Bulgaria received what was left. And throughout the later twentieth century, as the struggle for Macedonia took on new forms and fomented new conflicts, some distinct and contradictory images of ancient Macedonia rose from the earth again.

At a wide bend in the Skopje-Thessaloniki highway, the sprawling mound of Hellenistic, Roman, and Byzantine ruins finally came into view. At first glimpse, those ruins couldn't be called impressive; they seemed to be just a silent, natural feature of the landscape, rising above the slopes of a long, low mound whose grassy surface had been burnt brown by the hot summer sun. In fact, I might even have missed it were it not for the huge letters, S-T-O-B-I, set into the slopes in white painted stones, like a homemade sign for a truckstop restaurant. The tourist parking lot was empty, the small museum was shuttered, and the only sounds were the rustle of the wind and the muffled conversation of a work crew taking a lunch break in the shade of some trees by the nearby railroad line.

The elderly attendant in the small wooden gatehouse was sleeping, and when I managed to rouse him, he was visibly annoyed to have to rummage through the drawers of his desk to find the book of entrance tickets to the site. I paid my fee and entered the silent ruins of the ancient city. But I was without a guidebook, so the ruins told me no particular story. I wandered down the colonnaded main street, pausing every now and then to walk through the empty, weed-clogged rooms of Roman-period buildings whose once-brilliant floor mosaics were bleached to a dull greyness by exposure to the elements.

A century ago, most of those ruins were protected, lying safely under the Macedonian soil. Until the late nineteenth century, in fact, Macedonians didn't understand the full extent of Stobi's ruins. Until that time, they didn't have to dig for their history. History was the stuff of ancestors' legends, fondly told and retold in family tales. This ancient, abandoned city mound on the banks of the Vardar and Crna rivers was known only as *Pusto Gradsko,* "the Deserted Town." The story of its early history and sudden abandonment was a matter of belief in the supernatural, certainly not the raw material for serious historical scholarship—at least by the standards of the West. But Western scholarly standards soon arrived uninvited. The decline of the Ottoman Empire—the "Eastern Question"—attracted the agents and explorers of the Great Powers of Europe to the Balkans. And in 1858, just two years after the Crimean War had ended, the "deserted town" of medieval Macedonian legend was renamed. Johann Georg von Hahn, the Austrian consul-general in Thessaloniki, was the first to identify the ruins of Pusto Gradsko as the ancient city of Stobi—thereby beginning the expropriation from the local storytellers of the ownership and interpretation of this region's past.

Scattered references to Stobi in the writings of Greek and Roman authors provided von Hahn and subsequent European archaeologists with the basic outlines of Stobi's history and underlined the close connections of this Macedonian city with the culture of the Greco-Roman world. Mentioned first in connection with a military victory in the vicinity in 197 B.C. by the armies of King Philip V of Macedonia, Stobi became a district center when the Romans conquered Macedonia thirty years later. And by the end of the first century B.C., during the reign of Augustus, a period of spectacular urban growth began. By the end of the first century A.D., Stobi's population was granted the full legal and economic privileges of citizens of Rome.

Yet the city's greatest period of prosperity came after the triumph of Christianity: During the fourth and fifth centuries A.D., Stobi became the seat of Christian bishops who administered and watched

16

over an important diocese. Stobi's Bishop Budius had been invited to attend the first Ecumenical Council, convened at Nicaea in A.D. 325 by Constantine the Great. And later in the fourth century, the city was honored by a state visit of the Emperor Theodosius and apparently became the capital of the newly formed province of *Macedonia Salutaris*, or "Healthful Macedonia." In the closing centuries of antiquity, Stobi was the center of a far-reaching transformation that gave it a different character than it had possessed in the earlier pagan epoch, stretching back to the time of Alexander the Great.

This was the literary background, gleaned from the Greek and Latin sources. Yet after von Hahn's identification of the ancient city of Stobi with the area of ruins at the confluence of the Vardar and Crna rivers, its modern transformation could truly begin. The site proved to be a rich mine of the impressive architecture and artifacts that European antiquarians were so fond of collecting. Austria's zealous imperial involvement in the Balkans naturally gave the scholars of that country the initial advantage. In 1902, Professor Axel von Premerstein of the Imperial Museum of Vienna undertook the first full-scale excavations at Stobi, and he proudly shipped back to the museum his finds of architectural fragments, pottery, and inscriptions as freely exportable cultural property.

With the end of World War I, however, the imperial system of Europe crumbled, and Stobi's past was once again transformed. The creation of the "Kingdom of the Croats and the Slovenes" by the victorious Great Powers opened the antiquities of Stobi to renewed attack. But this time the attackers were not foreign expeditions, anxious to cart away Stobi's treasures. King Alexander I, patron of renewed excavations, saw in Stobi's ancient columns, inscriptions, and mosaic floors a means to bolster his royal prestige. Throughout nearly the entire turbulent interwar period, from 1924 to 1940, the National Museum of Belgrade—eventually renamed the Prince Paul Museum—stripped away the topsoil and rubble that blanketed the ancient city of Stobi to uncover its most prominent ancient monuments of grandeur and prosperity. In their restoration and presentation, they became monuments to the ruling house of Yugoslavia.

The royal connotation obviously presented a problem to the Yugoslav Communist party when it assumed control over Yugoslavia's past *and* present at the end of World War II. Although the nation's energies and resources were, for the most part, applied to the present, the meaning of the past needed some attention as well. In the early 1950s, the Conservation Institute of Macedonia, attached to the National Museum in the nearby city of Veles (later renamed Titov Veles), attempted to repair damage from the war and the elements, but their excavations were limited to a few random stabilizing probes. It was only in 1970 that the latest chapter in Stobi's ancient history began to be written. Beginning that year, a joint American-Yugoslav expedition, led by Professor James Wiseman of Boston University and Professor Djorde Mano-Zissi of the University of Belgrade, directed a multinational team of archaeologists, geologists, and students in the detailed reconstruction of the city's history.

The American and Yugoslav excavators had a much grander design than any of their predecessors as they concentrated on the city's "downtown" area—its forum—during the first few seasons of the dig. There, they cleared an unusually well-preserved Roman theatre and unexpectedly discovered a third-century A.D. *Who's Who* of Stobi: The individual seats in the theatre's lower rows still bore the carefully carved Greek names of season ticketholders. Other evidence of prosperity and Roman respectability came from the finds in a complex of workshops and villas. And surprising evidence of the prominence of Stobi's ancient Jewish community was uncovered in its well-appointed synagogue from the third and fourth centuries A.D. But the most impressive structure of all—and the scene of the most active work for the last few seasons—was a characteristic Christian structure that had dominated the skyline of Stobi in the fourth and fifth centuries A.D. It was a monumental church complex, dubbed "Bishop Philip's Basilica" by the archaeologists, who had found a Greek inscription honoring that bishop on one of its surviving entrance doorposts.

As I approached the ruins of that ancient basilica, I suddenly heard voices. The site wasn't deserted after all. The voices came from a deep trench, partially covered with a scaffolding of lumber and corrugated metal sheets. Soon the voices were interrupted by the banging of hammers, the sounds of lumber dropping, and occasional shouts. A small team of workmen was completing the construction of a shelter to protect Bishop Philip's Basilica from the coming winter rains. And as I walked toward the edge of the work area, I could see the need for protection: The exposed inner walls of the ancient structure still bore colorful paneled frescoes, at the foot of which lay an intricately patterned mosaic floor. Nearby stood an elaborate baptistery structure, with its circular baptismal font enclosed and protected by more frescoed walls and mosaic floors.

A young archaeologist stood at the edge of the excavation area, directing the preservation work. I introduced myself and began to speak with him about the significance of this site. The American participation in the expedition, he told me, had ended two years earlier, but some limited digging had continued under Yugoslav auspices, sponsored by the National Museum at the nearby city of Titov Veles and by the University of Skopje. The object of this continued archaeological work was to trace the structural history of the bishop's basilica, Stobi's most elaborate edifice during the Byzantine period. The finds here were certainly impressive, but there seemed to be something more basic at stake. And in listening to the archaeologist's description of Byzantine Stobi, I realized why Bishop Philip's Basilica—of all the possible sites in the ancient city—offered an especially meaningful modern symbol of ancient Macedonian history.

Bishop Philip's Basilica and the earlier church found beneath it evoked images quite different from phalanxes, conquest, and Alexander the Great. The excavation reinforced a dominating impression of Macedonia's communal life and early Christian piety. Scholars knew that Christianity had been established quite early in the city. But the young archaeologist now tried to expand on the implications of that as he stressed the significance of the ongoing work. The presence of a bishop at Stobi, he suggested, the visit of Theodosius, the mention of the city as the main city of the province, and the lavish basilica itself—all reflected Stobi's wholehearted acceptance of the new Christian way of life.

The meager remains of the Hellenistic period had, early on, discouraged the excavators from any hope that they could link Stobi with the period of Alexander the Great. This city's greatness had come centuries later, immediately preceding the great Slavic invasions of the fifth and sixth centuries A.D. At that time, the Christian tradition had sunk deep roots in Macedonia. And despite the dramatic political changes of the twentieth century, faith in the local Christian tradition remained one of the central elements of modern Macedonian nationality.

I nodded politely as the archaeologist stressed Stobi's importance. It was not—he wanted me to understand—just an outlying provincial city, but an important religious, economic, and cultural capital. Long after Alexander had faded into legend, the lively mix of peoples in northern Macedonia had created a new society. The sentiment seemed strangely familiar, uncannily modern. And as I listened to the archaeologist's interpretation of Stobi's historical importance, I sensed his deeper personal need to find his own place in history, to establish his own modern Macedonian identity in archaeological terms. Apparently he had found it at Stobi in the rubble of broken frescoes, mosaics, and building stones. In his own reconstruction of social change and regional culture in ancient Macedonia, he had fitted together a metaphorical portrait of *his* Macedonia today.

Yet there was clearly something more to the modern significance of Macedonia's history than just one man's longing for roots. About a hundred miles to the south, across the border in Greek Macedonia, I encountered a different historical reality. At the site of Vergina, onetime capital of the Macedonian kings, I discovered that archaeological claims about the true "essence" of ancient Macedonia were part of a modern struggle that remained painfully unresolved.

It took only a couple of hours to drive from Stobi across the Greek border, but as I approached the center of Thessaloniki, Greece's second-largest city, the atmosphere changed dramatically. Souvlaki stands, Western goods displayed in store windows, and loud bouzouki music booming from radios and tape players provided a sharp cultural contrast to the sounds and sights of the cities of Yugoslavia. And there was a conspicuous political difference: Election posters and spray-painted election graffiti were everywhere. The supporters of the two major parties, PASOK (the Greek socialist party headed by Prime Minister Andreas Papandreou) and Nea Demokrita ("New Democracy," the conservative party headed by Kostas Mitsotakis), were engaged in a bitter election campaign. Posters of the two parties' candidates covered almost every available concrete surface in the city. Loudspeakers blared from opposing party headquarters, and every now and then, pickup trucks covered with posters and fitted with sound systems passed down the main boulevards of the city playing patriotic Greek songs.

At stake in all the noise and excitement was a familiar political struggle. The supporters of the New Democracy party—with their blue-and-orange posters of the torch of freedom clenched tightly by a fist—were calling for a return to the original values so highly cherished in Greek history. They were fighting the internationalism of PASOK and stressing Greece's more conservative image. Here in Macedonia, however, conservative Greek nationalism was a relatively new thing. This part of the country had been annexed to Greece only in 1916, and few traces remained of the original population of Macedonian-speaking inhabitants. The population had largely been transformed within this century; many of the small towns around Thessaloniki had been established by Greek refugees from Turkey who were shifted here in a massive exchange of populations by the international agreement of 1923.

By now Macedonia was recognized as an inseparable part of the Greek nation, due in large measure to the efforts of Greek Macedonians, principally former president Constantine Karamanlis. Karamanlis was born in a small town northeast of Thessaloniki five years before southern Macedonia was annexed by Greece, and his attachment to his birthplace remained a constant feature of his long political career. His Macedonian Greek accent—at first an object of ridicule in the Parliament in Athens—later became his political trademark. In foreign relations, he made the most of his regional heritage, skillfully evoking powerful images of Macedonia's heroic past. On a state visit to Pakistan in 1977, he was hailed as the "first Macedonian leader" to come there since the time of Alexander the Great. And during the same year, there was ample cause for Greeks to look northward to Macedonia, for another son of the region, Professor Manolis Andronicos of the University of Thessaloniki, had unearthed there one of the most spectacular archaeological finds of the twentieth century.

Wanting to visit the site of the great discovery at Vergina in Greek Macedonia, I fortunately had arranged to meet some archaeologists who knew Professor Andronicos quite well. The next morning, I drove with them about fifty miles west across the flat Macedonian plain, again crossing the Vardar River, which I had followed from Yugoslavia but whose name was changed to the more classically Greek Axios here in Greece. The political posters and graffiti of the ongoing election campaign were in evidence even in the countryside, but as we arrived in the village of Vergina, the hilly, sometimes mountainous landscape seemed almost identical to that which I had seen in Yugoslav Macedonia. There seemed to be no question, though, about the importance of this place in *Greek* history. Vergina, originally named Aegeae, was the capital of the ancient Macedonian kingdom. And it was among the ruins and fields of this village that Professor Manolis Andronicos's archaeological career began.

In the late 1930s, as a student at the University of Thessaloniki, Andronicos had assisted Professor Konstantine Rhomaios in the excavation of a massive palace near Vergina—a palace later identified as the residence of one of the later Macedonian kings. The excavations there were suspended with the outbreak of World War II, but upon being appointed curator of antiquities for the region after the war, Andronicos resumed the search for archaeological evidence of the great age of Macedonia. While most Greek and foreign expeditions had concentrated their work in Attica, the Peloponnese, and the islands of the Aegean, Andronicos quietly worked his own archaeological pasture through the 1950s and 1960s, patiently looking for evidence of the ancient Macedonian culture, especially from the short-lived empire of Alexander the Great and his father, Philip, in the fourth century B.C.

Near the edge of the village of Vergina stood a great tumulus, or manmade mound, that had attracted the attention of explorers and antiquarians since the mid-nineteenth century. Its height of approximately forty feet and its diameter of almost 120 yards seemed suggestive of an ancient burial place. As early as 1952, Andronicos had dug into its center but had found nothing. A decade later, he attacked the mound with more determination, directing the excavation of a long trench through its center, and even though the only finds were smashed tombstones, he was not ready to abandon the site. For the third time, beginning in 1976, he directed an excavation team to dig into the mound, and this time he had some spectacular results.

The finds did not come immediately. At first he uncovered only more of the smashed marble tombstones, but their dates were suggestive. None were later than 274 B.C., the date of an attempt by Gallic mercenaries of King Pyrrhus of neighboring Epirus to sack the Macedonian royal tombs. The coincidence of ancient sources and the archaeological finds—however tenuous—seemed to suggest that the tumulus at Vergina did indeed contain the graves of ancient Macedonian kings. What he had not counted on, however, was the efforts by the later Macedonian kings to repair the damage done by the Gauls. The main tumulus was in fact meant to cover an earlier grave mound, and, after moving nearly forty thousand tons of earth from its center, Andronicos and his team finally uncovered an undisturbed tomb of an ancient Macedonian king.

The discovery of the royal tomb at Vergina created a sensation. The king's treasure of gold, silver, glass, and ivory objects—which were deposited in the tomb as burial offerings—sparked new scholarly interest in the culture of ancient Macedonia and its relationship to the art of Classical Greece. Professor Andronicos became an instant archaeological celebrity as, in subsequent years, the results of his long career of exploration in Macedonia became the inspiration for *The Search for Alexander*—a highly publicized touring museum exhibition and a docu-drama series on British and American television. But more than art appreciation was involved with the Vergina discoveries; there was also a dramatic human element. Andronicos believed he had found the tomb of no less a personage than Philip II of Macedon—father of Alexander the Great.

Our directions to the site of Andronicos's excavations were vague, and we drove past fields and through farmsteads until we finally reached a shallow valley just outside the village; within the valley was a barbed-wire enclosure, with warning signs to keep away casual onlookers. The tumulus itself was partially covered by a protective roof and surrounded by low, cinder-block buildings—the site resembling a tightly guarded military compound. The watchman on duty at the main gate was not sleeping. He had strict instructions not to let in any unauthorized visitors. And it was only after we passed a letter of introduction through the barbed-wire fence that he went off to find a member of the excavation staff to let us in.

Under a threatening afternoon sky, we passed a few minutes standing by the perimeter fence. There was no activity visible within the compound, just the long, low buildings and, within their circuit, a half-buried structure covered by a corrugated metal roof. The guard returned with a young man who motioned to him to unlock the gate. As we were finally allowed to enter, the young man introduced himself as Georghis, a staff member of Professor Andronicos's dig. Apparently used to giving guided tours of the site of the great discovery, he politely invited us to follow him into the main underground structure—through a narrow passageway and then down a steep path into a suitably funereal gloom.

It was difficult to visualize how the great tumulus had looked before the excavation; it had been thoroughly transformed by Andronicos's massive dig. The first tomb we entered was empty, and that was how it had been discovered—looted by the Gallic mercenaries in 274 B.C., Georghis explained. Although all the precious objects were removed by the ancient looters, several clues remained to suggest its occupant's identity. In the small burial chamber—about ten feet by twelve feet in size and now illuminated by a single bare light bulb—Georghis had set up a drawing table to copy the graceful fresco still dimly visible on the wall. The subject of the main composition was the abduction of the maiden Persephone by the underworld god Hades, a favorite Greek theme of the tragedy of death. The graceful depiction of the heroine of the story and the discovery here of fragments of an ivory comb indicated that this may well have been the burial place of a princess of the Macedonian royal family.

The small, empty tomb at the edge of the tumulus was merely the introduction; the centerpiece of the expedition lay ahead. Georghis led us along a dark, underground walkway onto a makeshift wooden balcony. As he stepped down into the excavation area, we waited in the darkness. And then suddenly, as he flipped a switch to illuminate the banks of floodlights above and behind us, there was blinding light.

The colors on the façade of the tomb at the center of the tumulus were shocking, not so much for their bright hues as for the fact that the elaborate decoration of the tomb entrance seemed perfectly preserved. The floodlights revealed a Doric façade of white Macedonian marble decorated with red, blue, and gold paint. The magnificent tomb, covered with earth soon after its construction and the burial of Philip, still maintained the brilliance it had been given by the skilled team of artists hastily assembled by the Macedonian royal family in the wake of Philip's assassination in a palace plot in the summer of 336 B.C.

A long black curtain hung across the top of the façade, and Georghis drew it back with a flourish, revealing the most spectacular element in the tomb's decoration. Painted on plaster applied to a brick face, a long and elaborate hunting scene extended across the entire width of the façade. On the extreme left, several naked figures could be seen spearing a frightened deer. Next came several more of the naked figures, who, together with their hunting dogs, had cornered a vicious-looking wild boar. On the right side of the panel were more naked hunters taunting a huge, standing black bear. And in the center of the painting were two mounted figures—none other than Alexander the Great and his father, King Philip, Georghis assured us—spearing a lion, the symbol of royalty.

This impressive painting was never intended to be left open for the benefit of casual admirers. It, like the grave goods found inside the sealed burial chambers, was intended for the benefit of the deceased alone. Inside the tomb, Andronicos and his team had discovered an unsurpassed collection of ancient armor, jewelry, bronzework, and carved ivory deposited around the precious gold container of ashes of the deceased. In fact, there were so many objects inside the tomb, and they were packed so thickly, that Andronicos had had to resort to an unorthodox, yet highly exacting, excavation technique to remove them all. Georghis explained the process. First the capstone was removed from the burial chamber's vaulted ceiling and the offering-strewn floor was photographed from above. A rectangular grid was drawn on the resulting photograph, and the team then descended into the tomb and sliced up the thick layers of offerings along the lines of the grid squares so that they could be reassembled in the laboratory and be peeled off layer by layer.

If there had been only gold vessels, pottery vases, and metal weapons, such a complicated procedure would have been unnecessary. But Andronicos and his team discovered that the king had been laid to rest with offerings of a far more perishable kind—offerings that at the time of our visit were still being analyzed, photographed, and studied in the nearby excavation laboratory. Georghis drew the curtain back over the façade painting and extinguished the banks of floodlights. Then we followed him out of the tumulus and into the laboratory building to see the still incompletely dissected organic layers. Andronicos and his team had already identified the remains of wreaths of flowers, leather objects, wooden furniture, and dozens of fragments of fabric, to which hundreds of delicate gold ornaments once were sewn.

The Vergina tomb and its offerings provided a portrait of Macedonian power and prosperity, executed in a style that was distinctively Greek. Whatever the racial origins or ethnic affinities of the ancient Macedonian people, it seemed quite clear that by the time of King Philip, they had begun the process of wholehearted cultural assimilation of the artistic and architectural styles of the south. The motifs of the tomb decorations brought to mind Classical Greek examples, and Professor Andronicos had even suggested that the tomb paintings themselves were executed by well-known fourth-century artists Nichomachus and Philoxenus of Eretria.

The archaeological work at Vergina obviously required a substantial budget, but Georghis surprised me when he revealed that time and painstaking effort—not money—were the main problem here. Excavation funds were generously provided by the Greek government—not the least of the reasons being that when Professor Andronicos discovered the tomb, Constantine Karamanlis, native of Greek Macedonia, was the prime minister. Karamanlis had a deep personal interest in demonstrating that Macedonia could boast an ancient Hellenic culture as impressive as that of the cities farther south, and he saw in the "Tomb of Philip" a way to enhance *both* Greek and Macedonian prestige. Its finds and its interpretation reinforced the traditional images of authority, prosperity, and power that his political successors in the conservative Nea Demokrita party were now attempting to uphold. Karamanlis, as prime minister and later as president, saw to it that Professor Andronicos's excavations would continue with full government support, even after his own term of office. And despite the occasional carping of scholars who still rejected some of Andronicos's specific historical claims for the tomb and its contents, King Philip of Macedon—a national father figure for the Greek nation, and especially for Greek Macedonians—had, through archaeology, miraculously risen from the grave.

As we left the lab and walked back along a gravel path past the great tumulus, Georghis suddenly spoke up again. Earlier, as we examined the wealth of finds from the tomb of Philip, Georghis's tone had been that of a detached art historian, commenting on the quality and style of the various objects the expedition had found. But now, his tone was unexpectedly emotional. Although I had not mentioned my earlier experience at Stobi, the modern conflict over Macedonia—and conflicting interpretations of the character of the ancient Macedonians—came up of its own accord. "Before you leave," Georghis announced with an odd, unprovoked defensiveness, "I want you to see some finds that will disprove all the false anti-Hellenistic propaganda that's coming from Yugoslavia these days."

Those finds were far more humble than the precious grave gifts of Philip's Tomb, but they had a clear significance in modern ethnic terms. Georghis unlocked the door to a metal shed near the edge of the excavations and I followed him inside. Grey metal shelves filled with pottery sherds and marble fragments lined the walls of the dark and drafty storeroom. On its bare concrete floor lay rows of ancient tombstones. The carved marble slabs had been one of the main clues that led to the discovery of the great tumulus; from their date, form, and location, Andronicos first realized that they marked the graves of the loyal Macedonian nobility who chose to be buried close to the royal tombs. Some of these ancient grave markers were in perfect condition, some broken and partially effaced. Many bore palmettes and classical-style bas-reliefs. A few were more modest. But the single point that Georghis wanted to stress about these small tomb monuments was that all of them were inscribed in Greek.

As Georghis walked up and down the rows of tombstones, he pointed out some of the names. The ancient Greek letters were carved into the marble with precision; like the characters in a first-year Greek textbook, they weren't difficult to read. Every now and then, Georghis would stop to run his finger along a line of carved letters on a particular tombstone, emphatically pronouncing the name of the deceased: Demetrios . . . Antigonos . . . Eugenes. . . . By the third or fourth dramatic reading, his point had become abundantly clear. Pronounced in Georghis's flowing, native Greek accent, the names sounded strangely familiar, not ancient at all. It was as if, there in the cold and gloom of the storeroom, Georghis was respectfully recalling the names of some recently departed relatives, members of a prosperous, conservative, northern Greek family.

"These people were Greeks," he insisted, tightening his voice to emphasize his point once again. I hadn't suspected that Greek archaeologists were even aware of the nationalist interpretation of finds in Yugoslavia. I would never have imagined that they took them so seriously. But Georghis apparently felt the need to refute any suggestion of Slavic heritage in ancient Macedonia with the cold, mathematical logic of archaeological chronology. Since the tombstones could all be dated by their style to the late fourth and early third centuries B.C.—the era of Philip, Alexander, and their immediate successors—the "Greekness" of Macedonia's population at the time of its greatest glory would seem, therefore, to be beyond dispute. And the frequent listing of the deceased's fathers and grandfathers with equally well-known Greek names pushed that purely "Greek" character of Macedonia even beyond the reign of Philip—into a more hazy heroic age.

For Georghis, Macedonia was no melting pot. Not now and not in the past. Any suggestion to the contrary, especially if it came from archaeologists in Yugoslavia, could be seen only as a calculated political attack. At Vergina, an ancient Greek name meant Greek nationality. Its discovery in association with the royal tombs at Vergina was a legitimate reason for modern Greek national pride. Despite the claims of ancient Athenian orators and modern Yugoslav historians, the excavators at Vergina felt confident that the Macedonians were fully Greek in both culture and ethnic identity during the golden age of Philip and Alexander.

Quite clearly, then, there were *two* ancient Macedonias existing side by side in the twentieth century. Here at Vergina was the royal Greek Macedonia, with its lavish funeral deposits and characteristic Greek names. Across the border in Yugoslavia was a pious, Byzantine

Macedonia, with its evidence of economic development, waves of immigration from central and eastern Europe, and resultant social change. Each of these modern archaeological themes offered a convincing validation of the present, a mirrorlike image of modern ideologies. And, for the first of many times, I realized that the past may not have an independent existence apart from the present. Its ancient texts, architecture, and artifacts—fragments of a living reality now dead—could only be brought back to life by taking on meanings in our own living reality. Modern Macedonian archaeology, born and matured in an era of conflicting nationalism and territorial conflict, could hardly help but transform ancient Macedonian ruins and tombs into powerful, emotion-laden metaphors of what Macedonia's future should be.

2

TURKEY

Searching for Troy

𝄢**I** had hoped that a visit to Troy would summon up some familiar images from childhood. I expected that a trip to the city of Priam, Paris, and Helen would awaken memories of grammar-school lessons, memories of grammar-school versions of famous Greek myths. But from the driver's seat of the Avis car I had rented at the Istanbul Hilton, the landscape around Troy seemed unpleasantly unfamiliar. It wasn't easy to call to mind strutting Greek and Trojan heroes. On one side lay rolling hills covered with fields and orchards, punctuated by the stone-and-cement clusters of modern Turkish villages. And on the other side, the sun's glare harshly silhouetted the silent traffic of freighters and tankers gliding past one another through the Dardanelles straits.

It wasn't particularly easy to get to the City of Legend. It took two full days of driving from Istanbul—across the massive Bosporus Bridge, clogged with morning rush-hour traffic; past a long stretch of nondescript apartment blocks, factories, and warehouses; and then through the small towns and farmland along most of the Asian shore of the Sea of Marmara. Çanakkale, the major town in the vicinity of Troy, proved to be the first of a series of disappointments. Its youth hostels, cheap hotels, and restaurants bearing the names of Homeric heroes seemed only to mock Troy's ancient reputation. And the campgrounds and motels clustered nearby along the coastline were, for the most part, rundown and modest. Despite its fame, Troy apparently was not one of Turkey's main tourist resorts.

Here, modern tragedy seemed to shoulder aside the romance of the ancient epic. I found it impossible to ignore the many grim reminders of the fighting that had raged on this battlefield of empires even in our own century. In the main square of Çanakkale, a grotesquely twisted artillery piece was set up as a World War I memorial; along the coastal highway south of the city stood many small, tombstonelike markers commemorating deadly encounters between the modern armies in their bloody struggle for control of the Dardanelles in 1915. And across the water, on the tip of the Gallipoli Peninsula, loomed the monuments to the tens of thousands of Turkish defenders and troops of the British, French, Australian, and New Zealand Expeditionary Force who lay buried, far from home, in the peninsula's vast war cemeteries. The gigantic Turkish war memorial rose through the haze on the horizon. Its stark, four-legged form was grim and frightening, a stylized Trojan horse whose sleek head and upper body had been cut off with extreme cruelty.

These disturbing images clashed with my fantasies. Even if the story of Troy was itself a tale of bloody and violent warfare, the families of the fallen no longer came to hear speeches or weep over graves. Troy's appeal was not the war but the discovery of the truth of the ancient legends—legends conveniently shorn of their vividly unpleasant memories. Even in the sixth grade, we were taught to believe that the Trojan War had a modern happy ending. As schoolchildren, we learned how that strange and stubborn character named Heinrich Schliemann devoted his life and fortune to digging up the fabled city and how he had discovered the treasure of Priam, its king. So I followed the road signs toward the mound of Hissarlik, where Schliemann made archaeological history and where, I hoped, the present could be safely ignored. About three miles down a winding side road, past more fields and the small village of Tevfikiye, I began to feel the excitement. The road came to an end in the midst of parking lots and souvenir shops—those sure modern signs of a famous site of antiquity. And after a walk of another half-mile down the access road, I finally recognized the familiar image I was seeking. From behind a grove of pine trees rose a huge wooden horse.

That contented-looking horse, recently built by the Turkish Ministry of Culture for the benefit of tourists, might have offended a few archaeological purists, but as the most famous symbol of the war between the Greeks and the Trojans, it conveyed attractive, romantic associations in a way that ruined buildings and superimposed debris layers never could. The story of Troy may have been a saga well known to the ancient Greeks and Romans, but, like the ruins of Hissarlik, it had come down to us in pieces, reconstructed by classical scholars from the surviving fragments of dozens of ancient texts. Homer's *Iliad* recounted the events of only a few weeks of a ten-year struggle, and the whole affair took at least twenty years altogether—if you count the ancient Miss Universe contest that started it all.

Archaeology, of course, could add nothing to the personal details of the story—the story of how Paris, son of Priam, the king of Troy, chose Aphrodite as the most beautiful of the goddesses, and of how Aphrodite enabled him to abduct Helen, wife of Menelaus, the Spartan king. Archaeology could not confirm the beauty of Helen, nor the depth of Achilles's rage. It could only provide a much less imaginative outline of the story, a reassurance that a violent confrontation between the Trojans and the Greeks probably took place at the end of the Mycenaean period, sometime during the thirteenth century B.C. The rest was beyond confirming or disproving—which is why the ambiguous ruins of Troy needed a modern horse. For here, I eventually came to discover, archaeology was not the handmaiden of history. It was the delivery boy of myth.

There was something compelling about the image of two national wills pitted against each other in combat over a matter of honor that had kept the memory of this ancient city alive for thousands of years. Thucydides called the siege of Troy the first great war waged by the Greeks as a nation. Euripides and Aeschylus elaborated on the specific details of the story with the reverence of biblical commentators. The story of Troy served the cause of early Greek patriotism, and that emotion was merely transferred to other patriots in other countries after Athens lost its position of dominance. While the Greeks long continued to sing the praises of Agamemnon, Odysseus, Ajax, and Achilles, other peoples came to revere the heroes who fought on the losing side.

From the ashes of Troy new empires were born—or at least that's how the story was read. Later patriots found or imagined that their own nations' destinies began with the fall and destruction of Troy. Despite the outcome of the battle, a select few of the Trojan survivors were later claimed proudly as founding fathers of new nations whose moment was yet to come on the stage of history. Aeneas, according to legend, wandered toward central Italy and founded a city called Roma. Antenor sailed with his followers up the Adriatic to the lagoons of Venice. And, farthest traveled of all, a mysterious Trojan named Brutus reportedly found a new home in the cold and rainy British Isles.

Imperial mythmaking, though, is no longer the main factor behind Troy's continuing attraction for tourists. In our own times, its patriotic significance is scarcely mentioned. Gone are the days when European statesmen and military leaders could inspire their listeners with the heroic images of the *Iliad*, as Lord Kitchener saw fit to do at the start of the bloody, doomed campaign for Gallipoli. Troy now lives primarily in the clichés and trademarks of popular culture: "Trojan horses," "apples of discord," condoms, and the anachronistically gladiatorial costumes of the University of Southern California marching band. It also lives, of course, in the compulsory reading of sixth-graders, high-schoolers, and undergraduates, who make their way through the masterpieces of Western literature with varying degrees of fairy-tale fascination and academic drudgery.

It's only in one small community that a passionate interest in the meaning of Troy still burns brightly. And there too it's more a question of modern patriotism than historical study; the archaeologists and classical scholars who tirelessly rehash the issues, occasionally spicing them with accusations of their opponents' dishonesty and malice, all acknowledge Troy as their spiritual home. For at the mound of Hissarlik, at the end of the nineteenth century, the modern techniques of archaeology were developed. And while the spiritual father of this enterprise was not a fleeing Trojan prince or Greek hero, but rather a self-made millionaire named Schliemann, he has become—like the massive wooden horse looming above the ruins of Hissarlik—one of the cartoonlike centerpieces of a new myth of Troy.

Tucked away in the corner of the dusty parking lot of the Helen and Paris Souvenir Shop stood a small plank cabin with a large sun-yellowed photo cutout of a slight and timid-looking man. Both the man and the cabin seemed out of place in the midst of the campers, tourist buses, and garish plastic snack-bar tables, but perhaps it was the strange contrast that drew a steady stream of souvenir shoppers to this unlikely monument. Unfortunately, disappointment awaited the curious, who might have hoped to find an authentic relic of Trojan history here.

THIS IS *NOT* SCHLIEMANN'S HOUSE, read the small, hand-lettered sign in English, French, and German, an apologetic message that went on to explain how the cabin structure was built a few years earlier by a German film company for a television docu-drama about the excavations of Troy. Despite the apology, though, the old movie set had obvious commercial value for the owners of the gift shop, for during the last century, Schliemann himself had pushed the antique Greek and Trojan heroes from center stage. His story was a part of the larger legend of the ancient city, and the members of the German film company were just some of the recent mythmakers who had taken a heroic myth as literally as any of the ancient poets of Troy had done.

Schliemann himself clearly encouraged the stories. His memoirs, published for the first time in his report of the Troy excavations, read like a fairy tale too good to be true. Born in the small town of Neubukow in Mecklenburg, Germany, in 1822, the son of a poor parish pastor, he began his business career in true Horatio Alger fashion—at the age of fourteen as a hardworking grocery boy. But seeing that his fortune would never be won in the sale of herring, butter, milk, salt, sugar, and vodka, he made his way to the port of Hamburg and signed on as a cabin boy on a brig bound for Venezuela. That brig went down in a December gale off Holland, but the cabin boy Schliemann miraculously was saved. Deciding to remain in the bustling metropolis of Amsterdam rather than risk the further uncertainties of a second sea voyage to South America, he began a spectacular rise to fame and fortune by taking a job as a messenger-clerk for the commodities firm of F.C. Quien and Son.

International trade—buying low and selling high across oceans and continents, conquering new markets through speculation, amassing huge windfall profits for predicting scarcity or sudden demand—proved to be young Schliemann's path to wealth and fame. His almost uncanny talent for language and his natural business acumen quickly set him apart from the other young clerks, who were content to sit behind their high wooden desks mindlessly stamping, sorting, and filing bills of exchange. Teaching himself Russian, and recognizing the lucrative possibilities of indigo speculation in the vast and largely untapped Russian market, Schliemann convinced the directors of B. H. Schröder & Co.—another Amsterdam firm—to appoint him as their agent in St. Petersburg. There, he proved that he was no ordinary ambitious twenty-four-year-old. After establishing himself as one of the shrewdest foreign traders in the czar's empire, he set his sights on the New World.

In 1851, at the height of the California Gold Rush, he opened a commercial bank in Sacramento and bought up more than a million dollars' worth of prospectors' gold dust in less than six months. And that wasn't the only profit Schliemann gained from his time in America. He proudly reported in his memoirs that since he had been a resident of California in 1850—when that state was admitted to the Union—he "joyfully embraced the opportunity of becoming a citizen of the United States." He apparently already had good reason to feel at home in America: Before leaving for California, he had spent some time in the nation's capital, and in a detailed diary entry he described a congenial evening spent at the White House in the company of President Millard Fillmore and his family.

Those colorful adventures would have been enough for most thirty-year-olds of any era, but Schliemann hadn't even begun the most famous phase of his career. Returning to Russia at the time of the Crimean War and slyly cornering the market in saltpeter, brimstone, and lead—the makings of ammunition—he continued to add to his profits in indigo as well. But for Schliemann wealth was not an end in itself; it was merely a means to gain honor and respectability. "I loved money indeed," he recalled in his memoirs, "but solely as a means of realizing the great idea of my life." Schliemann had gained a great fortune, but his social status as a mere merchant and speculator was something less than he would have liked. So in 1863, at age forty-one, he summarily liquidated his assets and retired from the sordid world of business to devote himself to a life of edifying world travel and to that most gentlemanly of Victorian pursuits—the study of ancient Greek.

Troy, Schliemann maintained, was always his obsession, even before he had become a businessman. From the time in his boyhood when his father had given him a Christmas present of Dr. Georg Ludwig Jerrer's *History of the World for Children*, with its vivid, melodramatic illustration of Troy sacked and burning, Schliemann claimed that he felt destined to dig up the proof that Homer's story was true. But Schliemann's childhood fantasy was to lead—at least at first—to scholarly scorn rather than his hoped-for social respectability. By the time he began his intensive private study of Homer, a thoroughly skeptical attitude toward the details of ancient Greek legend had become the dominant intellectual mood in European university lecture halls and gentlemen's clubs.

In light of detailed analysis of the inconsistencies and obvious reworking of the text of the *Iliad*, few classical scholars believed that the story of the siege and conquest of Troy—whatever its literary significance—had any greater historical basis than the Greeks' fables about the struggle between Zeus and the Titans or other figures of Greek mythology. Those myths, so the scholars believed, represented the childish stage of Hellenic culture; far more appealing was the image of Classical Athens, an elegant community of philosophers, orators, and art lovers—which was, of course, very much the way that the aristocrats and intellectuals of Europe liked to think of themselves. The violence, the plunder, and the greed of the Homeric heroes impressed the conservative classical scholars as disturbingly "un-Greek." So the Trojan War of the *Iliad* was dismissed as a fable, having little basis in fact.

But having an innocent, businessman's faith in the drama and violence of Homer, and—even more important—a successful speculator's fortune to support his archaeological obsession, Schliemann almost miraculously made the illustration in Dr. Jerrer's book come to life. After traveling to Greece and excavating what he later suggested might be the ashes of Odysseus and Penelope on the island of Ithaca, he traveled to Turkey and identified the mound of Hissarlik as the site most likely to contain the Trojan citadel sacked by the Greeks. And, after submitting his doctoral dissertation on the subject, written in ancient Greek, to the University of Rostock in Germany, Schliemann prepared to mount his own attack on the city of myth. He married a beautiful young Greek woman in Athens, returned to the mound of Hissarlik, and hired a gang of Turkish peasant workers. They dug, and he found.

The most dramatic moment in Schliemann's Troy excavations was first described in his own account of the digging; it has been continually elaborated in a succession of kitschy novels and films since that time. It occurred in the late spring of 1873, when, standing with the workers in a deep trench, he suddenly saw a glimmer of gold.

Quickly dismissing the workers for an unexpected rest break, he summoned his wife, Sophia. "In order to secure the treasure from my workmen and save it for archaeology," he wrote, "it was necessary to lose no time." Feverishly digging together to avoid detection, they uncovered an enormous cache of gold, silver, and copper vessels, ingots, and jewelry, which Sophia Schliemann excitedly wrapped up in her shawl.

This was the famous "Treasure of Priam," Schliemann's most important archaeological evidence that he had, in fact, discovered the ancient city of Troy. Its location was in the destruction debris of the next-to-lowest of nine superimposed levels—indicating its great antiquity. And the fact that the treasure was found in a chest apparently hastily dragged out of a nearby palace at the time of the city's destruction seemed to match perfectly the Homeric description of the Trojan royal family's fear and confusion at the time of their city's tragic fall to the Greeks.

Unfortunately, it is no longer possible to see Schliemann's famous treasure—at Troy or anywhere else. In 1873, Schliemann was so fearful that the Ottoman government would confiscate the precious ancient artifacts that he smuggled them out of the country—first to Athens, then in 1880 to the Imperial Museum in Berlin, where they remained safely stored for decades. But less than seventy years later, their location—even their existence—became uncertain, for the Trojan gold vessels and jewelry mysteriously disappeared in the spring of 1945. According to some accounts, they were destroyed in the intensive Allied bombing of Berlin at the end of World War II. Other, more sinister reports suggested (without any firm factual basis) that they were discovered by the arriving Soviet army and transported clandestinely back to Leningrad to be hidden away forever in a top-secret vault in the Soviet Union.

The fate of the objects, though, was not the focus of the archaeological controversy that arose later. Continuing excavations at the mound of Hissarlik after Schliemann's death in 1890 proved quite conclusively that "Troy II"—the level in which the treasure was found—had nothing to do with King Priam and should be dated to the Early Bronze Age (ca. 2500–ca. 2200 B.C.), about a thousand years before the generally accepted date for the Trojan War. Today, after more than a century of digging and study, the question has become far more basic, far more direct. Some scholars now claim that Schliemann's history-making discovery was the work of an overactive imagination. And a few even go so far as to claim that the so-called Treasure of Priam was nothing more than an elaborate hoax.

The first suspicions about Heinrich Schliemann's character began to surface in the mid-1960s, when a prominent New York psychoanalyst, Dr. William Niederland, trying his hand at psychohistory, spent a summer in the Gennadius Library in Athens, where Schliemann's private papers are kept. In reviewing about twelve thousand letters and unpublished journal entries, Niederland discovered that despite Schliemann's published tributes and fondness for his father, he repeatedly expressed great hatred for him in his diaries and letters to his sisters, angrily blaming Pastor Schliemann for his mother's premature death. And Schliemann seemed, in fact, to have been strangely obsessed with death from his earliest childhood, an obsession that grew throughout his later business career. In almost every foreign city he visited—Rome, Istanbul, New Orleans, and Sacramento, among many—he was strangely attracted to the cities' cemeteries, often taking the time and effort to examine modern death registers and to record in his journal the measurements and epitaphs of modern gravestones.

Niederland therefore suggested that Schliemann's obsession with archaeology was not an innocent and romantic quest to uncover the truth of an ancient legend, but an unconscious solution to one of the great psychological problems of his life. By embarking on a quixotic crusade to prove that Homer's Troy really existed, Schliemann defied and ultimately overturned the weight of scholarly opinion—which, Niederland contended, was the acting-out of a subconscious struggle with an authoritarian father figure he both feared and loathed. And by resurrecting ancient Troy and claiming for himself the treasure of its fabled King Priam, Schliemann symbolically succeeded in an even more heroic struggle—in reversing the effects of both death and time.

Niederland's observations were, for the most part, ignored by archaeologists and historians, but the initial Freudian analysis-at-a-distance soon gave way to far more damning charges—far more incriminating than subconscious Oedipal conflicts. The issue suddenly became one of professional honor. In 1972, at a festive gathering to commemorate the 150th anniversary of the birth of Heinrich Schliemann, Professor William Calder of the University of Colorado presented the audience of Schliemann admirers with some shocking evidence. In preparing his speech on the life and works of Schliemann, he had undertaken some archival research and had unexpectedly uncovered several glaring misrepresentations in the great man's autobiography.

His inquiries at the University of Rostock revealed that the doctoral dissertation in ancient Greek that Schliemann claimed to have submitted was never approved by any member of the faculty. A careful comparison of Schliemann's unpublished diary entries and the records of the United States Immigration and Naturalization Service indicated that his American citizenship was granted not by acclamation in California but by application in New York City—a full eighteen years after the date he claimed in his memoirs. And Calder's careful combing of the characteristically detailed social columns of contemporary Washington newspapers indicated that the sociable evening Schliemann claimed to have spent at the White House with the First Family simply never took place.

The cracks in the idol's statue grew wider as the unexpected extent of Schliemann's personal deceptions was gradually leaked to the scholarly public. Professor David Traill of the University of California, taking the lead from Calder, showed that the most memorable details of Schliemann's career in America—as he later so proudly recounted them—were a mixture of exaggeration and psychopathic fantasy. His experiences in California, at the time of the Gold Rush, were good examples. Traill proved that Schliemann's poignant, personal description of the Great Fire of 1851 in San Francisco was copied almost verbatim from a local newspaper, since he was in Sacramento when it occurred. And his sudden departure from the goldfields was not, as he claimed, necessitated by an attack of fever, but rather by fear of attack from an angry business partner whom he had apparently defrauded in the rough-and-tumble gold-dust trade.

The picture grew even darker as Traill dug deeper. His research in federal microfilm archives revealed that Schliemann's American citizenship not only was obtained later than he reported, but also was obtained by swearing falsely that he had been a longtime resident of the United States. And as a terrible, perhaps final, blow to the heartwarming saga of lifelong faith and dedication, Traill found direct evidence in Schliemann's letters that he had fabricated the charming story of the Christmas in Mecklenburg—of gazing at the illustrations in Jerrer's *History of the World for Children*, of bravely vowing, as an eight-year-old, that he would someday uncover the remains of Troy. At the time of the publication of the fully elaborated story, Traill explained, Schliemann was involved in a bitter battle over excavation rights to the mound of Hissarlik, and he brought forth his lifelong devotion to the "Trojan Question" as public testimony of his personal dedication to the site. But Traill could find no written evidence of Schliemann's interest in Homer *before* his arrival at Hissarlik. And even though a copy of Jerrer's *History* was indeed among Schliemann's possessions, Schliemann's signature on the title page proved, on the basis of handwriting analysis, to be not that of a boy growing up with romantic dreams in Mecklenburg—but of Schliemann as an adult.

Like a shark smelling blood, Traill quickly went in for the kill. At the 1981 annual meeting of the Archaeological Institute of America, he presented what he believed was evidence of Schliemann's ultimate dishonesty—in the story of the discovery of the Treasure of Priam itself. Glaring contradictions in the various published accounts of the date and even the precise location of the treasure first aroused his suspicions, as did the later testimony of Schliemann's personal servant, Yannakis, who claimed that the famous "treasure" contained no gold whatsoever and was found not in a wooden chest in the royal palace but in a tomb well outside the city walls. Most damning of all was the role played by Sophia Schliemann, who reportedly had stood faithfully by her husband, carefully wrapping the precious finds in her shawl. Schliemann lovingly recalled her help in his report of the excavations, claiming that it would have been "impossible for me to have removed the treasure without the help of my dear wife, who stood at my side." But this, too, was a myth just waiting to be shattered. Traill reconstructed the evidence in Schliemann's diaries and personal correspondence to prove that Sophia played no part whatsoever in the discovery. She was in Athens visiting her family at the time.

Traill's conclusion was that Schliemann simply invented the story of the Treasure of Priam, piecing together the collection from individual finds uncovered during all three seasons of the Hissarlik dig. Acknowledging the possibility that Schliemann also might have obtained some of the objects from sources other than excavation (his penchant for purchasing ancient artifacts from antiquities dealers was well documented in his diaries and account books), Traill nevertheless concluded that since the surviving drawings of the finds showed that they were all characteristic forms of the Early Bronze Age, they were probably, individually, authentic. The problem was that Heinrich Schliemann, recognizing what the public might want to be discovered at Troy, made *their* archaeological dream come true.

Before Schliemann, the Greek past was aloof and aristocratic, taken in prescribed doses like therapeutic mineral waters by well-educated ladies and gentlemen in university lecture halls and drafty museum galleries. Symmetry, order, and classical restraint were the values cherished most highly; wild tales of adventure and plunder were dismissed as disturbing fairy tales. But Schliemann was more in tune with the tenor of his times than most of the respectable scholars whose approval he sought. "In spite of his passion for Homer," wrote the art historian and archaeologist Adolf Furtwängler about Schliemann in 1881, "he is at heart a businessman and a speculator. He can never get rid of that." Yet Schliemann's success lay precisely in that identity, for his earlier career as a speculator and international commodities trader had immersed him in the romantic adventures of the nineteenth century—from the wilds of the California goldfields to the bloody, modern battlefields of the Crimean War. The era in which he lived was one of imperial conflict, of the clash of national wills to conquer territory. Military and commercial warriors—not philosopher-artists—were the heroes. Great treasures—and speculators' fortunes—were discovered and lost.

Schliemann's Troy captured the public imagination precisely because it mirrored popular Victorian sensibilities, highlighting the public taste for stories of wealth and empire, whether of Sir Walter Scott, Rudyard Kipling, Homer, or even Schliemann himself. At Hissarlik, the self-made man from Mecklenburg had uncovered a fabulous world of romance and riches lost in the heat of ancient battle and recovered by triumphant European archaeological technology. Schliemann's excavations evoked a past that both mimicked and celebrated the present; facts that hindered or obstructed the excitement of the story could be safely hidden or set aside. Yet the factor that Schliemann's latter-day critics failed to understand in their outrage at his deceptions was the reason for his continued popularity. Schliemann's success was in mythmaking, not science. His story of his life, his discoveries, and even of Troy was simply a late-Victorian dime novel of high adventure that sold very well.

Despite the recent, embarrassing revelations, Schliemann still had his defenders, as did the legend of Troy. The small-scale tourist industry near the mound of Hissarlik had continued to prosper. A modern-style shopping center with glitzy gift shops and a snack bar now offered serious competition to the older, tumbledown stands and creaky postcard racks on the opposite side of the access road. The romance and the legend offered a few local people a good living. The garish posters, ashtrays, and dishtowels printed with the images of ancient heroes and modern ruins; the Trojan Horse key chains; the cellophane-packaged slides; and the glossy, full-color guidebooks banked on the tourists' continuing faith in the story of Troy. Casting doubts on Heinrich Schliemann's version of the story profited no one at all.

The reluctance to attack Heinrich Schliemann openly seemed to be shared by at least some scholars, since many of those who had spent their careers analyzing and reinterpreting the archaeological finds from Hissarlik had their own interests and long-held conceptions at stake in the controversy. Professor Machteld Mellink of Bryn Mawr College, past president of the prestigious Archaeological Institute of America, accused Schliemann's latter-day critics of harboring a personal "vendetta" against him and ignoring the important scholarly contributions he had made to modern archaeology. The counterattack of Professor Donald Easton of Liverpool University was more pointed. In a series of detailed articles, he attempted to refute many of Traill's accusations, claiming that while Schliemann might occasionally have been prone to romanticization and exaggeration, the story of his discoveries was substantially reliable.

Of course, even the most ardent of Schliemann's scholarly supporters recognized that the debate about the archaeological evidence for the Trojan War was far from being settled. And with the steady accumulation of additional data from the entire Aegean region in the century since Schliemann's excavations, the debate had widened to include the far more provocative and troublesome question of the reason for the collapse of the Mediterranean civilizations of the Late Bronze Age.

On one point, all scholars seemed to be in agreement: The mound of Hissarlik was the most likely location for ancient Troy. Although the remains of other Bronze Age settlements had been located in the general vicinity, none possessed the strategic position, the impressive architecture, and the evidence of continuous occupation that would make them attractive alternatives for the site of the legendary city. But that was not to say that the location of Homeric Troy was certain; with the refinement of excavation techniques and the ever-more-detailed study of Hissarlik's superimposed layers, the problem had taken on a more vertical aspect. The question could be put simply: Which of the nine superimposed city levels at the mound of Hissarlik was besieged, conquered, and immortalized in the legends of the Trojan War?

Schliemann, of course, was initially confident that the second layer from the bottom—Troy II—was the city of Priam. The evidence of fire, destruction, and the treasure—whatever its origins—were his strongest arguments. But in his final seasons of excavation, when he gained the assistance of Wilhelm Dörpfeld, an experienced architect and field archaeologist, that confident initial identification collapsed. In the meantime, Schliemann's other excavations in Greece had undermined the dating. The characteristic painted pottery he found at Mycenae, the capital of Troy's great enemy Agamemnon, was completely different from the types of vessels found in Troy II. Many of the same types of Mycenaean vessels, however, were found considerably higher in Hissarlik's levels, in the layer called Troy VI. Dörpfeld therefore became convinced that Troy VI was the Homeric city. Unfortunately, Schliemann had already destroyed a large part of that city in his eagerness to get down to the level of Troy II.

After Schliemann's death in 1890, Dörpfeld carried on the Troy excavations, and his hypothesis gained strength as the impressiveness of the few surviving areas of Troy VI was revealed. Along the southern edge of the mound, largely untouched by Schliemann's work gangs, he uncovered a massive city wall with projecting bastions and well-built houses that contained the typical Mycenaean-style pottery. The dating seemed to indicate that this was indeed the city sacked by the forces of Agamemnon, and the sheer scale of the fortifications of this period confirmed the Homeric connection in many scholars' minds. By the turn of the century, few doubted that Priam's city had, in fact, been located. But times changed—and so, inevitably, did scholarly convictions. In the 1930s, when an expedition from the University of Cincinnati went to the site to excavate what was left of the ruins, Troy VI fell out of favor, supplanted by the stratum above it. The ancient stories of the city's siege and conquest were now associated with Troy VIIa.

Carl Blegen, one of the directors of the Cincinnati excavations, believed that the impressive fortifications of Troy VI were destroyed by an earthquake, not human attackers. The jagged cracks in some of this city's massive towers and the precarious, backward tilt of a section of the citadel wall seemed to him to be beyond the power of an invasion force armed mainly with bronze spears and swords. Yet in the remains of the next city, VIIa, Blegen distinguished some evidence that *did* appear to represent the preparations for a long and bitter siege. The tightly packed houses along the inside of the fortification walls seemed to suggest the presence of a much larger population seeking shelter, and in many of the modest houses of this stratum were an unusually large number of storejars and silos— apparently for emergency supplies. And the pottery types of VIIa also seemed right from a chronological standpoint. Since the time of Schliemann and Dörpfeld, the study of Mycenaean pottery had advanced considerably, due in large measure to the work of Blegen himself. And since Blegen believed that the Trojan War took place at the height of Mycenaean power—before the events that destroyed the equilibrium of the Late Bronze Age civilizations of the eastern Mediterranean—it seemed significant to him that Troy VIIa contained examples of pottery of the fully developed Late Bronze Age Mycenaean style.

"It is Settlement VIIa, then," wrote Blegen, "that must be recognized as the actual Troy, the ill-fated stronghold, the siege and capture of which caught the fancy and imagination of contemporary troubadours and bards who transmitted orally to their successors their songs about the heroes who fought in the war." Schliemann's faith, though displaced by five levels, seemed validated by the results of the University of Cincinnati dig. The Troy of legend—shown so vividly in Georg Ludwig Jerrer's *History of the World for Children*— was also a city that could be dug up.

But the story didn't end with Blegen. Although the relevance of archaeological evidence to the Trojan War stories continued to be a matter of faith for all but the most hard-bitten of scholars, by the mid-1980s, a growing number of the faithful were returning to Troy VI as the city of myth. The Age of Blegen at Troy was over, and, appropriately enough for the new epoch that was dawning, an alternative version of the ancient story was presented to the public on their television screens. Michael Wood of the BBC thought Troy might be a good subject for a documentary series, and in his slick, chatty, and often romantic personal version, *In Search of the Trojan War*, he suggested that Blegen's theory about Troy VIIa and the

Trojan War was at least partially influenced by the ominous realities—not of the Late Bronze Age, but of the wars of the twentieth century.

In Blegen's earlier identification of the humble buildings, storejars, and silos of level VIIa, Wood suggested, "Blegen inferred a war economy like the soup kitchens during the Blitz of London, the images of his own day." That wasn't, of course, the only reason why Wood rejected Blegen's theory; the recent recognition by some scholars that Troy VIIa contained some pottery types that *postdated* the destruction of the Mycenaean palaces in Greece made an attack by Agamemnon's armies seem highly unlikely. And Wood showed how the earlier city, Troy VI, may have, after all, been destroyed by human attackers. If an earthquake caused damage to the fortifications, Wood suggested, it might merely have helped the Greek cause along.

Once again, the impressive bastions of Troy VI received the aura of legend, a legend updated in the electronic age. Wood offered what he called some "plausible hypotheses" for the historical reality that lay at the heart of the story. Yet it was difficult to avoid suspecting that Wood—like Blegen and Schliemann before him—was in some sense merely reflecting contemporary concerns.

Wood's "Plausible Hypothesis No. 1" suggested that the sack of Troy may have come as the result of imperialistic aggression of an ominously modern kind. "The defense budget is massive and rising," wrote Wood, placing himself in Agamemnon's situation room in the palace at Mycenae, "bronze—like oil today—never gets cheaper, and if there were economic problems, it might have been difficult to obtain. . . . The king needs a foreign war." "Plausible Hypothesis No. 2" suggested an equally modern situation: a superpower conflict between the Mycenaeans and the Hittites of Asia Minor. The area around Troy was "in the Hittite diplomatic orbit," Wood told his viewers in the tone of a network anchorman, "and any interference there—'destabilisation,' as the Americans would call it these days— had to be countered." And Wood's last and most sweeping hypothesis, characterizing the Trojan War as the last, violent gasp of the Aegean Late Bronze Age civilization, evoked the familiar nightmares of modern industrial society—scarcity of natural resources, intensifying exploitation of the working classes, and social upheaval—all summed up under the distinctly late-twentieth-century rubric of "systems collapse."

Seen from this perspective, the most recent change of theory still kept the legend of Troy alive in the minds of the believers, merely updating some of the details. In the Age of Television, social and economic problems—not the beauty of Helen—were offered as the reasons for the launching of a thousand ships. The archaeological controversy had not dimmed the ardor of the scholars and television viewers who *wanted* to believe in the basic historical truth of the epic. The changes of detail, the modernization of metaphor, made belief relatively easy. And it seemed likely that even more surprising changes of detail would come in the future.

In a 1984 symposium on the Trojan War at Bryn Mawr College, for instance, Professor Calvert Watkins of Harvard presented what might be a new avenue of speculation about Troy's historical connection to the famous myth. The implications of his translation and analysis of a fragmentary religious text of the Late Bronze Age were far-reaching. Found at Boğazköy, the ancient Hittite capital near modern Ankara, the text contained instructions for a cult ritual, accompanied by epic verses to be chanted by a choir. In one of the verses, perhaps even the opening, the choir sang, "When they came from steep Wilusa," a phrase uncannily similar to "steep Ilios," an epithet repeatedly used by Homer to describe Troy. Watkins speculated that the fragmentary text might represent the beginning of an ancient epic in the Luvian language, another mythic story of Troy, a "Wilusiad." Even more surprising was the apparent sixteenth-century B.C. date of this poem; it raised the possibility that a literary epic about Trojan heroes was *already* ancient and well known throughout Asia Minor in the Late Bronze Age.

If that was the case—although Watkins himself was still hesitant to draw any definite conclusions—then it might be futile for scholars to seek the legendary Troy at Hissarlik in either level VI or level VIIa. Its true place might lie centuries before those cities were constructed. Who knows? Some later generation of archaeologists—having the benefit of new discoveries and with new reasons to update the legend—might again be singing the praises of that archaeological hero Heinrich Schliemann, the farsighted discoverer of the *Early Bronze Age siege of Troy II.* . . .

So what was I to make of all the conflicting interpretations and meanings as I walked into the ruins of Hissarlik past the huge wooden horse? I didn't have an answer. Although my visit to the site gave me a clearer mental picture of the various points of archaeological contention, I found only the cartoon images of my childhood—overlaid with a harmless, if discordant, modern reality.

The ancient topography of Troy had been transformed beyond all recognition. From the steep city overlooking the plain and the coastline, it had become an earth-and-stone dump heap, marked here and there by high hillocks of unexcavated rubble and scarred by eroded excavation pits. The Turkish Ministry of Culture had done the best it could to lay out signposted paths through the desolation, but it had to contend with the fact that the archaeologists who dug here—like warriors attacking an enemy city—were less concerned with what would be left after their triumph than with the obstacles that stood in their way. Sound, well-meaning intentions there surely were at the time of the excavations, but it was difficult to find the evidence now. The neat cottage built as headquarters for the University of Cincinnati expedition had sometime later been used as a small museum. But now even that was closed.

The arrow signs pointed the way down the path toward the more famous ruins, and at the path's end, some of the ancient landmarks came into view. The city wall and towers of Troy VI were the most impressive remains left standing after all the years of digging, yet they now served as an attraction, not a defense against strangers—a convenient motif for postcards and ashtrays, and for tourist snapshots. As I wandered by the fine ashlar blocks that had been jarred from their original positions (either by an earthquake or by Agamemnon's forces) I heard soft, poetic voices. Three young American tourists with their backpacks stacked beside them were sitting cross-legged on top of one of the ruined bastions reading aloud from a paperback Penguin edition of the *Iliad*.

It was late in the afternoon and the site was nearly deserted. There were no guided tours to follow in order to eavesdrop on the local guides' rendition of the story of Troy II, VI, or VIIa. So I walked onward through the eastern gate of the city, up some cement steps, and past the tightly packed house ruins of level VIIa. Pieces of some of the famous storejars were now scattered throughout the area, haphazardly collapsed in the muddy debris. The natural forces of exposure and erosion had done them more damage than the armies of Agamemnon or subsequent human invaders could ever have done. Only imagination and a talent for reading the architectural plans in the guidebooks could summon up Blegen's images of the impending-siege terror of the Trojans. Only an innocent faith that *this* was the Troy of Homer could restore this city level to life.

Farther along the path of attractions, on the bare marble platform of the Temple of Athena, from the ninth and latest of Troy's levels, the panorama of the flat Trojan plain was strikingly scenic in the fading light of sunset. But that beautiful, peaceful scenery needed an overlay of personal memory to summon up the mythic dimension. Was it right there on the nearby coast that the Greek longships were beached? Was it there that the funeral pyres for the fallen heroes were built, and there that Odysseus came up with his cunning horse-trick?

Where could I find the rich and well-built city praised by the ancient poets? I continued along the marked tourist paths, but the few remaining buildings from Troy II didn't seem to fit. The tiny citadel of the Early Bronze Age now lay at the bottom of Schliemann's great trench, dwarfed by overhanging mounds of debris and rubble. I could make out the forms of some of the houses from the low ruins of their foundation walls, but those empty remains were just mute evidence waiting to be given a modern layer of significance. And the significance, for me, was quite different from what the Turkish Ministry of Culture apparently had intended. In the shade of overgrown weeds and a fig tree, a weathered sign read, SPOT WHERE THE TREASURE OF PRIAM WAS FOUND.

The excavations of Troy, I knew, were a triumph of determination and hard digging, but the inherited power of the myth and its heroes was never completely ignored. Behind the interpretations of Schliemann, Dörpfeld, and Blegen lay visions of what the famous city cunningly conquered by Agamemnon's forces *should* look like, and

I think it was the same with every visitor who walked through the site. The image of Troy in each person's mind was subconsciously fitted to the ambiguous archaeological picture. And it was a perfect fit more often than not.

Fortunately, despite the current archaeological wrangling, there wasn't much at stake now in the discovery and interpretation of Troy's ruins. While scholars might argue bitterly about Schliemann's penchant for exaggeration, and while they might debate the significance of the pottery types found in Hissarlik's various levels, it was the romantic story of ancient heroism and modern discovery that most tourists came to see. Troy was no longer a symbol of patriotism and sacrifice; it had become just a fairy tale clothed, for reality's sake, in soil and stone.

Its modern use was innocuous, even amusing. And maybe that's why, as I left the ruins and walked back toward the parking lot and souvenir shops, I found the modern Trojan Horse the most familiar and comforting landmark at the site. Here was a truly cartoonlike image; it had been thoughtfully equipped with a steep staircase and open windows from which visitors could pose for souvenir snapshots. And even late in the afternoon on a slow day at Hissarlik, it revealed one of the inevitable effects of Troy's modern archaeological discovery. A few travel-weary tourists—not conquering warriors or heroes—now filled the belly of the huge wooden horse.

3

CYPRUS

Patterns in a Mosaic

🁢 ". . . **B**ut laughter-loving Aphrodite went to Cyprus, to Paphos, where her sacred precinct and her fragrant altar lie," wrote Homer in his account of a mythic tale told to Odysseus during his wanderings after the Trojan War. I, too, went to the island of Cyprus, although it was not to fall prey to the charms of Cyprus's most famous goddess; it was the clash of the past and the present that I had come to see. Now, as always, that island was a meeting place of cultures—as well as Aphrodite's home. Lying just forty miles south of mainland Turkey, less than eighty miles from the coast of Lebanon, and within easy sailing distance of the Greek islands of the Aegean, Cyprus had, throughout its long history, been both blessed with a vibrant local culture and saddled by the regrettably frequent inclination of neighboring powers to dominate the island's cultural and economic life.

The remains of ancient Cypriot culture—and the cultures of successive conquerors—lay scattered and buried throughout the island, yet the conflict of external and internal forces did not end in a hazily remembered heroic age. In 1974, following a Turkish invasion of the northern third of the island, Cyprus was violently partitioned into Greek and Turkish enclaves, destroying the fragile balance of power between the island's two most important ethnic communities. A heavily guarded barbed-wire boundary arose along the cease-fire line, dividing the island and running through the narrow streets of Nicosia, its capital. The pain of partition was keenly felt on both sides of the border; save for occasional, unsuccessful attempts at negotiation, the segregation of the Greek and Turkish communities was complete. And here, as elsewhere, the past possessed an almost mystical significance in a time of modern crisis. For many Greek Cypriots, the island's archaeological heritage had long provided a tangible rallying point for the future, an anchor for civic pride and national identity. Since the establishment of the Republic of Cyprus in 1960, its Department of Antiquities had been active in the discovery, preservation, and display of the island's archaeological heritage. And even though the 1974 war and the Turkish invasion had resulted in the loss of jurisdiction over the many important archaeological sites in the northern part of the island, archaeological activity in the Republic of Cyprus had steadily expanded. The excavation—and resurrection—of important sites of ancient Cypriot civilization in the southern part of the island continued to be sources of national pride.

The city of Paphos on the island's southwestern coast possessed a particularly rich ancient tradition—and particularly impressive archaeological remains. And because of my continuing interest in the *modern* meaning and significance of traditions and ruins, Dr. Demetrios Michaelides was a person I wanted to see. As the Paphos District inspector for the Cyprus Department of Antiquities, Michaelides was responsible for overseeing the excavation, restoration, and preservation of every significant trace of ancient Cypriot culture over the entire western third of the island, from the Rock of Aphrodite—the goddess's legendary birthplace—on the southwest coast to the barbed-wire boundary of the Turkish enclave on the northwest. His office at the Paphos Museum was filled with some of the most important finds from the half-dozen foreign expeditions conducted within his district during the previous summer, as well as the finds from the dozens of excavations he had personally conducted in and around the city of Paphos. History came to Michaelides in fragments, and it was his responsibility to see that those fragments were fitted into a meaningful pattern for the people of Paphos today.

That task was especially difficult, for as I learned during my visit, Paphos was in the midst of a dramatic transformation that had begun soon after the 1974 war. With an influx of Greek refugees from areas occupied by the Turkish army, Paphos had begun to emerge from its traditional isolation to become one of Cyprus's most rapidly growing cities. The government of Cyprus had encouraged foreign investment and the construction of a new highway from Limassol, and the opening of an international airport had suddenly made Paphos readily accessible to the outside world. Local developers and businessmen had taken advantage of the changing conditions: Paphos's sandy shoreline, its city center, and its suburbs were quickly being filled with newly constructed villas, shopping centers, offices, condominiums, and apartment hotels.

Much of that widespread construction took place near the site of the ancient city of Nea Paphos, whose extensive outlying cemeteries and impressive fortifications showed that this was not the first time in Paphos's long history that the city had experienced a building boom. During the Hellenistic and Roman periods (ca. 300 B.C. through ca. A.D. 400), Paphos was one of the Mediterranean's richest and most famous harbor cities. Its praises were sung not only by Homer, but also by such other prominent ancient authors as Diodorus Siculus, Cicero, Strabo, and Tacitus; from the time of the Roman Emperor Augustus in 15 B.C., Paphos's civic institutions began to receive direct imperial patronage. From its status as a small, inland Cypriot kingdom, Paphos rapidly became an active participant in a close-knit trade and cultural network begun by the Greeks and later greatly expanded by the Romans throughout the eastern Mediterranean.

This process began around 320 B.C., when Nikokles, an ambitious and farsighted ruler of the Paphian kingdom, moved his court from the old inland capital to an unoccupied peninsula, where he directed the construction of city walls, public buildings, and modern port facilities. There were, of course, good reasons why Nikokles's development plans at Nea Paphos—"New Paphos"—succeeded. The nearby mountains were thickly forested with exceptionally fine cedar for shipbuilding; the lush coastal plain was the site of the famous temple to Aphrodite; and the new city's well-built breakwater and harbor installations made Paphos a strategic base and a vital point of communication for the Ptolemies of Egypt and, later, the Romans in their struggle for control of the Middle East.

Today, at a time when the strategic location of Cyprus is once again of great interest to superpowers, the remains of that earlier period of Paphos's greatness have been revealed by extensive archaeological work. And a brief stroll from Michaelides's office through the galleries of the Paphos Museum showed me how archaeologists working in the city and its immediate vicinity had pieced together a story of steady progress brought about through ever-widening connections with the outside world. Just beyond the entrance were the pots, flint tools, and stone idols of the region's first human inhabitants, identified by many scholars as migrants from Asia Minor, who settled in the deep inland valleys around 3000 B.C. Next came a collection of Cypriot Bronze Age pottery and evidence of renewed overseas links: wine-mixing bowls and oil containers from Mycenaean Greece. Most prominent, of course, were the artifacts from Paphos's time of greatest prosperity in the Hellenistic and Roman periods. Among them were bronze *strigils*, used by Greek athletes at the city's gymnasium for scraping sweat and grime from their bodies; a fragmentary marble statue of Aphrodite retrieved from the sea near the modern lighthouse; and a wide selection of Greek and Roman vases, coins, and jewelry.

When I had a chance to sit down with Michaelides and learn about his professional background, I realized how well it suited him for his present job. Although he was only about forty, his career had already taken him throughout the Mediterranean, and he had established a reputation as a specialist in Greek and Roman art. Born in Nicosia, he gained his archaeological training at the Courtauld Institute and the Institute of Archaeology at the University of London. Later he served as assistant director of the British School at Rome. In that position, he had directed excavations at Otranto in southern Italy, but even before that, he gained some formative archaeological experience as a staff member in the large-scale excavations of the city of Benghazi in Libya in the early 1970s. There, beneath Benghazi's modern street levels, he helped to uncover the remains of the Hellenistic and Roman city of Berenike, which, like Paphos, prospered through its international trading links. In fact, his work on the mosaics of ancient Berenike became the subject of his doctoral dissertation, and, subsequently, the focus of his professional career.

When Michaelides spoke to me about the changing styles of Hellenistic and Roman mosaics, I sensed that he was really talking about the changes in culture itself. By tracing the appearance and spread of particular mosaic motifs throughout the various cities of the Mediterranean, and by noting the relative skillfulness with which the *musivarii*, or mosaic makers, executed their designs, Michaelides believed that it might be possible to reconstruct patterns of economic and social change as well. Although Michaelides's work at Berenike was only the beginning of a lifelong study, his return to Cyprus and his appointment to the post of inspector at Paphos in 1982 was another important step. For a scholar interested in ancient mosaics, Paphos was the ideal place to work and study, for the lower part of the city down by the seashore—Kato, or "Lower," Paphos—had provided archaeologists with some of the most spectacular examples of Hellenistic and Roman mosaic pavements found anywhere in the Mediterranean world.

The story of the discovery of the Paphos mosaics has its own irony, and here, once again, I found the past and the present to be inextricably intertwined. In 1962, just two years after the Republic of Cyprus gained its independence from Great Britain, Kato Paphos remained much the same as it had been for centuries: Only barely connected to the upper town of Ktima, it was a quiet fishing village in which the areas of marshland and ruins were far larger than the part that was occupied. The stones of an ancient breakwater could still be seen rising from the sea at low tide, but the harbor itself no longer sheltered any craft more substantial than the local fishermen's boats. The flat plain that extended from the village of Kato Paphos to the seashore was used by the inhabitants mainly for small-scale farming and sheep raising. Except for occasional fragments of marble sculpture and inscriptions that were turned up during plowing, there were few visible signs of the prosperity of Nea Paphos, the ancient Greek city that once had flourished here. That is, until a local Turkish landowner decided to level his fields.

In previous years, this landowner had enjoyed the good fortune of finding many well-drafted stones just beneath the surface, but no one had paid much attention to these discoveries, for such stones could be found throughout Kato Paphos, and for centuries they had provided plentiful building material for new houses and terrace walls. But when the landowner brought in a bulldozer for the much larger clearing operations, a find was uncovered that not even he could ignore.

When the bulldozer's scoop dug into the earth, it was clear that something out of the ordinary was here. Clumps of mosaic tiles— some bearing human figures, birds, and grapevines—lay scattered along the first furrow of freshly turned soil. When the officers of the district museum arrived to inspect the damage and reported their findings to the headquarters of the Department of Antiquities in Nicosia, they received instructions to stop all work at the site immediately and to clear it carefully, on the chance that the floor could be restored. When they started to dig, the work quickly became overwhelming. The room containing the mosaic was only a small part of a huge building, and the adjoining rooms were also paved with mosaic tiles. In light of their quantity and quality, legal proceedings were initiated to declare the property a site of archaeological importance, and the assistant director of the Cyprus Museum, Dr. Kyriakos Nicolaou, was called in from Nicosia to take over the dig.

Nicolaou's excavations, which continued for the next sixteen years, provided the first hard evidence for the opulence of Nea Paphos's past. The structure, which Nicolaou named "The House of Dionysos," contained more than seventy rooms in its surviving first story, more than twenty of which were paved with elaborate mosaics. The residence was built according to an architectural plan that was common throughout the Roman Empire; its central feature was an ornamental pool called an *impluvium*, surrounded by a colonnaded portico. On the western side of this central area was a large *tablinum*—the salon and reception room of every Roman patrician's home. The House of Dionysos obviously had been the residence of one of Nea Paphos's most wealthy inhabitants, and Nicolaou believed that the mosaics found in it revealed his artistic tastes, religious background, and perhaps his profession as well.

The bulldozer, it seems, had come right down on the *tablinum*, and although much of its floor was irreparably damaged, the parts that remained or could be reconstructed prominently featured the god Dionysos, and so gave the house its working name. In the center of the floor was a lively scene of a grape harvest, surrounded on three sides by a border of grapevines, and on the fourth side by an elaborate scene of Dionysos's triumphal parade. The god of wine was obviously the patron of the residents of this villa; in the portico itself was a mosaic scene depicting the discovery of wine. On the left, Dionysos was shown, in accordance with the well-known legend, teaching the art of winemaking to the aged King Ikarios of Athens. On the right was an oxcart overloaded with bulging wineskins, and beyond, a depiction of the inevitable aftereffects of this technological breakthrough. Two shepherds, shown falling to the ground in a drunken stupor, were identified by a caption set in black tiles on the pavement as OI PROTOI OINON PIONTES—"the first drinkers of wine."

From the evidence of the style of the mosaics, Nicolaou suggested that the house was constructed in the late second or early third century A.D., and he further hypothesized that it was the residence of a wealthy winegrower or wine merchant whose cultural connections lay firmly with the traditions of the Greco-Roman world. As the excavation proceeded, the entire complex of rooms was uncovered and mapped, with the private living quarters surrounding another pool to the east and the kitchens and workshops to the northwest. In all of the rooms that were paved with mosaics, the classical influences were obvious—among them, the mythic scenes of Hippolytus and Phaedra, Ganymede and the Eagle, and Narcissus blissfully gazing at himself. And in the entrance hall on the southern side of the house, a mosaic welcome mat bore the wishes of a gracious host: KAI SY ("And you") CHAIRE ("be well").

The excavation of the House of Dionysos was just the beginning of discovery in Kato Paphos, for it made clear to both Cypriot and foreign scholars the extent of the ancient treasures that could be found just beneath the surface. In 1965, a second project was begun nearby with the arrival of an archaeological team from the Polish Center for Mediterranean Archaeology in Cairo, which had received a permit to excavate a plot of land that lay to the southwest of the House of Dionysos. The director of the Polish excavations, Dr. Kazimierz Michalowski, was certainly no stranger to impressive Roman architecture, having already excavated at Alexandria in Egypt and at

Palmyra in Syria, but his finds at Paphos matched any that he had uncovered previously. The structure that he and his colleagues excavated proved to be the largest of its kind ever found on Cyprus, and in it were fragments of marble statuary and more of the elaborate mosaic pavements, which provided the building's cultural connections and date.

This structure clearly was not a private residence, but a public building. Around the four sides of a huge open courtyard or parade ground were complexes of distinct architectural units, including a monumental gateway on the eastern façade, a complete bathhouse on the southeast, and, in the center of the southern wing, a large reception room that terminated in a semicircular apse. As Dr. Wiktor Daszewski—who succeeded Michalowski as the director of the Polish excavations—searched for architectural parallels with other Roman buildings excavated around the Mediterranean, he eventually came to the conclusion that this structure was probably the residence and administrative headquarters of the Roman governors of Cyprus, who controlled the island's resources from the time of the Roman conquest in 58 B.C. until the shifting of the capital to the city of Salamis— just north of modern Famagusta—sometime during the fourth century A.D.

Here, too, the mosaic floors and their motifs suggested a modern archaeological name for this structure: "The Villa of Theseus." Along the entire southern edge of the courtyard ran a long, geometric-patterned mosaic that ended in a small chamber with a circular mosaic depiction of Theseus killing the Minotaur. And in the southern wing, in the central apse that Daszewski subsequently suggested might be the official reception room of the governor, was a scene showing the infant Achilles's first bath, watched proudly by his mother, Thetis, and his father, Peleus, and attended by two servant girls suggestively named Anatrophe and Ambrosia—"Upbringing" and "Immortality."

The discoveries at both the House of Dionysos and the Villa of Theseus provided Kato Paphos with its first two tourist attractions, and the officials of the Cyprus Department of Antiquities subsequently built protective roofs over the mosaics to ensure their preservation and appreciation by a growing stream of foreign visitors. But beyond the advantages for Paphos's tourist industry, the mosaic houses gave the local Greek population a tangible point of identification with their ancient cultural heritage. And in the summer of 1974, when the Turkish army was staging its amphibious landings on the northern coast of the island, the antiquities of Paphos gained a modern symbolic significance as well. A squadron of jet fighters of the Turkish air force swooped down over Kato Paphos, dropping bombs on the customs house and the medieval fort in the area of the harbor, and then on the mosaics in the House of Dionysos.

As I drove down toward the seashore with Demetrios Michaelides, I would never have suspected that the mosaics of Kato Paphos had been the focus of international conflict, at least from the surface appearance of things. The mosaics in the House of Dionysos had been completely restored and were now protected inside an impressive, villalike structure, far more substantial than the corrugated metal roof that shielded them before the Turkish attack. As we parked the car and walked through the nearby excavation areas to see the progress of the current digging, I discovered that the emphasis now was on a concerted, international effort to integrate the antiquities into the development of the modern city—not just to encourage additional excavations and the discovery of isolated, spectacular finds.

In its own way, this change in attitude came as a result of the Turkish bombing and the symbolic danger to the archaeological heritage caused by the Turkish occupation of northern Cyprus. With the antiquities sites in the northern part of the island beyond the control of the Department of Antiquities, intense efforts had been underway since 1974 to protect, preserve, and restore the most important sites over which the Republic of Cyprus government still had authority. This effort was not the project of the Greek Cypriots alone; the war damage to the mosaics began a process of international involvement in the archaeological exploration of Paphos. The reconstruction of the shelter over the House of Dionysos was, in fact, financed by the United Nations High Commissioner for Refugees. And in 1981, UNESCO entered the picture. After having sent a team of mosaic restoration experts to repair the war damage, the officials of that international organization responded with interest to a request by the government of Cyprus to include Paphos on UNESCO's

"World Heritage List." Although the mosaics were, at that time, the most impressive of the discoveries at Nea Paphos, they were not the only reason for the ancient city's inclusion in the worldwide effort to preserve outstanding archaeological monuments. Equally important was the role that Nea Paphos had played in the history, commerce, culture, and religion of the ancient Mediterranean world. After repeated visits of international experts and complicated negotiations over funding, UNESCO helped the Cyprus Department of Antiquities draw up a master plan for the protection and preservation of the city's antiquities.

As a first step in that wide-ranging program, Michaelides had undertaken the task of clearing the line of the ancient city walls. All around the area of modern Kato Paphos, vertically cut outcrops of bedrock marked the boundaries of the city's fortifications, established and maintained from the fourth century B.C. to the seventh century A.D. Over the intervening millennia, with the decline of the city, those ramparts had been filled with rubbish. Now Michaelides was supervising its clearance with a combination of careful excavation and the use of heavy earthmoving equipment. This project was intended to mark the boundaries of the planned archaeological park, but from another perspective, the raising of the city walls seemed to possess a clear modern significance—as an ironic repeat performance of the first act of King Nikokles when he established the city here in the fourth century B.C.

Just inside the line of fortifications lay the vast, empty fields of the northern section of Nea Paphos, which had gradually been purchased from their owners over the previous ten years by the Department of Antiquities. Chance finds and occasional excavations here had underlined this area's archaeological importance. On the plain below the hill on which a modern lighthouse stood—a hill that may have been the site of the ancient city's acropolis—the remains of the city's agora, or marketplace, had been partially excavated, and a nearby Roman-period odeion had been uncovered and restored for the presentation of modern performances. The discovery of an inscription that described the honors bestowed on the city's *gymnasiarch*—the director of the municipal gymnasium—was a clear indication that the most characteristic structure of every proper Hellenistic and Roman city could also be found somewhere in the immediate vicinity.

There were certainly indications of impressive ancient structures throughout the area. More than twenty years of excavation in Kato Paphos had taught the archaeologists working there how to recognize potential finds. As we walked across the open area, Michaelides pointed out to me that the surface there was noticeably uneven, a sure sign of buried walls. And if that weren't enough of an indication, the entire area was littered with ancient architectural elements. But Michaelides assured me that there were no immediate plans for excavation, no matter how promising the prospects. The Department of Antiquities was no longer reacting to sudden, unexpected discoveries. By purchasing the land and preventing construction, it had protected ancient Nea Paphos from any possible damage. There would be plenty of opportunity to uncover ancient monuments when the UNESCO master plan reached a more advanced stage.

That was not to say that no digging was going on in Kato Paphos; when we had first approached the area of the mosaic houses, I could see the steady progress that had been made in recent years. In addition to the excavation of remains from the Hellenistic and Roman eras, archaeological research had also concentrated on the later periods of the city's history. Near the church of Ayia Kyriaki within the built-up area of Kato Paphos, Athanasios Papageorgiou, the Department of Antiquities' curator of ancient monuments, had uncovered a succession of Byzantine churches beneath a level of Crusader structures. And at the mound of ruins known as *Saranda Kolones*— "The Forty Columns"—A.H.S. Megaw, the last British director of the Cyprus Department of Antiquities, had returned to complete his excavation of the Crusader castle that had dominated the harbor area in the twelfth century A.D.

For Demetrios Michaelides, though, the heart of the matter was still in the classical periods, and he led me to a fenced-in plot of land just to the west of the Villa of Theseus to show me the results of an excavation he had been conducting for three years. The fact that ancient mosaics could be found all over the area of Nea Paphos was certainly no secret; as early as 1942, a detachment of British troops stationed by the seashore was digging an air-raid shelter on this spot when the men uncovered an elaborate pavement depicting Hercules and the Nemean Lion, which they were instructed to re-cover. In 1962, during the excavations at the House of Dionysos, Kyriakos Nicolaou made some preliminary efforts to find that mosaic, but instead found another one—depicting an Amazon standing by her horse. It was only in 1978, with renewed excavations, that Nicolaou realized that *both* of those panels belonged to a single mosaic floor that had been executed with an artistry rivaling the pavements in the other mosaic houses of Nea Paphos.

When Michaelides took over the position of district inspector in 1982, that mosaic floor was something of an orphan—photographed and published by Nicolaou in various scholarly journals, but still lacking an architectural and historical context. For a mosaic specialist such as Michaelides, this was a personal challenge, a chance to fit this floor into the pattern of Paphos's cultural history that the other mosaic houses had already provided. And after three seasons of digging, "The House of Orpheus," as he now called it, was no longer an orphan. The pavement depicting the Amazon and Hercules proved to be just a side hall in another spacious Roman house, which was, like the House of Dionysos, built around an *impluvium* and a peristyle. In one of the rooms that led from this central area, Michaelides uncovered the elaborate mosaic floor that provided this house with its name.

According to Michaelides, the first elements to emerge were the animals. Clearing the mosaic inward from its edges, he distinguished depictions of a fox, bear, boar, bull, leopard, lion, partridge, tiger, deer, snake, eagle, and peacock—as well as the badly damaged remains of the depictions of two more birds. The individual members of this ancient menagerie seemingly had little to do with each other; each was shown almost as a cutout, with no attempt at a common background. But when Michaelides found the serene, stately image of Orpheus playing his harp at the center, the message of this mosaic became clear. Orpheus, according to the myth recorded by the Greek poet Pindar, was the greatest musician of all times. His harp was given to him personally by the god Apollo, and with it, Orpheus could make even wild beasts stop their fighting and sit quietly by his feet.

By the third century A.D., when the House of Orpheus was last occupied, the myth of Orpheus was interpreted in various ways. For some, it symbolized civilization's ability to still human passions. For others, it represented the triumph of Roman civilization over the world's "barbaric" peoples. And for yet others—probably the vast majority, according to Michaelides—scenes of Orpheus and the Animals provided a convenient artistic convention for displaying the same kinds of wild and exotic animals that were such popular attractions for spectacle and bloody combat in circuses and amphitheatres throughout the Roman Empire.

Michaelides realized that this mosaic might offer some indication of the extent of Roman prestige and power in Cyprus in this period, for the House of Orpheus itself lay in the shadow of the looming Roman governor's palace, just to the east. A significant clue, in fact, lay above Orpheus's head, near the top of the mosaic. The name of the person who had commissioned the decorative flooring was spelled out in Greek letters formed by black and red tiles. This was the first discovery of a homeowner's name in ancient Nea Paphos, and the name was clearly not of local origin.

The three-part Latin name, signifying its bearer's full Roman citizenship, was Gaius Pinnius Restitutus—perhaps, Michaelides suggested, a high Roman official or functionary who served in the Cypriot port. This example of the elaborate mosaic art of the city, although almost certainly conceived and pieced together by local Cypriot craftsmen, was meant to please a distinctly foreign taste. By the late second century A.D., the initiative of King Nikokles had long since faded into legend; it was *Roman* officials and merchants who now built their elegant homes in the wealthiest quarters of the ancient Cypriot city by the sea.

Michaelides had no simple explanation for the sudden destruction and abandonment of the House of Orpheus. As we stood in the empty, roofless rooms of the villa, surrounded by the mounds of excavated rubble, I couldn't help wondering whether the ancient destruction of this house and the rest of Nea Paphos wasn't—at least in some way—as significant as its fabled rise. Michaelides and his workers had, after all, begun to remove the tons of collapsed stone, broken pottery, and ash that covered the House of Orpheus, in order to reconstruct the villa's elegant architectural plan and to study its elaborate mosaic floors. And, as he readily admitted, neither the structure's ground plan nor its history was yet clear. Nonetheless, it seemed to me that the rubble of destruction that covered the villa might be something more than a mere archaeological obstruction. Could it, in some way, explain the ultimate consequences of the ancient municipal success story now being so eagerly memorialized?

Michaelides shook his head as he answered, quietly acknowledging that such sweeping questions may lie beyond the reach of modern archaeology. "We suspect that a severe earthquake struck Paphos sometime in the middle of the third century A.D.," he told me, "and since that date matches the date of the latest pottery types we found here, I suppose that the destruction should be connected to that event."

Somehow, that seismic deus ex machina seemed to be a convenient evasion. And in his tone of honest uncertainty, Michaelides almost admitted as much. The contrast between the elegant mosaics and the rubble that covered them was too stark for such a neat explanation. A sudden natural disaster alone did not explain why the wealthy Roman owners of the House of Orpheus did not return to their prized seaside location once the tremors had subsided. It didn't explain why the wealthy patricians of Paphos suddenly lost the determination—or the resources—to clear away the rubble and rebuild.

As we walked toward the car and passed the tour buses parked outside the House of Dionysos, I realized that something might be painfully missing from Paphos's presentation of its past. The portrait drawn there was of serene, almost static opulence, unchallenged by the vast majority of the people—the slaves, the women, the vinetenders, and even the poor drunkards who made it all possible. The message of the archaeological work in Nea Paphos was like a fairy tale, with all the unpleasantness of urban prosperity—both in the past and in the present—neatly concealed.

Only the wealthy owners of villas were represented, and, except for natural disasters, their position was secure. No social unrest was ever suggested as a reason for the destruction of their elegant houses, nor was the changing status of elites within the Roman Empire. Social explanations could only dim the radiance of Paphos's "golden age"— in the present as well as the past. The message conveyed to every visitor to ancient Paphos—and to those who would flock there when the restoration of the entire ancient city was completed—seemingly enshrined urbanization as a timeless virtue. And it suggested that Paphos's prosperity, once obtained, was somehow created without the constant labor of slaves, women, and workers, and that it was vulnerable only to acts of God. In fact, the archaeological picture provided by the already excavated remains of Nea Paphos offered a strange parallel to the advertising strategy of the local real estate developers who were building and selling vacation homes to foreign visitors in modern Paphos and its vicinity.

Of course I understood that this archaeological reconstruction was not *intentionally* meant to mislead visitors to Paphos. It was, as Michaelides later insisted to me, exactly what the tourists wanted to see. If one of the objectives of Paphos's modern development plans was the encouragement of income-producing tourism, then it was important, Michaelides suggested, to provide them with archaeo-logical attractions that stimulated their aesthetic sense and their historical imagination. The poor shacks of Nea Paphos's workers, servants, and slaves would never make an impression. "Even in an opulent house like the House of Dionysos," Michaelides related from personal experience, "the ordinary visitor does not stop to look at the bedrooms, which have ordinary floors of beaten earth."

I couldn't blame Michaelides for following the lead of the other scholars who had worked in the ruins of Nea Paphos. The rubble and debris of destruction overlying the Villa of Theseus and the House of Dionysos was as thick and dramatic as that which covered the House of Orpheus, and similar archaeological explanations pre-vailed. According to the excavators, both sites were ultimately de-stroyed by earthquakes. And both were abandoned by their owners, briefly occupied by poor squatters, then deserted forever to become covered with soil and overgrown with weeds.

Beyond the earthquakes and shattered walls, there was, of course, a wider context for the decline of Nea Paphos. By the late fourth century A.D., the Roman world had undergone a far-reaching transformation—in the acceptance of Christianity in place of classical traditions and, perhaps even more important, in the progressive breakdown of the Hellenistic and Roman overseas trade. The prosperity of Paphos, like that of the other Mediterranean harbor cities, was based on its vital economic connections, and when those networks began to disintegrate, natural disasters such as earthquakes might merely have helped the disintegration along.

In the fourth century A.D., the capital of Cyprus was shifted from Paphos to Salamis, a city located more advantageously to support itself on the agricultural produce of the island's rich eastern plain. And from that time, when agricultural self-sufficiency became more important than overseas commerce, the position of Paphos changed. No longer a city, it declined in importance to outsiders, but nonetheless remained a living community. And in that modest, yet self-sufficient existence, it eventually became the quiet fishing village seen by the officers and commercial agents of the British Empire when their Mediterranean fleet dropped anchor off the southwestern coast of Cyprus in 1799.

The archaeological rediscovery of Paphos's early period of expansion in the Hellenistic and Roman periods may not have been just an esoteric archaeological subject, neatly confinable to a remote and elegant past. In a metaphorical way, it both mimicked and justified Paphos's modern development. The arrival of the British fleet at the very end of the eighteenth century and their de facto annexation of Cyprus in 1878 as a strategic Middle Eastern outpost were the first steps in a process of growing economic and cultural connections to the West, a process that would ultimately result in Paphos's renaissance—some might say "coming back to life"—in the twentieth century.

For like King Nikokles in the fourth century B.C., the nineteenth-century British administrators of Paphos saw that its future lay in foreign connections. In 1891, the first modern carriage road was paved to connect the upper town with the harbor, and in 1908, the harbor itself was thoroughly dredged. Many years would pass before Paphos would have an international airport and be closely connected to the industrialized economies of the West. But the steadily increasing impact on Paphos of Western cultural traditions—among them, Western archaeological and historical understandings—was a clear sign that "Hellenization" in its modern incarnation was coming again to the city of Paphos.

Was this a rebirth or an externally imposed transformation? The answer to that probably depended on where the observer stood. For many of the inhabitants of the fishing village of Kato Paphos, their fate was removal—sometimes with handsome compensation, sometimes with none. By the 1980s, the once-quiet area of fields and pastures down by the seashore had become the preserve of a new elite of contractors, businessmen, and foreign developers. The archaeologists, too, had played an important ideological role in this transformation. Their discoveries, restored and presented to the public, helped to enshrine wealth and foreign connections as the cornerstones of Paphos's history.

But being a part of an international economy naturally required a certain payment, and, for Paphos, that cost was being exacted in the loss of its identity. The new beachfront hotels, the shopping malls, the vacation villas, and even the carefully restored historical monuments—all were characteristic artifacts of twentieth-century industrial society. And, as in the past, the same sources that offered Paphos its prosperity now also threatened to overwhelm it with imported myths, histories, and styles. In that respect, the last piece to be fitted into Paphos's archaeological pattern was the ultimate significance of the ongoing archaeological work itself.

Mosaics, once smashed, could be fitted together in new and different patterns. But for me, the ultimate significance of the restoration of ancient Nea Paphos remained disturbingly unclear. Were the ancient mosaic houses meant to become just stage scenery for a myth of urban rebirth and elegant living in the twentieth century? Or was there a lesson to be learned from the ancient city's rise *and* fall? It remained an open question, for me at least, whether the archaeological activity in Paphos would be merely another form of cultural assimilation, or whether Demetrios Michaelides and the other archaeologists working in Paphos could enable its modern inhabitants to maintain their own identity in the midst of Paphos's second great boom.

4

CYPRUS

Crusaders, Venetians, and Sugar Cane

◙ Just a few miles to the east of the outskirts of Paphos, the impact of modernization was more difficult to recognize. Off the main road to Limassol and up a hill overlooking the coast, the village of Kouklia was quiet. Its narrow streets and houses seemed ominously empty. Only the distant shouts of children playing and the muffled hum of the traffic passing on the highway broke the silence of the late autumn afternoon. Throughout the courtyards and open areas of the village, dark brown piles of grapes were drying and wrinkling into raisins; harvest time was already over here. The sun's glare reflected brilliantly off the calm Mediterranean and a pall-like haze of humidity rose from the coastal plain. I followed the signs through the narrow streets and past whitewashed houses to Kouklia's most famous tourist attraction. Just beyond the southern outskirts of the village were the ruins of the ancient Temple of Aphrodite, a sprawl of exposed pavements, weathered column bases, and massive stone blocks set on their ends along the low foundation walls. Yet the ruins of this famous ancient site of worship and pilgrimage seemed somehow out of place in this modern Cypriot village. Their impressiveness and historical reputation seemed discordant with Kouklia's modern realities.

A busload of French tourists was following their guide through the ruins, dutifully listening to a description of the importance of the cult of Aphrodite throughout antiquity. Here at the ancient temple, the guide explained, lay the "fragrant altar" described by Homer, and nearby on the coastline was the spot at which Aphrodite herself had emerged from the sea. The remains of Aphrodite's temple here at the site of the ancient city of Paleapaphos ("Old Paphos"), she continued, bore traces of the veneration of pilgrims from all over the Mediterranean for hundreds of years. From the Hellenistic period to the advent of Christianity, an annual procession of priests and supplicants would wind its way along the coast and up to this temple, bearing gifts of incense and sweet flowers to the goddess of love. The temple area had been continuously expanded and embellished by the reverent gifts of Hellenistic kings and Roman emperors, who built colonnades and paved courtyards. But only ruins now remained.

I had visited Kouklia twice in previous years with other archaeologists and with specific archaeological questions in mind. On an earlier visit, I had met the current excavators, Professor Franz Georg Maier and Dr. Marie-Louise von Wartburg of the University of Zürich, and had listened to their description of the site's early history. Few historical questions had been answered conclusively, but the Bronze Age origins of the temple seemed quite clear. According to legend, Old Paphos had been founded by King Agapenor, the leader of a contingent in Agamemnon's forces, on his way home from the Trojan War. And the hundreds of Mycenaean pottery fragments uncovered in the temple and in the tombs of the vicinity offered a clear confirmation of the site's connection with the culture of Bronze Age Greece. My archaeological questions to Maier had all been about those Mycenaean finds and Mycenaean connections; I had, at the time, no interest in, nor even an awareness of, the potential modern implications of his archaeological work. In one of his reports, however, he had hinted at a survival of the ancient tradition. The prayers and candles offered by the village women at a huge stone of the temple ruins—which they identified as *Panayia Galatariotissa*, or "the Milk-Giving Virgin"—seemed to be a faint echo of the ancient worship of Aphrodite as a mistress of fertility.

But now I had a different reason for coming to Kouklia; in the years since my first visit, I had learned that Maier and von Wartburg had discovered what might be a more significant link between Kouklia's past and present than even the veneration of its timeless goddess could provide. Although the digging season was over and they would not return until the following summer, I had come to see for myself the recently excavated ruins in both the temple and the vicinity of the village that had begun to shed new light on a long-overlooked facet of Cypriot archaeology. As Maier and von Wartburg had recognized, the history of Kouklia did not end with the abandonment of Aphrodite's temple—even though the interest of most archaeologists did.

In an effort to complete the archaeological picture from the Bronze Age to the present, they had not neglected the remains of more recent periods—"recent" at least by the standards of Near Eastern archaeology. Their excavations at Kouklia had revealed some surprising evidence of the agricultural life and economics of the village in a period when the Temple of Aphrodite had long been a ruin—during the Crusader period on Cyprus (A.D. 1192–1489), when the island was a family fief of the Lusignan "Kings of Jerusalem." The island of Cyprus, no less than the Holy Land, had become deeply enmeshed in the violent medieval struggles between European Crusaders, Byzantine emperors, and Muslim sultans for control of the Middle East. Conquered first from its Byzantine overlords in 1191 by Richard the Lion-Hearted, Cyprus briefly passed to the control of the Knights Templar and then to the family and followers of Guy de Lusignan, an embattled French nobleman whose claim to the throne of Jerusalem had been made hollow with the fall of the Holy City in 1187 to the forces of Saladin.

Guy's successors, a long line of French kings of the Lusignan line who stubbornly clung to the title of "King of Jerusalem," maintained their realm on Cyprus long after all of the Crusaders' territorial possessions in the Holy Land itself had been wrested away. Cyprus was the last major outpost of Crusader rule in the eastern Mediterranean, yet the discovery of archaeological finds from this period at Kouklia had a significance that far transcended the Lusignan era. Far more suggestive were their long-range economic implications: Maier and von Wartburg believed they had found evidence of a profound change that took place at this village—and across the entire island of Cyprus—that would affect the lives of its people for centuries to come.

That change was the widespread cultivation and processing of sugar cane, a lucrative commercial activity extensively documented in Lusignan court records and in the account books of the Venetians, who took over the island in 1489. Medieval historians had long been aware of its importance; for nearly 300 years—from around A.D. 1300 until the Ottoman conquest in 1571—"Cyprus" was synonymous with "sugar" in the eastern Mediterranean, and the impressive Crusader castles and cathedrals all over the island were clear evidence of the prosperity brought by the sugar-cane industry. Yet until Maier and von Wartburg's recent excavations at Kouklia, no archaeological remains of the island's medieval sugar industry had ever been thoroughly excavated and studied. No archaeologist had ever investigated the importance and impact of sugar—or, for that matter, any other cash crop in the development of Cypriot society. And although I initially assumed that this subject was no more than a brief historical footnote of no relevance to the present, the surprising discoveries of Maier and von Wartburg showed how the meteoric rise and catastrophic fall of medieval sugar production on Cyprus might offer a new perspective on the island's economic role in *many* periods of its history.

Crusader sugar was not Maier and von Wartburg's original incentive for digging at Kouklia. Like all their archaeological predecessors at the site, they were experienced classical scholars and were primarily interested in tracing the architectural history of the Temple of Aphrodite when they began extensive excavations there in 1973. At that time, the later eras of the site's history were considered to be of little or no archaeological significance. The earlier European excavators who dug at Kouklia in the nineteenth century had offered only brief, passing comments on the fragments of medieval pottery found in the uppermost levels of the temple ruins, or on the standing remains of a Gothic-style manor house nearby. Yet as Maier and von Wartburg cleared the surface of a previously unexcavated part of the ancient sanctuary, they recognized the overlooked archaeological richness of Kouklia's later history. Digging just below the surface, they quickly came upon masses of unusual and distinctive pottery vessels that gave an unexpected direction to their work.

Scattered throughout the area were fragments of hundreds of narrow clay jars and funnel-shaped "sugar cones"—containers into which the boiled syrup of sugar cane was poured and crystallized in a method of production described extensively in medieval texts. The previous explorers of the site had also found many examples of these in and around the temple, but in their haste to get down to the lower levels, they had failed to recognize the potential importance of this discovery. At the time of the 1888 excavations by the British-sponsored Cyprus Exploration Fund, the medieval remains overlying the ancient temple were even more extensive, yet they were regarded as an unpleasant obstruction that prevented easy access to the museum-quality finds below. The buildings of the Middle Ages, callously dismissed as just "a farm or monastery," were dismantled and completely removed. In retrospect, that clearing operation caused irreparable archaeological damage, for the cones, jars, and medieval stone structures were evidence of an important period in Kouklia's history—when it served as the center of an extensive Crusader sugar plantation and refinery.

Later generations of archaeologists in Europe and America came to recognize the value of industrial installations, and in the twentieth century, the burgeoning study of "industrial archaeology" began to shed new light on the technological development of Western civilization at such relatively unromantic locales as the ruins of watermills, foundries, factories, and plantation sites. In the Middle East and the classical world, little attention was paid to such monuments of drudgery; the myths and the heroic histories of the region provided a more romantic context for the archaeological work. Yet at Kouklia, the advantages of industrial archaeology were obvious, for Maier and von Wartburg had unwittingly selected an excavation area where the medieval remains provided an indication of the extent and complexity of the sugar industry on Cyprus.

They soon uncovered a kiln for the on-site production of the sugar cones and jars, and nearby, the specialized installations for another stage in the refining process. A series of stone platforms—previously identified as the bases for a Roman colonnade—seemed in fact to be the supports for the huge copper cauldrons used for boiling the sugarcane syrup. And the hearth emplacements were clearly part of an even larger system; a plaster-lined channel running through the temple ruins from a main aqueduct had provided the medieval sugar refiners with a steady supply of water for their industrial-scale boilery.

The discovery of the medieval sugar refinery in the ruins of the Temple of Aphrodite was just a beginning. As Maier and von Wartburg traced the line of the ruined aqueduct across the modern Paphos-Limassol highway down toward the coastal plain, they began to recognize the full extent of the medieval sugar plantation at Kouklia. At a distance of nearly a mile from the manor house and the main refinery, they discovered two ruined mill structures that had been powered by the downward rush of water from the main aqueduct. Around these ruined buildings lay thousands of clay jars and sugar-cone fragments scattered in the rubble and weeds. And as the excavation of the two mill structures proceeded, the story of Cypriot sugar began to take on a significance of more obvious relevance to modern Cyprus than the romantic dreams of Aphrodite's temple in the Hellenistic and Roman periods. The finds offered a vivid object lesson in economic development by providing some surprising evidence of the technological sources of the medieval Cypriot sugar industry, its main product, and perhaps even the reason for its final collapse.

In order to appreciate the significance of the finds at Kouklia, it's important to keep in mind just how exotic and unfamiliar sugar was to most Europeans of the Crusader period. Today, we live in a world sweetened from breakfast to bedtime with sugar, but it wasn't always that way. Until the late Middle Ages, honey was the main sweetening agent in Europe, and the products produced from the cane stalks of *Saccharum officinarum*—a plant native to India and Southeast Asia—were almost entirely unknown.

Burchard of Mount Zion, a German monk who traveled to the Holy Land in the thirteenth century, provided one of the earliest European accounts of sugar manufacture, an account that is noteworthy for its mix of fascination and surprise. Enumerating the strange plants cultivated by the Palestinian peasantry, Burchard noted that "sugar canes also grow there. These are like common canes only bigger. Within they are hollow, but full of a porous substance like that which one finds in rods of elder wood." Of no less interest to Burchard was the ingenious process by which the sugar was extracted, a process that he apparently watched himself. "The canes are gathered," the German monk continued, "cut in lengths of half a palm, and so are crushed in the press. The juice squeezed out of them is boiled in copper boilers, and, when thickened, is collected in baskets made of slender twigs. Soon after this it becomes dry and hard, and this is how sugar is made. Before it dries, a liquor oozes from it, called honey of sugar, which is very delicious and good for flavoring cakes. . . ."

Burchard's first encounter with the seductive charms of sugar took place in the Jordan Valley, then under Crusader rule. Beyond the boundaries of the Kingdom of Jerusalem, however, the manufacturing process was far more advanced. In most parts of the Islamic world, specially manufactured sugar cones—not crude twig baskets—were used to mold the crystallizing sugar into standardized, conical sugar "loaves." Matching clay jars collected what Burchard called "honey of sugar"—a by-product of the production process better known today as molasses.

The reason for the technological sophistication lay in the sheer scale of consumption, since for the confectioners and dessert lovers of the Islamic world, sugar's attractions were not nearly so surprising as they had been to the naïvely curious German monk. By the thirteenth century A.D., sugar refining was one of the major agricultural industries of the Middle East. Having first spread from India and Persia with the Muslim conquests, sugar had established an unrivaled reputation as a delicacy for both royal and common tables, and it was consumed in enormous quantities. By Burchard's time, it had become a standard feature of the lavish feasts and public celebrations of the Mamluk sultans of Egypt. At that time, the court in Cairo alone—according to the medieval Egyptian historian al-Maqrizi—consumed nearly three hundred tons of sugar a month.

This huge demand for sugar provided the economic raison d'être for extensive and elaborate irrigation systems, mills, and boileries throughout the Islamic world. Cultural and culinary barriers, however, initially hindered its spread to Europe; the Crusaders in the

Holy Land merely taxed the sugar refineries they found already operating there without developing much of a sweet tooth themselves. Maier and von Wartburg have come to believe that sugar production may have started on Cyprus in the early thirteenth century, but it was only after the destruction of the Crusader kingdom in Palestine in 1291 and the exile of the remaining princes and nobles to Cyprus that the Crusaders began to be involved in sugar. And even then, it was apparently not because of their own craving for sweetness, but because of an unusually sweet business opportunity.

"I came near a castle called Baffa, in the lordship of the king of Cyprus," wrote the Italian traveler Nicolai de Marthono in 1394, "in which castle is made a great quantity of sugar." It was clear that by Marthono's time—a century after Burchard—sugar was no longer a strange and exotic substance to Europeans, but a well-known trade commodity. Even though the Crusaders' calls for a new campaign to conquer the Holy Land were growing increasingly hollow, their economic involvement with Middle Eastern products had steadily intensified. Italian trading vessels now crisscrossed the eastern Mediterranean, unloading and picking up cargoes at ports controlled by the Mamluk rulers of Egypt. The boundary between Islam and Christendom had now been transformed into an arena of economic interaction—one in which sugar played an important role. In fact, one of the most famous Italian merchant handbooks of this period, *La Pratica della Mercatura*, written by the Florentine banker and international commodities trader Francesco Balducci Pegolotti, described three distinct grades of Cypriot sugar, their market value determined by the thoroughness of the refining process.

The most expensive sugar type was known as *muccaro* (from the Arabic word *mukarrar*, "refined"), produced from syrup that had been boiled three times. Slightly less expensive were the types produced from two boilings of syrup, among them *musciatto* (from the Arabic *muwassat*, "medium" grade). And the cheapest of all was the simple, crushed crystal sugar, *polvere di zucchero* (in Arabic, *qand*—the source of the English word *candy*), which was boiled only once.

The production and sale of these various grades of sugar supported the splendor and pomp of the Lusignan court at Nicosia, and its apparent profitability eventually brought the Venetians themselves into the production of sugar. First merely serving as agents and shippers for the Crusader kings of Cyprus, Venetian merchants were later granted some of the vast Cypriot plantations as private concessions; in that position, they came into direct conflict with the royal authorities. The most serious dispute, according to the legal archives of the Republic of Venice, occurred in 1468, when the officers of King James II of Cyprus diverted the water supply from the plantation of the Venetian Cornaro family at Episkopi to the neighboring royal sugar plantation at Kolossi, resulting in the destruction of the Venetians' entire crop and in a continuing legal dispute. But as the medieval records also revealed, the struggle for sugar could sometimes be bitter for the losers. In this case, the Crusaders were the losers, and the Cornaros eventually got their revenge.

Less than five years after the "sugar war" at Episkopi, King James II—seeing that his rule over the island was endangered by the hostile advance of the Mamluks of Egypt and by continuing conflict with the merchants of the Italian city-states—recognized that he needed an ally. A successful appeal for the diplomatic, economic, and military support of the Venetians, however costly to his honor and independence, would offer him at least a chance to keep his throne. So, forced by the unpleasant reality of his weakened position, the king married Caterina Cornaro, the teenage daughter of the prominent Venetian family, and made her, as it turned out, Cyprus's last queen. In 1489, after the death of James and the utter collapse of Lusignan power, she was persuaded by her Venetian friends and relatives to turn the island over to the Republic of Venice. The descendants of the Crusader nobility remained on the island, but their influence was eclipsed by a new class of Venetian colonial technocrats. And for the next century—until the coming of the Ottomans in 1571—Cyprus became little more than a huge Venetian plantation and sugar refinery.

It's not often that archaeologists have such a rich historical background with which to work, and rarely do they have such a clear opportunity to deepen that background with abundant archaeological finds. For the story of Cypriot sugar, as recorded in the medieval chronicles and account books, left many questions unanswered. No scholar was ever quite sure how the Cypriot plantations operated, and, no less important—since the European demand for sugar was still relatively insignificant—to whom the Crusaders and Venetians sold their Cypriot sugar loaves.

Sugar cane no longer grows on the coastal plain near Kouklia, and most of the fields are now planted with bananas, papayas, and mangoes—the Cypriot cash crops of the late twentieth century. Yet it's possible to reconstruct the main stages of production in the Crusader sugar industry, due to the archaeological discoveries of Maier and von Wartburg. The two medieval structures they excavated down on the coastal plain at the locality known as "Stavros" proved to be specialized installations for the milling of sugar cane. When I arrived several years after the excavations, they were not easy to locate. Medieval industrial ruins apparently held little attraction for tourists, and since the mills were far from the Temple of Aphrodite, I had to find them myself with the help of Maier and von Wartburg's published excavation map.

The Gothic manor house up on the crest of the hill was my landmark, and, once back on the Paphos-Limassol highway, I looked for a turnoff that might lead down toward the coastal plain. In just a few hundred yards, I spotted a gravel track that led past an old farm building. Turning onto it, I stopped my car by a long, low ruin to recheck the map, which indicated that a stretch of the aqueduct from the main refinery to the mills should have been located somewhere in the vicinity. I had difficulty, however, believing that this ruin was it. Still preserved to a height of almost eight feet and extending along a distance of more than a hundred yards, it seemed too well preserved to have been built by the Crusaders. But its connection with their sugar industry was unmistakable. As I walked along this ruin, I could see hundreds of fragments of clay sugar cones and jars embedded in the cement between its stones.

From the aqueduct, the gravel road led down the slope toward a grove of trees and a field of wild reeds whose waving, canelike appearance immediately brought to mind the profitable crop that once had grown here. A local man dressed in khaki work clothes, a broad-brimmed hat, and high boots was cutting down some stalks with an iron sickle; nearby, a woman in a full peasant dress and a kerchief tied tightly under her chin was gathering reed stalks while some raucous children were playing in the thick undergrowth. This family group, collecting raw material for mats and baskets, seemed surprised, even a little apprehensive, at the unusual arrival of a tourist. As I parked near their pickup truck, I waved to show that I had no sinister intentions. I was only interested—as they obviously knew most outsiders were—in the ruins of the past. Here the ruins were clearly separated from the present, and from the fields of wild reeds. A tall wire-mesh fence surrounded the larger of the mills that Maier and von Wartburg had uncovered. The gate, though closed, was unlocked. So, as the reed cutters went back to their business, I entered the excavation area and went about mine—to see for myself the evidence of the ancient processing of Cypriot sugar cane.

Weeds had already begun to obscure the details of the ruin, but the basic elements of the mill structure were clear. It had been built into the steep slope to maximize the power of the water flow from the main aqueduct, and it contained the remains of elaborate mill mechanisms. That, in itself, was hardly surprising for a mill of the Crusader period, for waterpower was one of the main factors behind Europe's first great "industrial revolution," from the eleventh to the fourteenth centuries A.D. From England to Italy, water mills began at that time to be used widely to grind grain, pump water, work bellows, and pound (or "full") freshly woven cloth.

For many historians, this precocious burst of industrial development in Europe was recognized as a hint of even greater potential achievements. Somehow the Europeans seemed to have a natural capacity for such development—the ingenious substitution of the carefully controlled forces of nature for the power of human or animal brawn. But in the case of the mills at Stavros, the capacity seemed quite clearly borrowed rather than inherited; the wheel mechanisms uncovered by Maier and von Wartburg were quite different from the predominant type of waterwheels used in Europe. Instead of being positioned vertically, they were of the characteristic horizontal Near Eastern turbine type.

In sharp contrast to the Gothic-style architecture of the manor house farther up the slope at Kouklia, the mills at Stavros were, in fact, thoroughly Near Eastern in plan. Their steep water chutes had been copied from contemporary Syrian and Palestinian models, and the use of a large, subsidiary, ox-driven grinding wheel was Egyptian in inspiration. Purely European technology, it seemed, was poorly equipped for the processing of sugar, and in this Crusader-period mill and refinery at Stavros, Maier and von Wartburg were able to reconstruct nearly the entire production process. Yet they did so by comparing their archaeological finds—not with the chronicles of any European traveler, merchant, or mechanic but with a treatise on sugar refining written by the Egyptian encyclopedist, historian, and naturalist Ahmad ibn al-Wahhab al-Nuwairi in the early fourteenth century.

Al-Nuwairi spent his whole life in public service in Egypt; he distinguished himself as an energetic and respected court official in the complex bureaucracy of the Mamluk sultan al-Malik al-Nasir. Toward the end of his career, al-Nuwairi recognized the need to collect all the practical knowledge that might be useful to administrators and scholars in the future. And since sugar was such an important commodity in Islamic civilization, he detailed the stages of its production in the botanical section of his nine-thousand-page encyclopedia, *Nihayat al-'Arab fi Funun al-Adab*—"The Aim of the Intelligent in the Art of Letters"—a work characteristic of the sophistication of Islamic culture at the time of Cyprus's great sugar boom.

According to al-Nuwairi, sugar refining was a methodical business involving a complex series of operations that began at harvest time. He related that after the cane stalks were harvested and cut into sections, they were pressed first in a large wheel to produce a moist mash. This mash was then squeezed in another wheel—most likely water-driven—to extract the syrup, which was collected in plaster-lined vats. From there, the syrup was poured into copper cauldrons and boiled to the desired thickness, after which it was poured into the clay sugar cones.

Initially, while the boiled syrup was still quite liquid, the opening at the bottom of each cone was plugged with pieces of cane. But when the evaporation and hardening of the raw sugar was almost completed, the plug was removed and the cones were inserted in jars to collect the thick molasses that dripped from the still-moist sugar loaves. As al-Nuwairi acknowledged, this method of production, by which both molasses and crystallized sugar were manufactured, was no recent innovation; it was well known and widely practiced throughout the Islamic world. But from a modern archaeological standpoint, the finds at Stavros and Kouklia provided new insight into the transfer of that technology across cultural barriers—a transfer of which al-Nuwairi initially may have been unaware. The excavations of Maier and von Wartburg revealed that the Frankish and the later Venetian lords of the Cypriot sugar plantations had apparently transplanted both the cane stalks and the time-tested processing technique.

The excavations had also revealed an even more surprising connection between the European sugar magnates of Cyprus and the world of Islam. Even at the time of my visit to the mill at Stavros, long after the excavations had ended, thousands of sugar-cone and bottle fragments lay scattered on the surrounding surface and were visible in the vertical debris layers around the dig's boundary. These discarded by-products of sugar manufacture provided telling evidence, for when von Wartburg counted and classified them, she was able to identify the main product of the Cypriot sugar industry. The three main types of matching cones and jars, in graded sizes, apparently represented the once-, twice-, and thrice-boiled sugar mentioned in the Italian merchant handbooks. The most unexpected discovery was that the largest and crudest of the molds—for the once-boiled sugar—were by far the most common types.

This finding was unexpected, for from the prices quoted in the medieval merchant handbooks, it might have been assumed that the Cypriot refiners would have taken the time to boil the bulk of their sugar more thoroughly. The fine *muccaro* and even the medium-grade *musciatto* were sold at substantially higher market prices than the rough *polvere*.

But wholesale prices alone apparently did not determine the economic role of Cypriot sugar, von Wartburg eventually realized, especially in light of the limited European demand. The concentration on the cheaper types had to be seen in a wider context of East-West trade relations—in response to a steep decline in the production of sugar within the Mamluk empire. Some modern Middle Eastern economic historians had already noted that in the fourteenth century the sultans of Egypt—who reserved to themselves a monopoly on sugar production—had concentrated increasingly on the finer types of sugar, leaving a vast gap in the market to be filled. The feasts and festivals in the great cities, towns, and villages of the Islamic world went on as before, and they still needed sugar to keep them sweet. So it is one of the most ironic findings of the excavations at Kouklia and Stavros that the Frankish knights and the merchants of Venice on Cyprus may have profited grandly by supplying cheap sugar to the bazaars of Cairo, Damascus, and Baghdad.

The reed cutters were gone by the time I finished my tour of the mill ruins at Stavros. As I returned to my car I noticed that their pickup truck had vanished and the field of wild reeds was silent again. Sugar, once grown here in industrial quantities, now played no significant role in the agricultural economy of the Kouklia region— or, for that matter, of any part of Cyprus. Its decline and fall as a major industry was catastrophically sudden. According to the evidence of the latest pottery types discovered in the excavations, Maier and von Wartburg determined that the mills and refineries were burned and abandoned in the late sixteenth century. This date was suspiciously close to that of the Turkish conquest of Cyprus in 1571— an event still mourned by the modern Greek community as the greatest tragedy in the island's history. And since travelers' accounts of the subsequent centuries reported that Cypriot sugar production declined to almost nothing, it seemed possible, even probable, that there was a close connection between the two events.

Naturally, the impact of the Ottoman conquest and the settlement of a substantial Turkish population on the island has significance for understanding the roots of the modern intercommunal conflict. With Cyprus now divided into two hostile ethnic communities—separated by a barbed-wire and minefield boundary since the 1974 invasion by the Turkish army—images of Turkish invaders, in whatever historical period, have a particularly violent, threatening character to the Greek Cypriots of the south. The conventional historical interpretations of the sixteenth-century Turkish conquest have meshed well with this modern understanding, in the assumption that the end of the island's medieval prosperity and its subsequent centuries of economic stagnation were brought about by the unwelcome advent of the forces of Islam.

But Maier and von Wartburg's excavations offered a different perspective in their hypothesis that the Turks may not, after all, have put an end to the Cypriot sugar industry. In fact, the decline and fall of Cypriot sugar and the decline of Cyprus's economic importance now seem to be related to commercial trends and innovations thousands of miles from Cyprus. And the collapse of the island's sugar industry may, in fact, have been one of the *causes*, rather than outcomes, of the Turkish conquest.

The investigation of the medieval sugar industry at Kouklia required that Maier and von Wartburg utilize some unfamiliar sources of historical background in addition to the chronicles of Crusaders, Venetians, and Mamluks. Their review of some previous historical and archaeological studies of sugar in other parts of the world helped in every stage of the research. The identification of the stone bases in the Temple of Aphrodite as supports for huge copper cauldrons came from a report on medieval sugar refining in Morocco; the manufacture and use of the sugar cones was understood through parallels from Persia and Sicily; and, surprisingly, the plan of the Stavros refinery could best be reconstructed with the help of a detailed seventeenth-century account of a French priest's travels in Brazil.

As far as I know, no Brazilian parallels had ever before been used in Cypriot archaeology, but the study of the development of the island's agricultural technology required a new approach. The rise and fall of Cypriot sugar was just one episode in sugar's spread from its original Southeast Asian homeland to the coffee cups, cakes, and candy bars of the twentieth-century industrialized world. And the pace and direction of that movement were determined by the ease of access to the essentials of its production: a favorable climate, water for irrigation, cheap plantation labor, and fuel for the boileries. The Mediterranean sunshine, springs, peasants, and forests of Cyprus were the keys to sugar success in the Middle Ages, as proven by the Crusaders and their Venetian successors. But all those elements were soon found in even greater abundance elsewhere, and the economic prominence of Cyprus was to be severely—even fatally—challenged with the discovery of the New World.

Far to the west, on the shores of the Atlantic Ocean, Portuguese explorers and their commerce-minded patrons may have been late in grasping the profitable possibilities of sugar, but when the Portuguese went into the business in the late fifteenth century, they completely transformed the nature of the industry. First establishing plantations in the Canary Islands and the Azores, they were soon able to produce sugar with local labor that was far cheaper even than that produced by the Venetians on the backs of the hard-pressed Cypriot peasantry. This, though, was just a small-scale experiment in comparison with what was to come. The real revolution in the sugar industry came in the early sixteenth century, when the Portuguese established their first plantations with West African slave labor in the vastness of Brazil.

It was no coincidence that the plan of a Brazilian sugar refinery drawn by Father Jean-Baptiste Labat in 1690 was similar in layout to the ruins at Kouklia. The methods of milling and boiling, even the forms of the sugar cones and jars, were transferred virtually unchanged from the Old World to the New. Only the scale of production was altered. The equatorial climate of the Portuguese colonies in the New World was even more favorable for cane cultivation, and the size of the labor force was limited only by the extent of the human harvest reaped along the coast of Africa by the Portuguese slave traders' ships. So with all Brazil a potential plantation, and with African slaves to grow, harvest, and process the sugar cane, only one factor was lacking. The Portuguese realized that they must now also cultivate a European demand.

Sugar had always been a high-prestige commodity in Islam, so why not in Christendom? Little by little, in the late Middle Ages, sugar had trickled into the European consciousness—as an exotic curiosity for the palates of the rich and powerful. Its significance, though, lay more in its acquisition from great distances and from seemingly hostile cultures rather than in the attraction of its sweetness alone. But the sweetness was ultimately made more alluring by naturalizing its social importance within Europe. In 1513, the gratifyingly malleable nature of sugar was demonstrated when King Manoel I of Portugal presented the new Pope Leo X with a life-sized sugar portrait statue of His Holiness, surrounded by twelve sugar cardinals and 300 sugar candles, each nearly five feet high. This promotion gimmick apparently succeeded in making sugar synonymous with public tribute and personal enjoyment—a ritual connection that lingers even today in our elaborate birthday and wedding cakes. More important, sugar became increasingly familiar to an ever-widening public in Europe as the competition for status between townsmen and nobles became increasingly sweet. And with sugar firmly established as an essential element of social life in Europe, the demand steadily soared. Whereas Cyprus's annual sugar output had been at most a few hundred tons, the Portuguese plantations in Brazil were, by the mid-sixteenth century, shipping out almost two thousand tons of refined sugar every year.

So the outside forces that put an end to the sugar industry of Cyprus began to be felt at least several decades *before* the Ottoman conquest. Cyprus's economic importance was soon buried in an avalanche of New World sugar that flowed onto the markets of both Europe and the Middle East. Maier and von Wartburg therefore came to recognize that the abandonment of the mills and the refinery at Kouklia was the result of international economics intertwined with local political and military change. The island's sugar industry, established in an entirely different commercial context, just could not compete with the shiploads of sugar—a certain cheap grade still mockingly called "Cyprus" sugar—from South America and, later, from the West Indies.

With the changing position of Cyprus in the European economy, a political realignment probably was inevitable. In 1571, despite desperate Venetian resistance, Cyprus fell to the Turks. The long rule of the island by Europeans ended soon after its profitability dropped. When the smoke had cleared and Ottoman officials were established in the manor house at Kouklia, new crops, such as cotton, were raised. And by the following century, the agricultural transformation of the island was total; it was American, not Cypriot, sugar that the rulers of the island used to sweeten their Turkish coffee.

The discoveries at Kouklia have already made an impression on other scholars working on Cyprus. In 1987, Maier and von Wartburg resumed the excavations at Stavros and uncovered the remains of an elaborate boilery structure where the sugar-cane syrup was refined.

The detailed ground plans of the various installations, the profiles of sugar cones and jars published in Maier and von Wartburg's excavation reports, and their study of the sugar mills' historical context now make it unlikely that other archaeologists working on the island will ever again completely ignore such archaeological evidence. The importance of industrial archaeology may not yet have caught on fully in Cyprus, yet at least some previously overlooked Crusader remains have become the object of considerable interest. At the sites of Episkopi and Kolossi near Limassol, where the great "sugar war" was waged in the fifteenth century, the remains of the competing Crusader and Venetian refineries are now being studied intensively. And at the castle of Saranda Kolones in the port of Paphos, the discovery of sugar-cone fragments in the Crusader levels has prompted the excavators to pursue the question of precisely when and how the Cypriot sugar industry began.

But beyond the specific questions of Crusader sugar, the work of Maier and von Wartburg at Kouklia has encouraged a number of scholars to investigate the same questions of agriculture, technology, and economics in other historical periods. Cyprus, as a natural geographical crossroads for Asia, Africa, and Europe, absorbed many cultural influences and experienced several periods of great prosperity. Perhaps the impressive remains of the Late Bronze Age foundation of the Temple of Aphrodite—or even of the lavishly decorated mosaic houses of Nea Paphos in the Hellenistic and Roman periods, or even the terminal buildings of Paphos's new international airport— are, like the Crusader castles, merely symptoms of larger economic trends whose fluctuations are the most significant factors in the course of Cypriot history.

The main emphasis of Cypriot archaeology—like the archaeology of every other region of the classical world—has long been directed at uncovering evidence of artistic influences and political events. This search has served the modern social function of illustrating accepted historical traditions and highlighting the achievements, even the cultural "character," of specific ethnic groups. Whether searching for ancient Macedonians, Mycenaeans, Minoans, Trojans, or Cypriots, the archaeologists have, in many cases, discovered what they have set out to find. The elaboration of ethnic history and of the exploits of ancient kings and generals may, however, merely echo the self-perceptions of ethnic groups and military leaders of the present day. More and more "things" are discovered and proudly exhibited in national museums, but basic perceptions of society and community remain the same. At Kouklia, I sensed that this emphasis could be changing. In the coming decades, archaeologists working in Greece, Turkey, and Cyprus might find that the most useful clues to understanding the region's historical development could be quite different from the aesthetically pleasing museum pieces that excavators had always been looking for.

That isn't to say that irrigation systems, watermills, and broken sugar cones were likely to replace Hellenistic mosaics and Roman temples on the tourist postcards and posters of Cyprus. It isn't to say that the rich tombs of Macedonian kings, the palaces of Bronze Age Crete and Greece, and even the romantic myths of Troy will no longer draw busloads of eager visitors. Myths of the past will always be pleasing to real estate developers and tour operators everywhere. It's just that excavations like those of Franz Georg Maier and Marie-Louise von Wartburg have demonstrated another way that archaeology can be useful: in exploring some of the powerful yet overlooked forces that created the world in which *we*—not ancient, mythic heroes—live.

5

ISRAEL

The Fall of Masada

Even though more than twenty years had passed since the end of Israel's most ambitious archaeological undertaking, the name of the site where it took place—Masada—still exerted an undeniably romantic appeal. For many Israelis and visitors to Israel, that isolated, flat-topped mountain in the Judean Desert remained the most visible symbol of the power and significance of modern archaeology. Excavations undertaken there from 1963 to 1965 revealed the magnificent fortress-palace of King Herod the Great of Judea (37–4 B.C.), as well as evidence for the later, tragically unsuccessful attempt by Jewish rebels to prevent Masada's capture by the Romans at the end of their Great Revolt against Rome in A.D. 74. For modern Israelis, deeply concerned with issues of sovereignty and independence, the finds at Masada had long offered a tangible link between the present and the past. The fact that after nearly two thousand years of exile Jews returned to reveal the splendor and the tragedy of an earlier national existence at that remote mountain in the Judean Desert made Masada a powerful political metaphor.

I had visited Masada at least a half-dozen times before, while studying and working in Israel, and now, as I came back to the country after being away for several years, I made the trip again. I was not alone in that journey. In the years since the end of the excavations, Masada had become one of Israel's most popular tourist attractions, easily accessible from Jerusalem by a scenic highway that winds along the western shore of the Dead Sea. Maintained by the Israel National Parks Authority as an historical monument, the visitors' complex at the foot of the mountain included every modern tourist convenience: a youth hostel, a museum, a cafeteria, and a row of the inevitable souvenir shops. A cable-car ride to the summit now made the difficult climb up Masada's steep eastern slope unnecessary for all but the hardiest visitors and student groups. This ease of access, the spectacular natural scenery, and the continuing popularity of the dramatic story of Masada had encouraged a steadily growing flow of tour groups and visitors whose buses, rented cars, and vans filled the parking lots at the foot of the mountain on almost any day of the year.

The excavated ruins on the summit of Masada were still carefully maintained and identified with signposts, but it was not pure archaeology that the majority of visitors had come to see. They came, rather, to participate in a modern pilgrimage ritual performed dozens of times every day. After stepping off the cable cars near the summit of the mountain, those visitors were transported back to the time of Masada's most famous and stirring events by the vivid descriptions of the local tourist guides. And for this dramatic retelling, the visible archaeological remains on the summit of Masada were not so much tangible proof of the story's historical accuracy as they were elaborate and persuasive stage scenery for a modern passion play of national rebirth.

The narrative of Masada's ancient rise and fall continued to be told in much the same manner as it was presented to the public at the time of the excavations, even though some of the original evidence had been questioned or reinterpreted on an archaeological level since that time. But I shouldn't have been surprised at the continuing appeal of an ancient legend. Having already glimpsed the modern power of the past in Yugoslavia, Greece, Turkey, and Cyprus, I should have realized that dates and historical facts were only a small part of Masada's mystique. Masada's story was such a meaningful parable for the modern, besieged State of Israel that it seemed to have a life of its own, quite apart from archaeology. And I even began to suspect that the discovery, preservation, and presentation of the mountain's archaeological remains might reveal as much about modern as about ancient Israeli history.

There's no question that Masada was an archaeological achievement. From a purely logistical standpoint, the excavations there were a triumph of organization and determination over the most difficult of natural conditions. Long before the parking lots were paved at the foot of the mountain and the cable cars were installed to ferry tour groups to its summit, Masada was a remote and isolated plateau, cut off by precipitous ravines from the towering limestone cliffs that line the western shore of the Dead Sea. The excavations were undertaken on the summit and steep slopes of the mountain, hundreds of feet above the surrounding terrain. Furthermore, the climate of this region is brutal and sometimes violent: dry and extremely hot in summer and subject to high winds and flash floods in winter. Yet beyond the physical obstacles lay the legend, for the remoteness and inaccessibility that made Masada's modern excavation so difficult were the same factors that made its reputation as an impregnable fortress unparalleled in antiquity.

Physical difficulties, however, did not stand in the way of the dig's director, the late Professor Yigael Yadin. As a former chief of staff of the Israel Defense Forces, he saw Masada as both an archaeological and a national challenge, and by gaining financial support and publicity from private and public institutions both in Israel and abroad, he was able to marshal enough public interest to see that the challenge was overcome. With the help of the Israeli army to clear a campsite at the foot of the mountain, and with the assistance of engineers from the National Water Authority to pipe drinking water to the site, Yadin and his staff supervised the work of hundreds of volunteers from twenty-eight countries through two years of almost continual digging. Due to their efforts and their discoveries, Masada became the most famous project in the history of Israeli archaeology, and—perhaps second only to the clearance of the tomb of Tutankhamun—the most publicized excavation in the twentieth century.

Beyond the spectacular natural setting and the enthusiasm of the volunteers, there was, of course, the ancient story of Masada that set it apart from most other archaeological digs. Few other sites in Israel—or, for that matter, in the entire eastern Mediterranean— could boast such a colorful cast of characters or such a spectacular closing scene. According to the first-century A.D. Jewish historian Josephus Flavius, whose writings are the main source of our knowledge about Masada's history, this mountain was chosen by the Roman client-king Herod as a secure place of refuge in case of either popular uprising or dynastic intrigue. Herod had ample reason to fear for his safety, for many Judeans considered him to be a usurper. He had, with Roman help, snatched the throne of Judea from the local Hasmonean, or Maccabean, dynasty. So, building on the foundations of a small outpost established earlier in the first century B.C. by his Hasmonean predecessors, King Herod spared no expense in the construction of a desert pleasure palace, a Judean Xanadu. His court architects, engineers, and master builders—not to mention a huge force of laborers—transformed the remote mountain in the wilderness into a luxurious, self-supporting residence for the king. And Josephus showed obvious admiration for this massive construction project in his detailed descriptions of Masada's lavish reception rooms, bathhouses, colonnades, and living quarters—as well as massive storerooms and water cisterns—that permitted Herod and his royal entourage to live elegantly and securely in otherwise-impossible terrain.

Yet the focus of Josephus's description of Masada was not the opulence of Herod's palace but the grim determination of its later occupants. He related how in A.D. 66, seventy years after the death of Herod, at the time of a popular uprising in Judea against the Roman imperial administration, a desperate group of Jewish rebels captured Masada from the small legionary garrison that had been posted there for many years. Using the remote fortress as a secure base of operations, the rebels continued to hold it even after the Great Revolt elsewhere in the country was brutally crushed by the Romans and the city and temple of Jerusalem had been destroyed. Because Masada was a self-sustaining fortress far out in the wilderness, the rebels held out for more than three years after the fall of

Jerusalem. Naturally, this caused the Romans some embarrassment, and by the autumn of A.D. 73, they were determined to put an end to it.

The new Roman governor of Judea, Flavius Silva, marched on Masada at the head of the Tenth Legion, the powerful force of veterans that had besieged and conquered Jerusalem. After establishing his field headquarters at the foot of Masada and making sure that his troops were properly provisioned, Silva ordered the construction of a siege wall around the entire mountain so that none of the defenders of Masada could escape. And with a slave force of captured Jewish rebels, Silva's engineers went to work. They spent several months in the slow, methodical construction of a massive earthen ramp up the western slope of the mountain—to provide a means of approach for their fearsome, ironclad siege tower and battering ram.

When the siege tower was finally moved into position and rolled up the steep ramp toward Masada's fortifications, it might have seemed that the conquest of the fortress would be quick. The huge battering ram made short work of the stone defensive wall built around the edge of the summit by Herod, but the Romans then discovered that the rebels had constructed a defensive wall of their own. Just behind the line of the old Herodian fortifications, they had laid down a double row of heavy timbers, inside which they piled freshly dug earth. This pliable wall proved far more resistant to the battering ram; repeated pounding of the wood and its earthen filling merely strengthened it. But Flavius Silva would not be repulsed so easily by this makeshift defensive stratagem. He ordered his troops manning the siege tower to hurl torches and shoot burning arrows at the timbers to set fire to the wooden wall. At first the flames and smoke blew into the faces of the Romans, but—"as if by divine providence," Josephus noted in his account of the final stage of the battle—the wind suddenly shifted and the zealots' last, hastily built line of defense was destroyed.

The Roman forces now felt confident of triumph, and they reportedly returned to their camps for the evening, intending to perform the coup de grace at daybreak. Yet, as Josephus explained to his readers, the defenders of Masada were determined at least to deprive the Romans of satisfaction in their military victory. In a stirring and now familiar passage, Josephus vividly described how the 960 men, women, and children holding out on Masada refused to suffer death at the hands of the Romans—or, even worse, the horrible fate of Roman captivity that had already befallen so many of their countrymen—preferring instead a bizarre mass suicide.

As recounted in Book VII of Josephus's *Jewish War*, the leader of the Masada rebels, Eleazar Ben-Yair, assembled his comrades in Herod's once-magnificent palace when it was obvious that the Roman siege forces could no longer be held back. Josephus's narrative recounts the details of Ben-Yair's attempts to convince the assembled fighting men that their deaths and the deaths of their wives and children would be preferable to lives as Roman slaves. God, it seemed, had forsaken their cause and they must now pay for their hubris in declaring holy war on the mightiest power on earth. And to convince the fainthearted that suicide was not really self-destruction, Ben-Yair declaimed eloquently on the immortality of the soul. So, with the conviction that they were taking the only honorable course available to them, the defenders of Masada went off to slay their families. And when that killing was completed, they gathered together all their supplies and personal possessions and set fire to the pile so the Romans would know that free choice—not starvation—had led them to take their own lives. The heads of families then held a grim lottery and chose ten men to slay all the others; by yet another fatal lottery, the ten survivors chose one man to slay the other nine and himself.

The following morning, when the Romans stormed the fortress expecting fierce resistance, they encountered only the silence of death. Being informed of what had happened on the previous night by two women and five children who had hidden themselves in an underground cistern, the Romans, according to Josephus, did not gloat over their victory. But, "encountering the mass of slain, instead of exulting as over enemies, they admired the nobility of their resolve and the contempt of death displayed by so many in carrying it, unwavering, into execution." So ended, according to Josephus, the last episode of the Great Revolt.

That was the dramatic story that lay behind the Masada excavations, yet what Yadin and his staff uncovered surpassed even the most optimistic expectations of finding a link between the written history and the archaeological evidence. Josephus's descriptions of the physical layout of Masada proved to be uncannily accurate. Beneath the rubble of collapsed walls at various places on Masada's summit, the excavators uncovered the reception rooms, bathhouses, and storerooms of the luxurious Herodian palaces, substantially as Josephus had described them. The most elaborate structure, the northern palace, was built on three levels on the dizzying heights of Masada's sheer northern face. And the arid climate of the site had preserved the vivid wall frescoes and carved plaster that had decorated its various rooms. Even more meaningful to the members of the Israeli expedition than the proof of the accuracy of Josephus's descriptions were the many archaeological indications of the events that had transpired on the mountain at the end of the Great Revolt.

Throughout the rooms of the Herodian palaces and administration buildings, the excavators found evidence of a later, far less opulent occupation. Crude mud and stone walls partitioned the halls and large rooms of the royal residences into smaller, less elegant chambers. In many of these makeshift rooms, the team found clay ovens and collections of personal possessions that seemed to represent the habitations of individual family groups. Yet the most evocative evidence came from the dozens of small cells built into the Herodian fortification wall. Clearing the debris from the floors of these small chambers, the team found cooking vessels, combs, coins, baskets, and even scraps of wool fabric and leather sandals. "As we excavated these casemate rooms," Yadin later reported, "we found ourselves recapturing the daily lives of the Zealots, and we stood awed by what had taken place in the final moments before the suicide."

Previous archaeological surveys of the surrounding area had already identified the remains of the eight Roman siege camps at the foot of the mountain and the Roman siege ramp on its western side. But it was the continued digging on the summit itself that brought to light the ultimate effects of the Roman siege. Throughout the rooms of the later occupation, the excavators noted thick layers of ash, charred beams, and blackened stones—traces of an intense conflagration that marked the end of the squatter occupation at the site. There was little question that those squatters were Jewish, as indicated by their construction of a synagogue and ritual baths and by their use of biblical scrolls, including fragments from the Books of Psalms and Leviticus. And there was no doubt that the destruction of their settlement had taken place at the end of the Great Revolt, as indicated by the catapult stones, Roman-period arrowheads, and the latest coins found in the destruction debris. These coins bore a date in Hebrew characters equivalent to A.D. 70—the year in which the city and temple of Jerusalem were destroyed.

Even more striking evidence came from the lower terrace of Herod's northern palace, where Yadin and his staff were led to believe that they had found the remains of some of the last Masada defenders, whose death had come just as Josephus had described. Beneath the collapsed rubble of the Herodian colonnade were the skeleton of a young man, surrounded by scales of armor and fragments of a prayer shawl, and the skeletons of a child and a young woman, whose leather sandals and long plaited hair were perfectly preserved after two thousand years in the arid desert air. "There could be no doubt," Yadin later stated, "that what our eyes beheld were the remains of some of the defenders of Masada."

In a cave on the southern face of the mountain, another group of excavators came upon an even more grisly discovery: a heap of twenty-five skeletons jumbled with the remains of clothing and personal possessions. Later anthropological analysis at the Hebrew University Medical School seemed to indicate that these were not the remains of Roman soldiers or Byzantine monks who were known to have occupied the area later, but perhaps more of the Masada defenders. The skeletons in the cave were the remains of a surprisingly heterogeneous collection of people who met their deaths suddenly— men, women, and children ranging in age from eight to seventy, as well as the skeleton of an unborn child.

But the most dramatic discovery of all came during the clearance of the debris near Masada's storerooms, where the volunteers discovered eleven unique *ostraca*, inscribed potsherds. Ostraca, in themselves, were relatively common finds at Masada, for it seems that the final occupants used them as coins or tokens for the efficient distribution of food and other supplies. But these ostraca were different. Instead of the usual letter or symbol, each of them bore a personal name. And since one of the names was "Ben-Yair," Yadin and his staff felt sure they had found the lots cast by the last Jewish rebels at Masada at the time of their mass suicide.

In 1965, the Masada excavations finally came to an end; for the scholars who had long speculated on the reliability of Josephus, Yadin's discoveries were truly astonishing in their quantity, state of preservation, and close correspondence to the ancient saga of the Masada siege. For the people of Israel, who had watched with fascination as the Yadin expedition undertook the challenge of excavating under the most difficult of conditions, the modern archaeological recovery of the finds from the time of the zealot occupation of the fortress—perhaps even the lots and some of the bodies of the defenders—seemed to be nothing short of a national miracle.

On an archaeological level, however, the Masada story didn't end in 1965. Despite the emotional, almost religious veneration that came to be associated with the story in Israel in the years that followed Yadin's excavations, doubts eventually began to surface in some scholarly circles about the ultimate significance of his archaeological finds. The famous ostraca, for instance, presented a numerical problem; besides the fact of the commonness of such artifacts on Masada, the ones bearing personal names were eleven in number, not Josephus's explicitly stated ten. With regard to the human remains, there were also some troubling questions. Josephus reported that the mass suicide of all 960 defenders took place in Herod's palace, yet the excavators found only three skeletons there. As for the twenty-five skeletons found in the cave on the southern cliff, even though Yadin identified them as the remains of the rebels, there is some indication that he himself wasn't so sure. In an interview with the *Jerusalem Post* on November 6, 1982, Yadin admitted that he couldn't even vouch for their being Jewish, since they had been found together with the bones of pigs. Most likely, they were, in fact, some of the defenders of Masada who were killed in battle with the Romans and tossed into a cave that the conquerors of Masada later used as a kitchen dump. But of the planned suicide, there were no clear archaeological indications, save only that which an imaginative faith in the literal truth of Josephus could provide.

That isn't to say that much of Josephus's account of the fall of Masada wasn't accurate; regarding the dimensions and physical layout of the fortress, the excavations proved that his description was substantially correct. And while the remains of the siegeworks and ramp also validated his account of the Roman conquest, his narrative of the grim decision taken by the defenders on the eve of their defeat—despite Yadin's poetic description—still seemed open to dispute. The archaeological evidence of the bodies in several places and the scattered traces of burning and small heaps of personal possessions all over the summit seemed, in fact, to contradict Josephus's account of all the supplies piled together as an act of defiance toward the enemy, and of the palace alone set alight by the last survivor before he took his own life. These discrepancies eventually led one American scholar, Shaye D. Cohen, to suggest a new interpretation of the evidence, based less on archaeology than on a reexamination of Josephus Flavius's personal motivations for composing his tale.

Cohen's credentials as a scholar of Josephus are impeccable. His book on the first-century A.D. author's life and background, *Josephus in Galilee and Rome*, is considered a standard work in the field. In it, Cohen described how Josephus, a scion of a prominent Jerusalem family, was placed in charge of the defense of Galilee at the outbreak of the revolt against Rome in A.D. 66, and how he defected to the Roman side a year later when his Galilean troops were brutally defeated by the Roman forces and he realized the rebel cause was doomed. Becoming the personal protégé of the emperor-to-be Vespasian, he adopted the family name of the Flavians, and after the war was over, he was set to work in comfortable surroundings in Rome to write the definitive history of the Great Revolt. His purpose was apparently not only to record the events faithfully, but also to demonstrate to the Roman reading public that the uprising in Judea was not an expression of the entire Jewish people, but the misguided work of irresponsible troublemakers who called themselves "Zealots" and "Sicarii." It was the latter group that made its last stand at Masada.

The *Sicarii*—or "knife-wielders"—adopted their name from their favorite means of political persuasion, and their reputation was anything but heroic in their own time. According to Josephus's testimony, they terrorized any Judeans who opposed the rebellion—using the tactics of assassination, arson, and theft. After killing the Roman garrison and taking control of the fortress at Masada at the outbreak of the revolt, they continued their violent ways. They did not come to the aid of their rebel colleagues in Jerusalem when the city was under siege by the Tenth Roman Legion but preferred to remain at their desert hideaway, maintaining themselves by preying on the surrounding populace. During the festival of Passover in A.D. 68, for example, they raided the nearby settlement of Ein Gedi, carrying off the inhabitants' crops and livestock. Their victims in this encounter were not the hated Romans, but—according to Josephus—more than 700 innocent Jewish men, women, and children.

This criminal background is not what might be expected of national heroes, yet Cohen explained why he believes Josephus gave the story the dramatic ending so beloved of visitors to the site today. According to Cohen, the story of the mass suicide served Josephus's polemical purpose: to have the Sicarii make a collective admission of guilt. This was the theme that Josephus wanted to make clear to his readers—how the idea of rebelling against Rome was a tragic mistake, and how, after coming to that realization, the Sicarii felt compelled to accept the verdict of history. Of course, it might legitimately be asked how Josephus could have known the precise text of Ben-Yair's speech if his only informants had been the two women and five children who had been hiding in an underground cistern at the time. Or how, for that matter, he could have known the precise order of the casting of the lots and the killing of the families if all the participants in that grisly ritual had died. But all these components of Josephus's story are easily understandable, Cohen argued, when they are seen in their proper literary context, for he showed that far from being a unique event in Jewish history, the story of the collective suicide was an example of what had become, by Josephus's time, a common—even hackneyed—literary motif.

In his article "Masada: Literary Tradition, Archaeological Remains, and the Credibility of Josephus," published in the 1982 *Journal of Jewish Studies*, a volume intended as a tribute to Professor Yadin, Cohen presented some highly incriminating literary evidence. In an attempt to show the popularity of the suicide theme in antiquity,

Cohen assembled reports of sixteen other incidents strikingly similar to the Masada story that were recorded in the writings of such prominent classical authors as Herodotus, Pliny, Appian, Plutarch, Xenophon, and Polybius. Spanning a period from the sixth to the first centuries B.C., these historians described how, facing imminent defeat, such diverse peoples as Lycians, Phocians, Taochians, Sidonians, Cappadocians, Isaurians, Spaniards, Greeks, Gauls, and Illyrians sacrificed their lives and their property rather than allow them to fall into the hands of their victorious enemies. Examining the doubtful authenticity of several of his examples, Cohen pointed out that the ancient historians "regularly sacrificed 'historical truth' for the sake of art and effect."

For Josephus, basing his own history on such classical models, the use of this collective suicide motif must have been an obvious way to end his account of the Great Revolt. The other stories, which may have served as his literary models, were always highly elaborated with gruesome details of death and dedication, and they served to underline the heroism of the defenders, even if their cause was misguided or doomed. After having placed the blame for the Great Revolt on the irresponsible Sicarii, Josephus could at least have endowed them with a final act of collective heroism as an elegant and literarily acceptable climax.

There was one glaring inconsistency in the story that seemed to Cohen to provide the key to understanding the events that actually took place at the climax of the Masada siege. Just as the final line of the zealots' fortifications was destroyed in the violent conflagration, the Romans—after carrying on their siege for several months—unexpectedly returned to their camps for the night. "Why withdraw when victory was so close?" Cohen asked his readers. The answer, to him, was simple. The Romans probably pressed on and conquered the fortress immediately, slaying all the rebels they could find. It was Josephus the historian, taking literary license, who inserted the dramatic pause so that he could describe the Masada defenders discussing and deciding on their fate.

The slaughter on Masada was undoubtedly horrifying, and few of the defenders could have escaped. And although there is the strong possibility that some of them might have taken their own lives as *individuals*, Cohen sincerely doubted that the speeches, the lottery, and the calculated killing of whole families ever occurred. These incidents materialized much later, in the creative imagination of a Jewish historian who sought to impress his educated audience with a chronicle written in an acceptable literary style. "Josephus needs no apology for these inventions and embellishments," Cohen noted, "since practically all historians of antiquity did such things." But, seen in that light, the Masada story takes on a new meaning as a literary device, well known in the first century A.D., that has perhaps been taken far too literally in modern times.

In 1968, three years after the completion of the Masada excavations, the government of Israel reburied the twenty-eight skeletons found on the summit of the mountain with full military honors under headstones used for the fallen of the Israel Defense Forces in the recent Israeli-Arab wars. The summit of the mountain itself became the scene of an annual swearing-in ceremony for the new recruits of the Israeli tank corps, who vowed every year under the light of torches that "Masada shall not fall again." Stamps, coins, and posters were issued to commemorate the achievement of the excavations and their importance to modern Israeli society. And Yigael Yadin, the director of the excavations, was well aware of the significance of this juxtaposition of the present and the past. "The echo of your oath this night," he proclaimed at one of the armored-division ceremonies at Masada, "will resound through the encampments of our foes! Its significance is not less powerful than all our armaments!"

Yadin's personal account of the Masada excavations quickly became a best-seller. *Masada: Herod's Fortress and the Zealots' Last Stand*, first published in English by Random House in 1966, was eventually translated into French, German, Italian, and Hebrew, and rewritten in a special children's edition as well. The site of Masada was restored and opened to the public, a symbol for the rebirth of the modern nation and its connection to a heroic past. Yet, in time, voices of criticism began to be heard, especially in the years after the 1967 war, when Israel was no longer seen so clearly as an underdog.

The initial uncritical acceptance of the Masada story began to give way to new interpretations, not all of them strictly archaeological. And in a 1971 article in *Newsweek* magazine, the American columnist Stewart Alsop first popularized the phrase "The Masada Complex" to describe what he saw as Israel's emerging diplomatic inflexibility. Writing at a time of diplomatic and military deadlock between Egypt and Israel, Alsop observed that the national acceptance of suicide rather than survival might, under the dangerous conditions in the Middle East, become a tragically self-fulfilling prophecy. But his observation was not taken as constructive criticism. By the early 1970s, Masada had gained an almost mystical significance in the Israeli consciousness, and in 1973, on an official visit to Washington to celebrate the twenty-fifth anniversary of the State of Israel's existence, Prime Minister Golda Meir finally had her chance to confront Alsop directly. The matter of Masada came up unexpectedly during a question period following a lunch at the Washington Press Club.

After responding to some routine reporters' questions, the Israeli prime minister turned toward Alsop and spoke her mind. "And you, Mr. Alsop," she said from the podium, "you say we have a Masada complex. It is true. We do have a Masada complex. We have a pogrom complex. We have a Hitler complex." Alsop was temporarily silenced. Challenging the significance of the Masada story as revealed by the excavations was seen at the time as tantamount to challenging Israel's right and reason for national existence in the modern world.

Today, more than fifteen years after that encounter, and almost twenty-five years after Yadin's excavations, the Masada complex is no longer mentioned so frequently. That, of course, is of little concern to the visitors who still flock to the site, for the symbol and slogan "Masada shall not fall again"—now mass produced and offered for sale on sweatshirts, coffee mugs, and ashtrays in the souvenir stands at the foot of the mountain—have a life of their own.

At the time of the excavations, Masada served to instill Israelis with a self-image of heroism and sacrifice when the country felt itself under the threat of imminent attack. And even though the times have changed and Israel now faces different challenges, Masada's impressive position, the vista over the Dead Sea, and the well-practiced story all conspire to exert their unique effect. A nation often chooses its past by the way it sees its present. In the case of Masada, scholarly doubts have little influence in undercutting the popularity of a dramatic story that once seemed so much in tune with its times. The tale of mass suicide on the remote mountain in the Judean Desert, so beloved of tourists to Israel, therefore continues to be both a complex historical problem and a clear manifestation of a modern state of mind.

6

ISRAEL

Fighting a Losing Battle

I could see that Dr. Amos Kloner was angry. From his small, crowded office at the Department of Antiquities in Jerusalem, he seemed to be waging a noble, if largely futile, campaign. Outside, the tourists who passed every day through the elegant promenade entrance to the Israel Museum were blissfully unaware of the seamier side of archaeology in Israel. They came, like reverent pilgrims, to view the Dead Sea Scrolls, to admire the relics of Jewish history in the Land of the Bible, and to be impressed yet again with the country's poetic resurrection of the past. Yet Kloner and many of his colleagues knew that the national fascination with archaeology concealed a less pleasant reality in which the country's antiquities were under attack.

It was surprising to learn that in a nation so publicly applauded for its devotion to the remains of the Israelite and Canaanite cultures, and for its reverence for the ominous message of Masada, the intentional destruction and vandalization of archaeological sites in some parts of the country was a problem that had gotten out of control. According to Kloner, farmers and construction crews working in rural areas often bulldozed the remains of ancient settlements, with little fear that the budget-strained and understaffed Department of Antiquities would even be aware of what they had done. And even more serious was the irreparable damage caused by a new breed of antiquities vandals who systematically ransacked ancient cemeteries and burial caves for the salable artifacts they contained.

As a result, preventing the destruction of antiquities had become a major part of Kloner's job. He was a district officer for the Israel Department of Antiquities in a region called the Shephelah—literally, "the foothills"—a narrow stretch of territory extending north-to-south for approximately sixty miles along the border between the country's highlands and its coastal plain. From 1948 to 1967, the central sector of that area was on the frontline of armed conflict; its Jewish and Arab settlements confronted each other across the heavily guarded Israeli-Jordanian ceasefire line. But since the 1967 war and the Israeli occupation of the West Bank, the rapid spread of new settlements and a rash of robbing for profit had made the Shephelah the scene of some of the most extensive archaeological devastation in the entire country.

So Kloner had invited me to join him in a visit to the area—to see for myself the extent of the destruction and to understand his difficulties in bringing it to a halt. As we left behind the traffic lights, city streets, and apartment buildings of modern Jerusalem, making our way toward the Shephelah, the scenery became deceptively peaceful. The region's rolling hills, broad valleys, and fields had been greened by the first winter rains. Less than fifteen miles southwest of the outskirts of Jerusalem, we entered a patchwork landscape of modern settlements, biblical landmarks, and archaeological ruins. Here, the past was inextricably mixed with the present, and the mix was a suggestive one. In the vicinity of the modern town of Beth Shemesh, which housed the jetfighter assembly plants of the Israel Aircraft Industries, was Tel Zorah, site of an ancient Israelite town mentioned in the Book of Judges as the birthplace of an earlier military resource—Samson, hero of the tribe of Dan. About five miles south of Beth Shemesh was the broad Elah Valley, the scene of David's legendary encounter with Goliath. And just beyond that, Kloner pointed out the imposing mound of Tel Azeqa, where—according to the Book of Joshua—the Israelite forces routed a threatening coalition of Canaanite kings.

But the biblical triumphs of the ancient Israelites against their Canaanite and Philistine enemies constituted only one chapter of the Shephelah's long history. A succession of later conquerors also left their mark on the land. The Assyrians, Babylonians, Persians, Greeks, and Romans all understood that the conquest of this region was vital to their control of both the coast and the hill country, and the tangible evidence of their attempts to civilize and develop the Shephelah could still be found scattered on the surface and concealed in the buried levels of its archaeological sites. As we passed the modern *moshav*, or collective farm, of Givat Yeshayahu, Kloner called my attention to a line of five recently restored Roman milestones that had originally been erected at the end of the second century A.D.—during the reign of the Emperor Septimius Severus—to commemorate the initial paving of the road that still ran this way.

Kloner was himself particularly interested in the impressive remains of the Roman-Byzantine era, a period of more than six and a half centuries during which the density of the population and the utilization of the Shephelah's resources reached levels that were not equaled until modern times. The Roman governors of the imperial province of Palaestina, he explained, were among the most successful conquerors of this region, devoting considerable effort and tax revenues to bolstering the province's strategic position on the eastern border of the empire. In areas such as the Shephelah—where the Jewish population had been almost completely wiped out in unsuccessful revolts against imperial authority in A.D. 70 and again in A.D. 135—the Roman governors offered generous land grants to demobilized legionnaires, constructed aqueducts and administrative centers, and established a network of highways to ensure economic development and internal security.

Those roads continued to be used to connect the capital city of Jerusalem to the southern part of the country long after the Roman Empire had collapsed. Through the subsequent centuries of Early Islamic, Crusader, Mamluk, Ottoman, and British occupation, the roads continued to protect and control movement from the hills down to the coastal plain. The most recent struggle to control these roads took place in 1948, soon after the establishment of the State of Israel, with the repulse of an invading Egyptian force and the conquest of the strategic junction at Beth Guvrin. Yet even after Israel's War of Independence had ended, the struggle was still far from over. The cease-fire line with Jordan—the "Green Line" delineated in painstaking negotiations at the 1949 Rhodes Peace Conference—divided this part of the Shephelah into hostile Israeli and Arab enclaves. And with that Green Line becoming a focus of continuing tension and military confrontation, even the ancient Roman road that crossed it received a new name.

"Back in the fifties," Kloner told me as we turned southeast at Kibbutz Beth Guvrin and drove toward the hill country to the east, "we used to call this stretch of highway 'Texas Road.' It was close to the border then and there was a serious problem with terrorists— we called them 'infiltrators' then. This was the Wild West of Israel; every couple of weeks there'd be an encounter between the settlers and the infiltrators from across the Green Line. Gunfights, murders, and surprise attacks. But that's all in the past now."

Now the struggle had shifted. Since the 1967 war and the Israeli occupation of the entire West Bank, the former border was no longer guarded. The Green Line was not even marked on most topographical maps. As we drove through the open barbed-wire gate of the former border moshav of Amaziah, Kloner remarked how dramatically the situation here had changed. Amaziah was established in 1955 at the height of the tension, and the twenty-five families who worked its fields suffered repeated attacks by infiltrators from the Arab villages to the east. Violence had now given way to economic expansion and to the establishment of new Jewish settlements. Just three years earlier, the people of Amaziah had ceded some of their lands to a new moshav called Sheqef, established on a nearby ridge that once was divided by the Green Line.

Sheqef was the place where Kloner and I were to begin our tour of the area, for this settlement had become the temporary headquarters of his campaign to put an end to the destruction and vandalization of the region's antiquities. The most intense robbing took place in and around the nearby Arab villages—which were, between 1948 and 1967, the home bases of the shadowy infiltrators who crossed the Green Line to attack the settlements in Israeli territory. Now, new tactics had to be adopted in the battle over the region's antiquities. Because of the steadily worsening archaeological situation in the area, Kloner had recruited a team of local men to serve as "antiquities police." Yet their task was as difficult as it was potentially dangerous. Even though they were equipped with a Jeep, guns, and police power to arrest anyone found intentionally damaging an archaeological site, they were often forced into direct confrontations with many local inhabitants—both Israeli and Arab—who viewed the strict enforcement of the antiquities laws as an attack on their rights to the land.

While the antiquities patrol was dispatched to put an end to the destruction, Kloner had authorized another team to cover the same territory to map, record, and classify what was left. In other areas of Israel, archaeologists had for years been conducting detailed surveys, but the extent of the surviving ancient remains in this part of the Shephelah was still largely unknown. The last large-scale archaeological explorations here were made by the French Orientalist Victor Guérin and the military surveyors of the British Palestine Exploration Fund in the late nineteenth century. Needless to say, archaeological techniques and knowledge had been refined considerably since the time of the last explorations, and although the robbing and devastation continued to be a serious problem, the survey team had already made some important discoveries.

As we drove down the main street of Sheqef, past rows of prefabricated houses, barns, and sheds for agricultural equipment, Kloner spotted the Jeeps of the two teams parked in front of the community house. We stopped, got out, and Kloner made the introductions. Two of the members of the antiquities patrol were settlers at Sheqef; Haim Ben-Saadon and Shimon Kadoori, both in their twenties, had come here with their young families to farm. The third member of the team, Ismail Suwaiti, a resident of the neighboring Arab village of Beit Awwah, was away for the morning, but Ben-Saadon and Kadoori assured Kloner that he would be back later in the afternoon.

The two members of the survey team were from the nearby communal agricultural settlements of Kibbutz Gath and Kibbutz Kfar Menachem. They were Yehuda Dagan, a professional archaeologist in his late thirties, and Zvi Katznelson, a man in his seventies who was "a farmer in an earlier incarnation," Kloner jokingly said. The introductions were brief, since Ben-Saadon and Kadoori had some problems they wanted to discuss immediately with Kloner. The territory they patrolled had few paved roads, and I overheard something about a broken axle. Kloner frowned and shook his head in exasperation at the delay this would cause in their work.

Fortunately, the survey team had no such problems. Dagan and Katznelson were to be our guides on a tour of the area. Kloner and I climbed into their Jeep and headed across the old Green Line toward the Arab village of Beit Awwah, where the antiquities robbing had recently been particularly intense. The border line, though now invisible, still marked a dividing line between conflicting cultures. As we bumped along the rocky track that led down from the ridge of Sheqef, I began to sense that the struggle of Amos Kloner to protect the region's antiquities from attacks by local farmers and villagers was part of a far wider conflict, one whose ultimate stakes were not archaeological at all.

Dagan and Katznelson seemed at first glance to be an odd couple; the difference in ages made them look less like teammates than like father and son. But in their attachment to this region—and in their involvement in its recent history—the two men shared much. Dagan was raised at nearby Kibbutz Gal On, a small settlement whose members had helped to repulse the attack of the Egyptian army in 1948. He had spent nearly his entire life living and working in the Shephelah, and his archaeological interests and experience were evidence of his continued connection to the land. After completing his degree in archaeology at Tel Aviv University, he returned to the area with his young family to become a member of another communal settlement, Kibbutz Gath. When Kloner asked him to conduct the archaeological survey, Dagan asked Katznelson, a retired senior kibbutz member and lifelong settler in the region, to help with the work.

As he drove the Jeep along the rocky track, Dagan proudly described the recent work of the survey while Katznelson remained silent, content to let his younger partner, the professional archaeologist, do the talking today. This time of year—early December—Dagan explained, offered the best conditions for exploration, since the recent, first rains of the season had washed away all the surface dust. Later in the winter, with more frequent, steady rains, the growth of a thick groundcover of thistles and weeds would make it impossible to look for potsherds, and many ancient settlements that could otherwise be spotted would be easy to overlook. But the forces of nature were not the only problems that Dagan and Katznelson confronted. On both sides of us were newly plowed agricultural fields surrounded by high piles of boulders and fieldstones. Those fields had been cleared recently by bulldozers, and the farmers of this region—both Israeli and Arab—seldom stopped to check whether the thick, reddish soil beneath the bulldozers' scoops contained any archaeological remains.

Dagan drove the Jeep up over a small hill just across the Green Line from Sheqef, where he came to a stop. From this observation point, he wanted to give us a general introduction to the area. We circled him as he unfolded a detailed topographical map, which was dappled with colored dots designating the ancient settlements of the various historical periods that he and Katznelson had found. And there were many. The precise boundaries of their survey extended across the former Jordanian border, from the rolling hills of the Shephelah up to the rugged, rocky slopes of the Hebron Hills to the east. Although Katznelson and Dagan had explored only about six square kilometers out of a total of sixty, they had already discovered more ancient sites than were previously known in the entire area.

"So far we've found archaeological remains from three main periods," Dagan told us. "Middle Bronze Age I, Iron Age, and the Roman-Byzantine Era. The most important conclusion I can make at this point is that this area was much more intensively settled in those periods than we imagined it to be." Opposite us in the valley was a low hill that appeared to be covered with the same sort of fieldstones that the settlers of Sheqef had recently cleared from their new fields. But as Dagan pointed out the various details, I began to recognize the doorsills, corners, and even main streets of a sizable ancient town. Time and nature had caused the stone structures to collapse and blend into the bare landscape of the surrounding hillsides. After mapping the ground plans of the surviving buildings and collecting the characteristic pottery sherds scattered among the ruins, Dagan had been able to identify it as a large Iron Age farming village, from the time of the ancient Judean kings. For the last two-and-a-half millennia, that village had remained a biblical ghost town.

On the summits of hillocks throughout the area, Dagan explained, there were other Iron Age villages in equally remarkable states of preservation. And in the valleys were the remains of many settlements of the later Hellenistic, Roman, and Byzantine periods. Dagan reported, however, that he had found almost no trace of Early Islamic, Crusader, or Mamluk occupation at any of the sites he surveyed. This indicated to him that there had been a dramatic drop in settled population here from the time of the Muslim conquest of the country in A.D. 638 until relatively recent times.

That long period of desolation now seemed to be over. The human landscape was once again changing as the settled population of the region grew. To our west was the new Israeli settlement of Sheqef, and to the east was the sprawling Arab village of Beit Awwah, with its new villas and farm buildings of stone, cement, and cinder block extending across the slopes of the surrounding hillsides.

Dagan had not registered the precise sites and description of this modern demographic development on his otherwise-detailed survey maps. His archaeological training had accustomed him to the neat separation of the present from the past. Yet the current flurry of building was—for Dagan and Katznelson and the other inhabitants of the region—hardly less important than the expansion of settlement of the Roman-Byzantine era, the biblical period, or the Middle Bronze Age. It provided the backdrop against which their struggle to preserve the region's antiquities was being undertaken. It even seemed to suggest that the present conflict in the Shephelah was just a continuation of the conflicts preserved in the archaeological remains. For no region of this country—not even this part of the Shephelah—was ever a permanent wasteland or permanently deserted territory. Although centuries may have passed between the peaks of cultures—between periods of expansion and intensive building—the builders were always, in some sense, taking over land that had been settled previously. The current wave of expansion was perhaps different only in the power of the tools with which the inhabitants could clear the landscape and in the pervasive evidence of its effects.

The present boom had begun only recently, for according to the reports of the early European explorers who passed through this area, the agricultural land here was mostly uncultivated and unoccupied as late as the mid-nineteenth century. The only Ottoman presence was a small garrison at the Beth Guvrin road junction, and the *mukhtars*, or village chiefs, of the town of Dura in the Hebron Hills had become the rulers of the hill country and this part of the Shephelah. The Dura mukhtars, according to tradition, exacted such a heavy tribute from the local Arab farmers that it effectively discouraged the establishment of new villages or even the expansion of the few existing fields. But in 1917, with the coming of the British and the imposition of a strong central government, the mukhtars of Dura lost most of their power. Many *fellahin*, or rural peasants, no longer bound by law and convention to their village overlords, set out on their own to farm unclaimed land in the surrounding territory. This population movement resulted in the establishment of scores of new villages; in fact, on the eve of the 1948 war, immigrants from the Dura area had established ninety-nine "daughter villages" in the Hebron Hills and the Shephelah, many of them on the sites of ancient settlements that had been unoccupied for more than 1,300 years.

That expansion was suddenly halted in 1948, when the area became a restricted border territory facing the newly created State of Israel. The war affected the nearby village of Beit Awwah severely; much of the land that supported its existence was suddenly out of reach on the other side of the Green Line. But because it possessed a strategic position as the easternmost of the "daughter villages" of Dura, Beit Awwah became one of the most important centers for the infiltrators, who used the village as a staging ground and headquarters for attacks against the Israeli settlements in the vicinity.

But since 1967, with the opening of the border and the inevitable assimilation of the region into the rapidly developing Israeli economy, the process of demographic growth in and around Beit Awwah had resumed with a vengeance. And *that* was the real problem that Dagan and Katznelson and the men of the antiquities patrol were facing.

The growing Arab population and the expanding Israeli settlements were engaged in a struggle for the area's limited resources, and that struggle was being waged by the relentless clearing and cultivation of new agricultural fields. The laws that protected antiquities sites— even the formalities of land ownership and registration—were regularly plowed under in each community's rush to stake a claim. Of course, the power of the two sides was not equal, but that did not lessen the intensity of the fight.

"What's really going on here these days," Dagan told us as he rolled up his survey map and we got back into the Jeep to continue our tour, "is a battle for land."

The olive grove at Rassem en-Naqur seemed a natural part of the landscape, but Dagan took us there to illustrate his ominous point. This site, located about a kilometer south of Beit Awwah, was marked on earlier survey maps as an ancient ruin. But now no ruins could be seen. A series of terraces containing rows of young olive trees extended down the sloping hillside, with each terrace neatly bounded by a stone retaining wall. Yet as we began to walk through the terraces, Dagan pointed out the telltale signs of destruction. The soft, newly plowed soil was filled with thousands of fragments of ancient pottery vessels, and the stones of the terrace walls included many ancient architectural elements, some of them bearing the scrape marks of a bulldozer's scoop.

As we walked among the olive trees, Kloner reached down to pick up a thick chunk of marble. It was a fragment of a marble chancel screen, a typical artifact of the elaborate Byzantine churches of Palestine. A few yards away, Dagan picked up a clump of ancient mortar still bearing the colored stone tiles that had once been part of an elaborate mosaic floor. In another section of the olive grove, they pointed out the remains of a neatly plastered water channel and the bulldozed opening of an ancient water reservoir, now partially covered by one of the retaining walls. Until a few weeks before—when the site was bulldozed and planted—the remains of the 1,500-year-old Byzantine agricultural monastery were far more complete. But the study of the agricultural organization and prosperity of the region in an earlier period was obviously of less significance to the villagers of Beit Awwah than prosperity is today. Most of the undeveloped land here to the east of the old Green Line was registered as property of the Jordanian government, and its status under Israeli administration was unclear. So the Ottoman tradition of squatters' rights still possessed the force of custom, if not of either Jordanian or Israeli law. The villager who had planted this olive grove knew that the authorities, at least for the time being, would probably not take the time or the trouble to uproot his *fait accompli*.

Kloner suggested that Dagan take the fragment of the chancel screen and the mosaic and a few representative sherds of Byzantine pottery, bag them, and label them to record at least a typical selection of artifacts from the destroyed site. Now that the ancient settlement levels were bulldozed and the hill was planted with olive trees, the Department of Antiquities could do little more than to protest to the village authorities, since the culprit was not caught in the act.

As we drove toward Beit Awwah, past more newly planted olive groves, Dagan said that he wanted to show us another of his recent discoveries, but this time he drove slowly past it, preferring not to stop. Scanning the line of the terrace wall that fronted on the rutted dirt roadway, he pointed out two stone columns embedded in a newly built wall. "Those were the markers for Mile Twelve," he told us, "milestones placed on the Roman road from Eleutheropolis to Hebron. The distance is right, and those columns are heavy, so they must have been found somewhere near here."

Kloner asked Dagan if he had checked the milestones for ancient Latin or Greek inscriptions that might provide the precise date for the construction of this branch of the road. But Dagan insisted that it was probably wiser not to show too much interest. He had learned from bitter personal experience that a conspicuous curiosity about ancient stones by an official of the Department of Antiquities could have a disastrous effect around here. On two occasions—once on the Israeli side of the Green Line and once on former Jordanian territory—he had apparently been spotted by villagers as he moved milestones to check for inscriptions, only to find on his return to the spot that they had been destroyed or taken away.

In this region, I could see, ancient stones were building blocks for the future, not relics to be revered or placed in museum displays. Dagan described how when the first villagers of the Masalmi clan of

Dura arrived here during the British Mandate period, they began to construct their new agricultural community from ancient remains. Those remains were still visible, but as we drove down the main street of the village, it was difficult to separate the new from the old. The few shops—whose open fronts displayed used furniture and kitchen appliances, fresh vegetables, sacks of grain, and farm equipment—were themselves constructed of ancient stones set in modern concrete. In another part of the village, the crumbling apse of a Byzantine church served as a shelter for goats. And close by, a herd of dairy cows contentedly chewed their cuds in the shadows of a large, ancient burial cave.

We did not stop in the village, but continued toward its eastern outskirts, where, overlooking a broad and fertile valley, the road came to a dead end. Farther to the east were the Hebron Hills, stony and barren, rising steeply toward the country's central mountain range. The dull thud of artillery and the screeching of jets off in the distance indicated that army training maneuvers were underway in the vicinity. Kloner, Dagan, Katznelson, and I climbed a ridge through yet another newly planted olive grove for a better look at the landscape.

"It's amazing how this valley is changing almost daily," Dagan told us as he pointed out several agricultural fields that had not existed only a few weeks earlier. In his earlier explorations of the valley, Dagan had located several previously unknown agricultural settlements of the Middle Bronze Age, but now they were gone. There was little to do but map those sites' approximate locations and to collect samples of the freshly crushed pottery that lay scattered in the fields. No force short of constant military surveillance or forced expropriation of territory could completely end the destruction of the region's antiquities. In this age of rapid economic development, only the prosperous and secure could afford to pay attention to archaeological preservation. And the villagers of Beit Awwah, in their struggle to expand or be overwhelmed by the changing economic and political conditions, had other priorities.

During the time that we were exploring the fields and ruins around Beit Awwah, the day had become pleasantly warm, but as we drove up through the hills toward the small village of et-Tabaqa, we bundled up in our winter coats. From an altitude of about 500 meters above sea level in the vicinity of Beit Awwah, we were climbing to the 900-meter level on the mountainous plateau. And the change in landscape was as striking as the changes in altitude and temperature; from the rolling hills and fertile valleys of the Shephelah, we were now ascending through rocky and barren terrain. Here and there along the roadside, we passed bulldozers spewing thick black exhaust as they cleared surface boulders and fieldstones in the preparation of new agricultural fields. But the higher we climbed, the less frequent was the evidence of modern expansion. As we turned off the main road and finally arrived in et-Tabaqa, I felt as if we had traveled backward in time.

Our reason for making this side excursion was to visit yet another of Dagan and Katznelson's newly discovered archaeological sites. This region, they explained, was one of the most remote in the entire country, and while its antiquities were not in immediate danger, they felt that it was important to locate and record all evidence of ancient ruins before the inevitable wave of development and archaeological destruction reached here. On an isolated hilltop to the west of the village, they had discovered the remains of a previously unknown Middle Bronze Age settlement overlooking the Shephelah and, beyond it, the coastal plain. Its strategic location was of obvious interest for understanding the settlement patterns of that period, for its apparently fortified character contrasted sharply with the open, agricultural settlements of the same period in the foothills below. Yet as we drove through et-Tabaqa toward this Middle Bronze Age settlement, I couldn't help but think of more recent periods of the country's history.

The isolated village of et-Tabaqa seemed strangely familiar. Its appearance immediately reminded me of the romantic engravings of other Palestinian villages that I had seen in the yellowed, brittle pages of nineteenth-century European travel books. The square, stone houses on both sides of the main street had no electricity, and beside each stood a beehive-shaped mud oven for baking bread. And while the principal artery of Beit Awwah had at least the benefit of asphalt, et-Tabaqa's main street was only a rutted dirt track bounded on both sides by high stone walls. The nineteenth-century European explorers of this region believed that its living inhabitants—not only its ruins—preserved some important traditions from ancient times. Their descriptions of their experiences among the Palestinian peasantry tended toward biblical romanticism—every girl at the well was a "Rachel" and every shepherd boy was a "David" peacefully tending his flocks. Yet times had changed, even if this village's outward appearance had not. The sight of an Israeli Jeep stirred obvious interest for the villagers; we were uninvited visitors from a different place and a different time. Many of the inhabitants came running out to the wall as we passed by their houses: veiled women with babies, barefooted children, and the few men too old to work in the cities or fields.

We silently acknowledged the friendly waves of the people of et-Tabaqa and, leaving the village behind us, drove out to a ridge overlooking the Shephelah, passing scattered groves of ancient olive trees. Stopping near an isolated cluster of houses, Dagan parked the Jeep at the foot of the hill where he and Katznelson had found the Middle Bronze Age settlement, and we began the long climb to the top. The sky here was cloudy, threatening to continue the winter rainy season that had begun a few weeks earlier. As we made our way up the rocky slope along a winding footpath toward the ruins, we came upon a small field plowed with irregular furrows from which the first sprouts of winter wheat poked through like new grass. Wondering whether I should walk across it, I turned to Kloner, who turned to Katznelson, the retired farmer from Kibbutz Gath. "Never mind," he told us, as he walked ahead, "these sprouts are very strong.

"This is how all the fields in this country used to be," he said as we followed him across the furrows, "small enough to be plowed and planted by a single farmer after the first rain. The fellahin used to wait for that sign to begin the winter agricultural season, but now it just doesn't pay to work that way." In order to make enough money to support a family, a farmer's fields had to be much larger than the traditional plots—a size that only a bulldozer could clear and a tractor could plow. That simple summary explained a great deal about the current situation in the area. All the bulldozing we had seen was neither a destructive urge to level ancient settlements nor a crude hunger for land. Faced with the increasing dependence of the West

Bank on the Israeli economy, the people here had to raise crops for income, not just for subsistence. So in all but the most remote and marginal parts of the region, the traditional farming methods of the Palestinian fellahin—so lovingly described by the nineteenth-century explorers as quaint biblical relics—were being abandoned and supplanted by a new way of life.

And even here, in one of the remotest regions of the country, the future was clear. Stretched out below us was a panoramic landscape encompassing almost the entire coastal plain of the country—from the Gaza Strip on the south to the northern suburbs of Tel Aviv. From this windswept vantage point, the rich farming land to the west appeared like an undulating blanket of green fields and hills, crisscrossed by modern roads and highways and dotted with modern settlements and towns. So much had been achieved there since the establishment of the State of Israel in 1948. And the development went on as the kibbutzim and agricultural settlements continued to prosper and grow. Before us lay the evidence of the power of a modern Western society that had gained recognition and support for its efforts to reclaim the land. The old way of life had retreated or had been swept eastward into the hills. Before us, to the west, was the future. Behind us, to the east, were the traditional villages and towns of the West Bank, awaiting an uncertain fate in the face of the inexorable wave of progress that could transform them, too, into archaeological remains.

Near the summit of the hill lay the huge boulders marking the boundaries of the Middle Bronze Age settlement whose location Dagan had carefully registered on his topographical maps. Little was left except the collapsed stones and a scatter of potsherds; the reason for its abandonment and the disappearance of its inhabitants around 2000 B.C. was unclear. Yet nearby, a dilapidated *maqam*, or Muslim shrine, offered a more recent lesson about the passing of a civilization. All through the country, these square stone structures with white-washed domes could still be seen guarding fertile valleys, roads, and springs, and ancient cemeteries. This one, I learned, was the shrine of a local figure of legend, Sheikh Ahmad al-Abd, "Ahmad the Slave." According to tradition, he was the guardian of the agricultural prosperity of the region. He appeared to the people of the surrounding villages as a benevolent apparition, a large black man wearing a glowing green turban on his phantomlike head. As late as the 1920s, his *barakah*, or power to promote good fortune, was held in such high esteem by the local people that they regularly stored their plows and farm implements in his maqam to ensure a good harvest for themselves.

But the Slave now seemed to have lost his power and couldn't be counted on anymore. The interior of the shrine was filled with rubbish and the dome had partially crumbled, leaving a ragged wound in its weathered surface open to the sky. The history and tradition that this shrine once preserved were irrelevant in an era of cash-crop farming and bulldozer-cleared fields. Katznelson looked toward the ruin and shook his head silently. "It's the same story with almost all the maqams of the area," he told us. "The people don't seem to care about them anymore." Progress had transformed the shrine of the Slave into a garbage dump. The past of this region was now claimed by other pilgrims—twentieth-century archaeologists, with their Jeeps and topographical maps.

"I have just one more site I want to show you," Dagan told us as we drove down through the hills on the main road from et-Tabaqa toward Beit Awwah. "And when you see it, you'll understand the *real* battle we're fighting here." At last we had come to the heart of the matter—to the aspect of the archaeological destruction that made Kloner and his team members so mad. Here, the issue was not merely the need of farmers to expand the area of cultivation, or even the relentless transformation of lifestyles. As Kloner had told me back in his office in Jerusalem, he and the men of the antiquities patrol also faced a determined enemy who knew very well the importance of antiquities in the Israeli consciousness, and knew precisely where the treasures could be found.

Those enemies were professional antiquities robbers, skilled teams of local diggers whose knowledge of the area enabled them to uncover and plunder ancient settlements and cemeteries that even the most detailed explorations of the survey team had failed to locate and protect. The work of these robbers customarily was thorough; they would sift through the soil of the ancient sites they attacked, discarding all relics and fragments they thought to be worthless and concentrating on readily salable artifacts, such as ancient jewelry and coins. Directed by local gang leaders, they destroyed archaeological sites by the dozens, leaving behind little of value. The scale of their plunder was shocking: On several occasions, the men of the antiquities patrol had stopped and searched suspicious vehicles, only to find and confiscate carefully packed boxes of ancient pottery vessels and bags of coins in quantities that would have pleased the director of almost any legitimate archaeological dig.

The fight to stop this kind of destruction could easily turn violent, for picks and shovels could become weapons when these robbers were cornered in a tomb cave with no escape route. Kloner described how the antiquities patrol had recently faced such encounters, and had even succeeded in apprehending a few illegal diggers. But such success—if it could be called that—was the exception rather than the rule. The resources of the antiquities patrol were too limited and the rewards to be gained from antiquities theft too attractive to put a permanent dent in the activity. For many of the inhabitants of this area with no land of their own to farm, antiquities robbing offered an alternative to factory jobs or menial work in the large cities of Israel across the old Green Line. In fact, it was in Israel that they had learned of the possibilities. The elegant antiquities shops of Tel Aviv and Jerusalem, whose customers were willing to pay high prices for pieces of history, offered the antiquities robbers of the Shephelah a comfortable livelihood that made occasional encounters with a few Department of Antiquities officers an acceptable professional risk.

Dagan was anxious to show us what a site looked like after the robbers had departed. The site he had in mind was called Qasr Wadi es-Samiyeh, "the castle of the Samiyeh Valley," located in a rich farming district just a few miles from Beit Awwah's northern outskirts. As we drove along the winding road toward the ancient settlement, I could see that bulldozers had been working here recently. New fields of reddish earth cleared of surface stones lay on both sides of the road. But side by side with these new agricultural operations were small plots of the traditional type. Spotting a familiar landmark in this changing landscape, Dagan pulled the Jeep off the road and parked by an isolated farmhouse. Katznelson volunteered to remain behind to watch over the Jeep and its contents as Kloner and I followed Dagan up into the fields past an ancient-looking well. No one emerged from the farmhouse; our only greeting was the vicious barking of a dog, which strained desperately at its tether in the farmyard and bared its fangs at our approach.

The site of Qasr Wadi es-Samiyeh, Dagan explained, contained the remains of an extensive farming complex of the first century A.D. It apparently had been owned and inhabited by Jews in the last century or so before the beginning of the Great Revolt against the Romans in A.D. 66. So far in our tour of the area, Dagan had shown us newly discovered sites from the Bronze Age, the Iron Age, and the Roman-Byzantine era, but none from the period of Herod the Great and the Revolt against the Romans—an historical era whose dominant, popular image was of Jewish independence in this country and the events that led to its tragic loss. The remains of this period were, of course, of special interest to modern Israel. Masada was but one modern archaeological shrine that commemorated its centrality to Jewish history. Little was known of the nature and character of Herodian-era Jewish settlements in this part of the Shephelah. And now little could be learned at Qasr Wadi es-Samiyeh. Dagan almost apologized for the fact that there was not as much to be seen here as there had been only a few weeks earlier.

When we finally reached the top of the hill, all I could see was a tumble of huge stones surrounded by heaps of freshly turned earth. It was as if a bulldozer had completely destroyed the complex of ancient structures; the squared, ashlar stones that once had been the main walls of the building were completely dismantled and lay in disorder. Nearby, the entrances to some subterranean rock-cut chamber tombs were open, in the midst of piles of freshly dug earth. But this was clearly not a case of a bulldozer's destruction during the preparation of an agricultural field. Beside the piles of carefully sifted earth were accumulations of cigarette butts and crumbled cigarette boxes, indicating that some person or persons had been digging steadily here over an extended period of time. Kloner picked up a piece of a recently smashed storejar from a pile of similar fragments that seemed to have been intentionally smashed on the ground. He then rummaged through another pile of shattered finds and picked up a sherd of a measuring vessel of stone typical of the Herodian period, and recognized by scholars to have conformed to Jewish purity law. "So this is all they left us," he said with a frown.

"By working a site like this for a week or two," Kloner explained, "professional antiquities robbers can make a good living for themselves. They're only interested in marketable items, and at a site like this, they could find dozens of ancient coins. But in order to get them, they have to dig up every bit of the site."

The retail prices charged for those artifacts in Israeli antiquities shops offer a clear incentive for the effort, even if the amounts received by the diggers are considerably less. The most common bronze coins of the Herodian period, for instance, could each bring $5 to $50, depending on their condition; bronze coins minted during the Bar Kochba Revolt against the Romans might get from $50 to $250. And the real treasures are the silver shekels of the First Revolt against the Romans, worth $500 to $1,500—with especially rare examples bringing ten times that amount. The value of these coins was a function of their desirability to collectors in Israel and throughout the world, who had come to associate them with the most heroic chapters of ancient Jewish history. But for the people of the region of Wadi es-Samiyeh, the relics had much more concrete significance. The average yearly per capita consumption on the West Bank was listed by the Israel Central Bureau of Statistics as around $1,200, so coins looted from illegal excavations were hard and completely tax-free currency.

As we walked back down to the Jeep, passing along the edge of one of the small agricultural plots, we now noticed someone had been watching us: an elderly farmer laboriously turning the earth with a donkey and a small iron plow. Kloner walked through the furrows toward the farmer and identified himself as an officer of the Department of Antiquities. The old man looked startled as Kloner asked him whether he knew anything about the illegal destruction of the ancient settlement at the edge of his field. But Kloner knew that this farmer probably was not one of the culprits. He, too, was a victim of the present; his was a vanishing way of life. The farmer pulled his donkey to a stop and just shrugged his shoulders. "I don't know anything about destruction," he told Kloner. "I come here every morning from Dura. I just mind my own business and work the land."

When we arrived back in Sheqef, the three men of the antiquities patrol were waiting. Haim Ben-Saadon and Shimon Kadoori, the young Israeli settlers, were now joined by Ismail Suwaiti of Beit Awwah, the third member of the team. During the day, Ben-Saadon had managed to arrange for a tow truck from a neighboring town to take the patrol Jeep away for the necessary repairs. But for the time being, at least, the patrol would be grounded. Even though Suwaiti had brought new reports of robbing and destruction of antiquities in the vicinity, there was nothing they could do right away.

Kloner seemed uncharacteristically discouraged when we started on the trip back to Jerusalem, and he admitted his fears that, despite all his efforts, the attempt to stop the destruction of the area's antiquities was having little effect. Despite occasional arrests and even more occasional convictions, he was dealing with antagonists whose determination to succeed was at least as strong as his. Even when the Jeep of the antiquities patrol was in good working order, the team members faced a problem larger than they could possibly handle. To the farmers and builders of the Shephelah, ancient remains were dangerous and time-wasting obstructions in an age when farmers had to expand their fields to survive. And for the increasingly sophisticated and well-organized antiquities robbers of the area, the ancient Jewish coins, pottery lamps, and other artifacts that lay buried beneath the ground were a valuable resource whose sale might permit them to escape a life of menial city jobs.

The antiquities robbers, with money rather than territory at stake, merely responded with ever-greater watchfulness, aware of the new rules of the cat-and-mouse game. Continued profits could be ensured by posting a lookout, camouflaging their excavations with piles of bushes and brambles, and digging only at night. "They're getting so clever these days," Kloner told me, with the dispirited tone of a crusader sensing imminent defeat at the hands of the infidels. "They know exactly when I'm in the area, and you can be sure that if I were approaching a site where they were working, they'd be gone by the time I got there."

Kloner found some classical music on the car radio as we traveled through the biblical landscape toward Jerusalem. But even the most soothing of concertos couldn't help him take his mind off the unpleasant realities he faced every day. When we reached the Elah Valley, where David fought Goliath, Kloner turned off the main highway onto a side road. We were now beyond the Green Line, in pre-1967 Israel, and even here the archaeological devastation went on. A few weeks earlier, Kloner told me, he had spotted a Roman milestone half-buried here by the side of the road. Fearing the worst, he now drove slowly up and down that road several times to locate it and check on its condition, but it had vanished. The culprits—whether of the nearby Arab villages or of the nearby Israeli settlements—had once again demonstrated the utter powerlessness of the Israel Department of Antiquities. "Someone must have picked it up and taken it," Kloner said with resignation. "It's probably cemented in a wall now or lying in somebody's yard."

To a certain extent, Amos Kloner might have been justified in his pessimism that nothing could be done to stop the destruction of antiquities in the Shephelah. But it seemed to me that the situation was not just one of hard economic realities triumphing over a noble, if futile, attempt to preserve the region's archaeological heritage. There were two sides to the coin of antiquities destruction. There were two sides to economic progress as well. Since 1967, this part of the Shephelah had undergone a great transformation, no less profound than the changes in rulers and civilizations preserved in the mute evidence of the region's archaeological remains. The traditional way of life of the Arab villages of the area was being replaced by another, and that process would continue no matter what the final resolution of the Arab-Israeli conflict would be. The villagers' traditional ties with their past were being broken; feeding the historical fascination of others at least had the advantage of providing short-term prosperity. But in the long term, the prospects were grimmer. In losing their link to the land's ancient treasures—yet not having the resources or the know-how to establish their own archaeological connection—the local Arab villagers, trying to survive under new economic conditions, seemed to be in the process of waging a losing battle themselves.

7

ISRAEL

A Modern Cult of Relics

◨ The antiquities robbing in Israel's Shephelah region was clearly part of a larger problem, and by the spring of 1986, that problem had become difficult to ignore, even in Jerusalem. The whole question of antiquities robbing and the trade in ancient artifacts had become—for the archaeologists at the Department of Antiquities and the various universities—a subject of agitated discussion and debate. The flashpoint came in early April, in anticipation of the opening of a much-publicized new exhibit at the Israel Museum. In fact, for all the angry condemnations and self-serving excuses I heard on the evening of the official opening, I was beginning to think that the exhibition of the Dayan Collection at the Israel Museum would be either the most welcome—or the most disgraceful—archaeological event to happen in the country for years.

The publicity announcements of the museum curators waxed rhapsodic about the importance of the collection. More than a thousand objects ranging from the Neolithic period (ca. 7500–4500 B.C.) to the Byzantine period (fourth to seventh centuries A.D.) recently obtained by the museum were to be displayed; the opening was to be an evening of lectures and gala ceremonies. Posters began to appear around Jerusalem advertising the event with full-color photographs of the centerpiece of the exhibition—a collection of twenty-two ancient human-shaped clay sarcophagi. While there were few archaeologists in Israel who questioned the exhibit's immense archaeological value, there were many who questioned the way that many of the individual artifacts in the Dayan Collection had reached their display cases.

On the evening of the opening, the long-awaited confrontation finally came. The demonstrators standing outside the main entrance to the museum held hand-lettered placards that succinctly stated their objections to the planned festivities. THE DAYAN COLLECTION IS "HOT" read one of them. ARCHAEOLOGY, NOT RELICOLOGY! and CRIME PAYS! read two more. One of the three dozen or so young archaeologists involved in the protest handed out mimeographed copies of the passage from the antiquities law that forbade private excavations and the unlicensed sale of ancient artifacts, and that empowered—even instructed—the director of the Israel Department of Antiquities to confiscate such illegally obtained archaeological finds.

Some of the arriving guests dutifully accepted the mimeographed handouts, but few showed any great sympathy with the cause. Moshe Dayan, former chief of staff, defense and foreign minister—the man with the black eyepatch who for a time was a symbol of the State of Israel—was a figure who, even after his death in 1981, still aroused strong emotions. And in this case, the controversy centered on Dayan's love for collecting archaeological objects, a passion so deep that he often organized his own illegal artifact-hunting digs. Fifteen years earlier, in 1971, a public outcry had been raised about those digs and about the failure of either the police or the Department of Antiquities to put an end to them. And now, with the validation that the museum exhibition gave to the Dayan Collection, the outcry was being raised again.

The guest of honor at the opening was Dayan's widow, Rachel. Arriving in a limousine at the main gate of the museum, she glanced toward the demonstrators with obvious annoyance. Her feelings were apparently shared by some of the museum curators who had worked so hard to make the evening a success. Dr. Yaakov Meshorer nervously watched from inside the entrance as TV camera crews illuminated the protestors' placards. His assistant, Dr. Rivka Merhav, shook her head in anger. This evening was meant to be one of celebration, not controversy. Moshe Dayan and his antiquities had become part of the folk mythology of modern Israel, and it annoyed the promoters of the exhibition to have embarrassing questions raised.

Historically speaking, it's difficult to determine precisely when Moshe Dayan first became interested in archaeology—if that is what his passion for collecting could be called. In an interview published a few days before the opening of the exhibition, his first wife, Ruth, recalled that his interest had been aroused in the early 1950s, when Dayan, then chief of staff of the Israeli army, first experienced the pleasure of digging at archaeological sites and miraculously discovering ancient pottery. Even then, of course, such activity was illegal, but Dayan was only one of many such archaeological amateurs. Archaeology in Israel had by that time already become something of a public ritual—not a strictly academic activity, but rather a tangible means of communion between the people and the land.

Long before the excavations of Masada, archaeological discoveries of ancient Jewish sites throughout the country had offered a poetic validation for modern Jewish settlement. Ancient artifacts came to possess the power of sacred relics in a new cult of veneration for the ancestors. For the many Israelis who eagerly collected them, those artifacts were much more than mere *objets d'art*; they came to symbolize a new, secular attachment to this ancient land. But few archaeology buffs in Israel had the resources and influence that Dayan possessed. In his position as chief of staff, he could mobilize military equipment and personnel to help him pursue his hobby. Selecting sites carefully, with the discernment of a seasoned "pot hunter," he gradually filled his suburban Tel Aviv home and garden with his vast collection of antiquities.

Through the years, Dayan's archaeological passion, like many of his other personal excesses, was overlooked by his political allies and loudly condemned by his political foes. The sometimes-exaggerated tales of his archaeological adventures became a part of the legend of the man. Soon after the 1956 Sinai Campaign, during the brief Israeli occupation of the peninsula, Dayan commissioned a military helicopter—so one famous story goes—to remove a massive granite stele from the ancient Egyptian temple of Serabit al-Khadem. At other sites, it was reported, he didn't hesitate to use army bulldozers to speed the work along. The most famous story of all certainly wasn't legend. During his "excavations" in the burial caves of Azor, near Tel Aviv, the underground chamber in which he was working suddenly collapsed, nearly killing the then–chief of staff.

A fear for Dayan's personal safety was not, however, the primary objection to his digging. Suspicions were aroused about questionable business dealings as well. Digging was not Dayan's only means of obtaining new relics for his collection; he was a familiar presence in many of the country's antiquities shops. Sometimes he bought. Sometimes he traded. And, despite his innocent protestations of an unsullied love for the country's ancient heritage—which he described at length in his book *Living with the Bible*—a number of Dayan's pieces, some of which were specially autographed and designated as coming from his personal collection, began to garner high prices on the international antiquities market.

The biggest uproar, if it can be called that, came in 1971. *Haolam Hazeh*, a Tel Aviv weekly famous both for its bare-breasted pinup girls and for its combatively leftist political leanings, published a series of articles exposing Dayan's unauthorized and unlicensed antiquities dealings—and condemning the authorities for doing nothing to stop them. The articles were written by the popular novelist and political gadfly Dan Ben-Amotz, who, with his acid wit and flair for self-promotion, submitted a complaint to the Tel Aviv police to investigate Dayan's dealings and, if necessary, confiscate his loot. But the police refused to do anything, the director of the Department of Antiquities made some nervous excuses, and Dayan went on with his digs. "I think morals are all right," Dayan was reported to have said in response to the articles and to the brief uproar that resulted, "but what I can't stand are people who have to preach them all the time."

At the time of Dayan's death in 1981, his collection was enormous, occupying, in addition to prominently positioned display cases and pedestals, a specially built storeroom and restoration workshop attached to his home. Some of the larger pieces—architectural fragments, ancient millstones, and clay storejars—were impressively displayed in his outdoor "archaeological garden," which served as the scene for countless diplomatic and political receptions during his tenure as minister of defense and, later, as minister of foreign affairs. Yet perhaps the most controversial aspect of Dayan's archaeological career was not the process of collecting but the final disposition of his treasure after his death. Despite his constant assurances that, in the end, his collection would be given to the Israel Museum in Jerusalem, his will did not mention any such gift. Instead, his vast accumulation of artifacts was placed on public sale and *purchased* for the museum by a wealthy New York patron and friend of the late general—with the sale proceeds of a million dollars going to Mrs. Rachel Dayan. So with financial insult added to years of archaeological injury, it was easy to understand why some people were upset on the evening of the gala opening of *The Dayan Collection: A Man and His Land*.

Although I'd heard all about the extent of Dayan's archaeological collection, I'll have to admit that I was astounded by the quantity and beauty of the objects when I walked down the main flight of stairs in the foyer of the Israel Museum and entered the special exhibition hall. Carefully arranged on dramatically lit platforms and in glass cases were dozens of complete bowls, jugs, juglets, storejars, incense stands, plates, dishes, stone mortars, goblets, pitchers, and chalices in a dazzling variety of shapes, textures, and colors—displayed with the calculated flair of a chic housewares store.

Other, less pleasant metaphors came to mind as I wandered past the glass cases and display areas featuring the delicately fashioned figurines of gods, goddesses, animals, and monsters; alabaster, bronze, glass, and faïence vessels; rare house-shaped burial containers of the Chalcolithic period; finely carved limestone busts; and huge, Egyptian-style clay mummy cases of the Late Bronze Age. What appeared to be a police display of the loot of a gang of antiquities burglars was, in fact, the work of only one man. My amazement must have been evident, for an archaeologist who had chosen to ignore the boycott and join the celebration approached me and smiled slyly.

"You know," he told me in a knowing whisper, "there were plenty of items that never got to this display."

The small protest outside had clearly not dampened the attendance; hundreds of invited guests filled the museum's auditorium to listen to a lecture by Professor Trude Dothan of the Hebrew University on her excavations at the site of Deir el-Balah, south of Gaza, where Dayan had earlier undertaken his own explorations and had obtained the twenty-two mummy cases that were now the centerpieces of the exhibition. In the lecture itself, Dayan's unauthorized digging was passed over quietly and tactfully. Outside the auditorium, the overflow crowd watched the lecture on closed-circuit TV while others milled around the display cases or gravitated toward the tables where glossy Dayan Collection catalogs and posters were being sold.

Dr. Martin Weyl, the director of the Israel Museum, stood nearby, in high spirits. Chatting with friends and museum patrons, he seemed gratified by the turnout and untroubled by second thoughts. "I think the controversy is wonderful," he told me with the self-assurance of an off-Broadway impresario on opening night. "Outside, the younger generation is questioning the moral standards of their elders. That's how culture matures and develops. It's my goal to provoke discussion like this."

"But don't you think this exhibit condones illegal activity?" Weyl shook his head, almost puzzled by my question. "Not at all," he answered casually as he waved to another guest. "My job is to collect and exhibit. The Department of Antiquities gave permission for the sale of this collection. It's not my job to enforce the antiquities laws."

The current antiquities laws of the State of Israel were certainly part of the problem, and for *that*, Moshe Dayan was not to blame. The fact was, if you wanted to buy a piece of history, Israel was one of the best places in the world to come. Sixty-one antiquities shops, licensed by the Department of Antiquities and conveniently located at hotels and tourist centers throughout the country, offered genuine archaeological artifacts to suit every tourist's pocketbook. And the merchandise was not only the precious coins so eagerly mined in rural regions such as the Shephelah. For about thirty dollars, visitors to Israel could buy a clay oil lamp from the time of King David or a small clay bottle from the time of Jesus; ancient jewelry, painted pottery vessels, and marble statues were considerably more. Some came neatly mounted on olivewood display stands; others were neatly encased in Plexiglas. But whatever their price and packaging, antiquities were among the most popular souvenirs of a trip to the Holy Land. They offered pilgrims and tourists alike an often irresistible opportunity to take home a tangible relic of the biblical past.

This situation presented a sharp contrast with that of the other countries of the eastern Mediterranean, where archaeological remains were no less plentiful. Greece, in its long-standing campaign to regain possession of the Elgin Marbles from the British Museum, had made the prohibition of antiquities sales and export part of its patriotic policy. Turkey had gone even further in its enforcement measures, with baggage searches of tourists leaving the country and ominous warning signs at all archaeological sites. And Egypt, long plundered by Western visitors in search of pharaonic knickknacks, was now attempting to stop the outward flow of relics, even if that decision came more than a hundred years too late.

In recent decades, the issue of private antiquities dealing and export had become a matter of concern to archaeologists all over the world. As early as 1970, in response to reports of widespread illicit digging for salable artifacts and the resultant destruction of archaeological sites in many countries, the members of UNESCO drafted and adopted an international convention aimed at discouraging the profitable trade in cultural property. The subsequent international effort to put an end to the sale of illegally obtained antiquities had achieved something less than total success. But the larger ethical issue at stake had at least been made clear in many archaeological circles: To condone large-scale trade in antiquities obtained from questionable or unknown sources was to condone the unrestricted plunder of the world's cultural heritage.

The State of Israel faced an uncomfortable dilemma with regard to private antiquities dealing—not only because the sale of ancient artifacts to tourists brought in substantial foreign exchange revenues every year. The image of the rebirth of a modern nation in an ancient land was an important, symbolic expression of Israel's identity and reason for existence. And every time an artifact was bought or presented to a foreign visitor, that message was succinctly conveyed. Nor was this just a matter related to run-of-the-mill tourists; the romantic juxtaposition of past and present was encouraged even on the highest levels of government. British Prime Minister Margaret Thatcher, during her 1986 official visit, was obviously touched to receive a Bronze Age Canaanite scimitar from the Speaker of the Knesset and an Iron Age Israelite oil jar from Prime Minister Shimon Peres. And in the following year, John Cardinal O'Connor of New York City proudly showed the reporters and photographers traveling with him the authentic Byzantine oil lamp—with an early Christian inscription—that he had received.

At the time, no one was too concerned about the origins of those diplomatic gifts, but the chances were they had come a long way. Purchased from licensed antiquities dealers, they probably had passed through the hands of several middlemen—each time rising in price, if not in value—since the time of their discovery by some anonymous peasant who had the luck to stumble on an ancient tomb cave. Hundreds of tombs throughout the country were being opened and plundered every year to provide merchandise for the antiquities market, so it's not hard to understand why a number of Israeli archaeologists, outraged by the positive publicity that the Dayan Collection received, soon embarked on an outspoken campaign to change the country's antiquities laws.

Maybe the Emperor Constantine was really the guilty party for the current attitude toward archaeology-as-relic-hunting in the Land of the Bible. From the time he recognized Christianity as an accepted religion in the Roman Empire in the early fourth century A.D., the small province of Palaestina became the "Holy Land" for an enormous mass of faithful, and all its ancient remains were imbued with a corresponding holiness. The Jews had, of course, held a special devotion to the country for centuries, but it was manifested in their study and recitation of national history and in their custom of pilgrimage. For the Christians, history and pilgrimage continued to be important, but they were eventually overlaid with a devotion to tangible relics as well.

Bones of saints, garments and shrouds of New Testament figures, even the cross on which Jesus was crucified were discovered, bought and sold, and highly prized for their spiritual and healing power. Useful for both biblical contemplation and as talismans to ward off ill health and bad fortune, ancient artifacts from the Holy Land quickly became status symbols for simple Christian pilgrims and wealthy aristocrats alike. They also became the focus of intensive and lucrative—if somewhat less than scientific—archaeological activity. By the end of the fourth century, the export, or "translation," of relics from the Holy Land had reached enormous proportions. Bones, stones, and ancient linen became objects of devotion in churches and wealthy homes throughout Europe. And pieces of the most precious relic of all—the True Cross—were carried as far afield as Italy, North Africa, Asia Minor, and Gaul.

To a large extent, this international market in relics was encouraged by church officials, for it became an important source of revenue for the monastic and religious establishments in the Holy Land. There was also a wider political significance, for the popularity of the cult of relics reinforced the prestige and influence of Palestine in the theological controversies that became matters of state in the Byzantine Empire. But the sheer scale of export eventually created a problem; the relics of the Holy Land were not an easily renewable resource. Even the True Cross itself, long a dependable source of sacred splinters, was beginning to lose substance by the beginning of the fifth century A.D. Since a halt to all export—and the political and economic power that it brought—was unthinkable, the bishop of Jerusalem wisely proclaimed a miracle: The True Cross, he reported to the faithful, had the wondrous capacity of regenerating itself.

Whatever the historical comparison between the Byzantine cult of relics and the modern antiquities market, no one was talking about miraculous regeneration in Israel these days. I had seen for myself in the Shephelah how extensive the robbing had been. And the Shephelah was only one small region. Whole districts—particularly on the West Bank—had been ravaged. Caves, settlement sites, and cemeteries have been systematically plundered for salable artifacts. Additional funds had recently been made available to the Department of Antiquities for an ambitious enforcement campaign. Intensive patrols of archaeological sites—in the West Bank and the Galilee as well as the Shephelah—had resulted in the arrest of a number of antiquities robbers. Yet the antiquities trade went on.

It didn't really matter, though, how many diggers were arrested, for there were many other peasants and farmers in the rural areas of the country who would quickly take their place. During the previous two years, Department of Antiquities officers had learned a great deal about the mechanics of the modern antiquities trade. In some areas, the activity was well coordinated, with local middlemen—aware of which types of artifacts were currently popular—hiring gangs of laborers to attack specific sites. And after their harvest of relics, the trail of the middlemen led to the big cities—sometimes in vans filled with crates of ancient pottery—where the loot would be delivered to the antiquities shops.

And here was the stage of the merchandising process that was the most difficult for the Department of Antiquities to control. The licensed antiquities dealers in Israel were legally prohibited from obtaining new merchandise from illegal excavations; only those objects *already* in private collections were permitted for sale. Each dealer was required to maintain a detailed inventory of his merchandise, with a record of the source of each item. Unfortunately, private collectors were under no such obligation, so it was easy enough for both the dealer and his supplier to falsify the records and merely claim that the newly obtained antiquities had been in private hands for decades. Previous ownership was next to impossible to disprove.

That's why even the most dedicated officers of the Department of Antiquities knew that they were dealing only with the symptoms of a much larger problem in their arrests and occasional convictions of antiquities thieves. As long as a guest at the Tel Aviv Hilton, or even a transit passenger browsing in the duty-free shop at Ben Gurion Airport, could buy an ancient souvenir of his or her trip to Israel, the free flow of money resulting from such purchases would continue to destroy the country's archaeological heritage.

The members of the governing body of archaeological activity in Israel, the Archaeological Council, had been placed in a difficult position by some of their colleagues. A growing number of archaeologists were now demanding not only that the Dayan Collection be confiscated as state property but that the country's antiquities shops be closed. The Archaeological Council, legally empowered to advise the minister of education on archaeological policy and antiquities legislation, had long been hesitant to act on this matter. Its twenty-six members—drawn from museums, universities, and public institutions—represented a wide spectrum of interests, and not all of those interests were, strictly speaking, scholarly.

Some of the interests were personal: A number of the council members had been helped in their careers by being given permission to study and publish scholarly studies of especially important artifacts from private collections. Other interests were professional: The representatives of Israel's museums were naturally interested in encouraging the continued donation of ancient artifacts from private benefactors. Over the years, therefore, a cozy, if quiet, relationship had developed between collectors and dealers and some of the most prominent members of the archaeological establishment. Illicitly excavated artifacts were regularly exhibited and studied with little or no investigation of their source. And, as a result of the moral status quo that had been established, the Archaeological Council had repeatedly vetoed any proposed changes to the antiquities laws.

In the spring of 1986, however, the force of public opinion finally upset this arrangement. The controversy surrounding the Israel Museum's purchase of the Dayan Collection provided a springboard for action. The boycott and picketing of the gala opening of the Dayan Collection received wide media attention, but the young archaeologists' crusade against antiquities dealing in Israel did not stop there. In the months that followed, they succeeded in convincing a majority of their colleagues that great harm was being done to the ancient remains of the country by the sheer scale of the antiquities trade. They circulated petitions, lobbied politicians, and finally achieved through the force of political pressure what mere moralizing had never done. In the summer of 1986, when the Archaeological Council held its meeting, the members finally, if reluctantly, passed a resolution recommending that the sale and export of antiquities from Israel be banned.

With that vote, the legislative machinery was set in motion. Taking his cue from the Archaeological Council, the minister of education instructed his legal counsel to begin drafting a new law. Hearings were scheduled in the Knesset, the younger archaeologists savored their triumph, and the future of the country's antiquities dealers looked bleak. Unfortunately, the would-be reformers underestimated their opponents. The antiquities dealers had friends in high places, and emotional appeals could be used to defend *their* point of view as well. The sale and export of antiquities had long had an important social function in modern Israel, and it was on that basis that the defenders of the antiquities trade mounted their counterattack.

The preliminary hearing of the Knesset Education Committee on the new legislation was something of a disaster, at least from the reformers' point of view. First, representatives of the Department of Antiquities and the Association of Archaeologists in Israel presented their by-now-familiar litany of reports of destroyed sites and fears for the future of the country's ancient heritage. But after they had finished, the Education Committee members heard some equally persuasive arguments. One of the senior curators of the Israel Museum expressed his belief that a ban on antiquities dealing would do considerable damage. As long as the antiquities shops were subject to government supervision, he argued, there was at least the possibility that archaeologists would be aware of new discoveries.

What about the Dead Sea Scrolls? They were purchased from illegal excavators. Was it wrong to make every effort to obtain them for the State of Israel and the scholarly world? The scrolls were just one example, the curator contended, and there were many more that came to mind. Antiquities trading was simply a fact of life, he continued, an activity that was impossible to eradicate completely, even in countries with truly draconian antiquities laws. If the shops in Israel were to be closed by legal order, the curator warned, the trading would merely continue underground. And, since collectors obviously would be afraid to reveal their new acquisitions to scholars, many important artifacts would be lost to archaeology.

In the weeks that followed the hearing, the momentum against reform began to pick up speed. The dealers and their supporters formed the Antiquities Trade Protection Association and, in newspaper and radio interviews, several prominent public figures proclaimed their strong opposition to any change in the antiquities law. The initial vote of the Archaeological Council had not been unanimous, and there was a chance that it might be reversed when the council was convened again. Three of its best-known members, Jerusalem mayor Teddy Kollek, Haifa industrialist Reuben Hecht, and former Supreme Court Justice Haim Etzioni (all of them avid antiquities collectors), now lent the full weight of their prestige to halting any legislative action and to preserving, at all costs, the antiquities trade.

Mayor Kollek, in particular, had never been known to back off from a political fistfight, and in his position as chairman of the board of directors of the Israel Museum, he had always viewed the archaeological reformers with disdain. In the ceremonies at the opening of the Dayan Collection, he had characterized their angry protest outside the main entrance as "the yapping of small dogs." Now that their threat was more serious, he himself went on the attack. In an interview in the glossy, upscale magazine *Monitin*, he put forth a counterproposal with something for everyone. Instead of prohibiting antiquities dealing, he suggested, the State of Israel should become an antiquities dealer itself.

By placing on sale the thousands of duplicate pottery vessels in its storerooms, the Department of Antiquities could, Kollek argued, achieve three valuable objectives at once. The massive influx of artifacts on the world market would, at least according to the mayor, stimulate international interest in the archaeology of Israel, lower the market value to the point that much of the present robbing would be unprofitable, and provide a new source of funding for the preservation and protection of archaeological sites. This proposal raised some troubling ethical issues that the mayor did not bother to address; it was highly questionable whether government employees had the right to dispose of national cultural property, much less determine its going price. But Kollek's proposal was quickly seen as a tactical maneuver by many political observers, for he had, in the meantime, taken a more direct approach to heading off any official change in the antiquities laws.

His personal intervention with his old friend Yitzhak Navon, the minister of education and culture, resulted in a sudden, unexpected suspension of the legislative process. The ministry counsel was instructed to stop, at least temporarily, the drafting of the new antiquities regulations. With the support of Hecht and Etzioni and virtually all of the country's museum curators, Kollek called for a new meeting of the Archaeological Council, to reconsider their previous note.

The archaeological reformers continued their protests, yet with other, more pressing diplomatic and military matters facing the country, public interest in the matter slowly faded away. Two years later, in 1988, the issue still had not been settled and the future of the antiquities trade in Israel was unclear. For despite the repeated calls for action in the Knesset and the intensifying efforts of the Department of Antiquities to put an end to the robbing, the sale and veneration of relics remained a familiar part of the Israeli scene.

The modern political and ideological power of the ancient relics was undeniable; that power had been used by both the supporters and the opponents of the antiquities trade. But the controversy over the Dayan Collection and the subsequent legislative battle symbolized a more profound disagreement about the modern ideological use of the past. With no foreseeable conclusion to the wrangling, it remained an open question whether in the future the antiquities of Israel would be viewed as a precious, finite resource—to be handled and interpreted only by experts—or whether, like the bones, shrouds, and True Cross of the Byzantine period, their usefulness would lie in how widely they were dispersed.

8

EGYPT

Strangers in the Land

The traffic in downtown Cairo was frightening on that February morning. The rush hour that had begun before dawn was still well under way. An unceasing stream of Fiat, Mercedes, Volkswagen, and Peugeot passenger cars, buses, motorcycles, lorries, and pickups whirled around the huge stone monument in the center of *Midan al-Tahrir*, "Liberation Square." There were no sidewalks to protect the workers and tourists who wanted to walk alongside the traffic, much less crosswalks for them to get to the other side. What protection there was lay in numbers; so I joined a small group of scrambling risk-takers, wading into the dangerous flow of oncoming vehicles, skipping across the jagged potholes in the pavement, and navigating around the concrete-and-girder pilings and construction debris of the still-unfinished Cairo subway.

I was on my way—I hoped—to escape from the present, into the more sedate and reassuring charms of Egypt's glorious past. I wanted to meet Professor Manfred Bietak, the director of the Austrian Archaeological Institute in Cairo, a scholar who seemed to me to be both a symbol and a spokesman for the younger generation of foreign archaeologists working in Egypt today. Bietak had established a reputation among his colleagues as an innovative and influential scholar whose economic and cultural approach to ancient civilization has already begun to challenge some of the accepted understandings of ancient Egyptian history. He and his staff had been digging at the rich site of Tell el-Dab'a in the eastern Nile Delta for almost two decades. When I first learned of the goals and significance of those Austrian excavations, I suspected that Manfred Bietak's brand of archaeology might be as revealing about the role of foreigners in the modern economy and culture of Egypt as it was useful for explaining Egypt's past.

It wasn't easy to make contact with Bietak; I had his telephone number but no street address. For two full days at the start of my trip through Egypt, I had tried without success to call him, and was almost ready to give up the search. The phone number I had been given apparently wasn't working, but it was out of order a different way each time I tried. The line was busy for all of the first day; there was no answer for most of the second. When I finally got through to a puzzled Egyptian family in the late afternoon, they angrily denied any connection whatsoever to Austrian archaeology.

I would have been surprised, even shocked, if they *had* heard of Bietak, for despite the intimate association of archaeology and Egypt in the Western imagination, the digging of the archaeologists goes on in a world quite isolated from the nation's modern realities. Tell el-Dab'a, site of the Austrian excavations, is far from the crowded streets of Cairo. It's located almost sixty miles to the northeast, in the midst of the labyrinthine Nile channels and waterlogged fields, on the outskirts of the sleepy delta town of Qantir. In ancient times, though, this site was of more than passing interest to many Egyptians; this part of the delta then was Egypt's most vulnerable border, a region that permitted easy access by outsiders along the eastern or Pelusiac branch of the Nile. The superimposed settlement levels, cemeteries, palaces, and temples that Bietak and his team had uncovered at Tell el-Dab'a testified to its ancient prominence. Here, they believed, once stood the ancient city of Avaris, the capital of one of the most mysterious groups of outsiders ever to penetrate the border—the foreign "Hyksos" kings of Egypt, who ruled the country from around 1670 to 1560 B.C.

Before coming to Egypt, I had become interested in the Hyksos "problem" that Bietak and his team were investigating at Tell el-

Dab'a—as yet another example of a search for the mysterious origins of an ancient ethnic group. As was the case with the Macedonians, the Mycenaeans, the Minoans, and the Israelites, time-honored national myths and legends had long concealed the Hyksos' true identity. In Egypt, however, the Hyksos were hardly beloved, nor were they seen as national forefathers in any sense. In fact, outright hatred of the Hyksos had been a standard theme in Egyptian historiography for thousands of years.

According to the most complete historical account, preserved in the writings of the third-century B.C. Egyptian priest Manetho, the Hyksos were "a people of ignoble origin from the east" who suddenly invaded the country, "then savagely burnt the cities, razed the temples of the gods to the ground, and treated the whole of the native population with the utmost cruelty, massacring some and carrying off the wives and children of others into slavery." They established their capital of Avaris in the delta, a strongly fortified city garrisoned by an incredible, obviously legendary force of 240,000 armed men. During the successive reigns of six Hyksos kings, lasting more than a century, they held Egypt under oppression until they were finally defeated in battle and expelled from the country by a native Egyptian dynasty. The fact that those invaders were less civilized than the Egyptians (and possibly were nomads) was seemingly reinforced by Manetho's explanation of the derivation of the name "Hyksos" as a combination of the ancient Egyptian words *hyk* and *sos*, whose meaning was "shepherd kings."

As modern exploration and excavation in Egypt proceeded in the nineteenth century, evidence was found of Hyksos-hatred in even earlier historical periods. Early in the century, the British Museum acquired a folktale written on papyrus that described the comical discomfort of a wicked Hyksos king named Apophis who could not sleep at night because of the bellowing of the Nile hippopotamuses 500 miles to the south in Thebes. And an inscription found in 1908 at Thebes—the capital of the local dynasts who ultimately destroyed the Hyksos rule—detailed the first stages of the battle between the Hyksos and the Thebans, in which the Egyptian forces sailed down the Nile and handed the foreigners a bitter defeat. A later find at el-Kab indicated that with the rise of the 18th Egyptian Dynasty, around 1580 B.C., that campaign became a rout. A tomb inscription of an officer in the service of Pharaoh Ahmose described the sack of Avaris and the Egyptian pursuit of the defeated Hyksos into southern Palestine.

Other ancient inscriptions revealed that long after the invaders were expelled from the country, their evil reputation remained. Nearly a century after the fall of Avaris, Queen Hatshepsut, in her dedication of a temple, boasted that she had "restored what was ruined and raised up what was previously neglected," for when the Hyksos had governed the country, "they ruled without Re, none of them acting according to the god's command."

Ancient Egyptian hatred of the Hyksos was obvious, yet there was considerable confusion in the ancient accounts regarding the Hyksos' origins and identity. The various preserved versions of Manetho's writings suggested that they may have been Phoenicians, Arabs, or even biblical patriarchs. But at the end of the nineteenth century, a time when racial explanations for history were fashionable among European scholars, the Hyksos were perceived somewhat more favorably by those scholars—if not by the Egyptians themselves. First, the British Egyptologist Francis Griffith turned his attention to the name "Hyksos" and concluded that it had nothing to do with shepherds. He suggested that the ancient hieroglyphic symbols transliterated as "Hyksos" actually meant "rulers of foreign countries," and it didn't take long for some of his colleagues to identify the Hyksos as a group of the world's most "natural" rulers—the ancient Aryans.

The evidence was, of course, quickly forthcoming, since many of the scholars knew more or less what they wanted to find. The pioneering British archaeologist Flinders Petrie identified certain metal weapons found in levels ascribed to the Hyksos as products of a distinctly "northern" culture, whose bearers, he suggested, had migrated southward from the Caucasus. The association of horses with Hyksos burials seemed to bolster the theory of an Aryan origin, since horsemanship was at that time still believed to be a characteristic European forte. And in the 1930s, when archaeologists of the Oriental Institute of the University of Chicago excavated "Hyksos" levels at the mound of Megiddo in Palestine, the staff anthropologists seemed to observe clear "alpine" characteristics in some of the skulls.

So the Hyksos, at least according to late-nineteenth-century European racial dogma, succeeded in conquering Egypt because of their supposed racial superiority. As was the case with the German tribes who overran the Roman Empire, a "pure" and "vigorous" people— so the European historians assumed—overwhelmed a sophisticated society in decline.

By the 1980s, though, such racially deterministic concepts—born in an era of European expansion and empire—had long gone out of fashion, and Professor Manfred Bietak's explanation of Hyksos origins seemed to me more in tune with the times. The era of international trade and international development had dawned in modern Egypt, as well as in the study of its past. Bietak's excavations at the site of the Hyksos capital of Avaris had convinced him that the phenomenon of Hyksos rule was a natural development of economic trends *within* Egyptian society, and that the Hyksos "conquest" of Egypt could, in fact, be explained as easily in cultural and economic terms as their "fall."

"The real processes of history," Bietak would later tell me, "are more complex than political concepts." He completely rejected the idea that the rise to power of the Hyksos was based on sheer military might, racial vigor, or innate technological superiority. In his published articles on the Hyksos, he had implicitly taken the role of their protector. Bietak had come to believe that the traditional view of the Hyksos as evil and violent intruders was merely self-serving political propaganda developed by subsequent Egyptian dynasties to explain away the true circumstances of Hyksos rule. Xenophobia may have been as effective a political weapon in antiquity as it is in the present, and Bietak argued persuasively that for modern scholars to take it at face value betrayed a dangerously unsophisticated approach to the far more subtle mechanics of history.

It's not difficult to understand why Bietak had a natural distrust of purely political explanations for historical changes; he had begun his professional career in the early 1960s on the Aswan High Dam Rescue Project, the massive scientific undertaking that is now recognized as a turning point in Egyptian archaeology. With the damming of the Nile above Aswan, the ruins of much of ancient Nubia would be submerged beneath the waters of the newly created Lake

Nasser, and thereby lost forever to archaeology. While earlier foreign expeditions to Egypt had concentrated primarily on monumental architecture, museum-quality artifacts, and hieroglyphic inscriptions, the scholars from the forty nations who came to Egypt under UNESCO auspices had no such luxury in their choice of finds. Racing against the rising waters of Lake Nasser, they mapped, excavated, and studied hundreds of ancient remains, ranging from the gigantic temple of Abu Simbel to the nearly invisible campsites of the Paleolithic period. Their goal was to recover as much archaeological information as quickly as possible. Yet, at the same time, they began to recognize some of the economic factors that the potentates of ancient Egypt had preferred not to stress in their official histories.

Bietak's role in this project, undertaken as part of the Austrian contribution to the international rescue effort, was to map and excavate the ancient Nubian settlements and cemeteries along the desolate gorge of the Nile Valley as it wound its way toward the Sudan border. The archaeological challenge was enormous, since earlier scholars had done only limited work on the rise and development of the Nubian culture as an independent entity. Bietak's predecessors had concentrated primarily on the region's connection to Egypt as a source of manpower and valuable raw materials, and in that sense they had shared ancient Egypt's imperialistic viewpoint. But Bietak's reconstruction of the development of this African civilization was not based primarily on the scattered references to raids, trade missions, and conquests in Nubia recorded on bombastic pharaonic dedicatory inscriptions and tomb reliefs. By tracing the appearance and distribution of distinctive artifacts in Nubian settlement levels and cemeteries, he discovered a more complex historical situation. He was able to show how movements of people, products, and ideas—not only the political and military policies of the kings of Egypt—affected the course of Nubia's history.

More than twenty years had passed since Bietak ended his work in southern Egypt, but his recent articles suggested that his approach to the question of the Hyksos at Tell el-Dab'a was essentially the same. Although the written sources on the history of the Hyksos provided a vivid and seemingly coherent account of the Hyksos rule in Egypt, the archaeological finds from Tell el-Dab'a offered quite a different perspective. From the start of the excavations, Bietak's strategy was to discover the economic and cultural function of the Hyksos capital and then to draw broader historical conclusions about the Hyksos themselves. Not unexpectedly, Bietak's reconstruction was a radical departure from all previous theories. Instead of finding a huge encampment of warlike invaders who cruelly subjugated the people of Egypt, Bietak and his excavation team had uncovered the remains of a flourishing, expanding community of merchants and craftsmen whose prosperity was based not on invasion and conquest, but on peaceful interaction through trade.

The resentment of foreign influence in Egypt, from the time of the Hyksos all the way to the present era of resurgent Islamic fundamentalism, seemed to be a continuing theme in its history. I wanted to meet Bietak and learn something more of the finds from Tell el-Dabʻa about the nature of ancient foreigners in Egypt than the architectural plans and pottery profiles already published in his technical reports. But modern Cairo's telephone technology—installed by more recent foreigners—had betrayed me. With only one day left before I was scheduled to take the overnight train almost 500 miles up the Nile to Luxor, I scrambled with the other pedestrians across Liberation Square and headed for the Cairo Museum for one last attempt at locating Professor Manfred Bietak.

Beyond the newsstands, hawkers, and tourist shills, the grounds of the museum seemed quiet. It wasn't that the exhaust fumes and honking of the traffic were suddenly blocked at the entrance; it was rather that I knew I was about to enter a cathedral of sacred and sedate antiquity established here in one of the world's most mammoth and occasionally unruly cities, a shrine to the comfort that Western ideas of "history" can sometimes bring. Those ideas had been transported to Egypt by Western scholars in the company of far more practical commercial agents and military men. The idea of a national museum was suggested to the Khedive of Egypt, Said Pasha, in the 1850s by the French Egyptologist Auguste Mariette—at the same time that another Frenchman, Ferdinand de Lesseps, was making the pasha's head spin with dreamlike plans for "modernization" and a canal from the Mediterranean to the Gulf of Suez.

Both Frenchmen ultimately achieved their objectives, and their efforts transformed Egypt's identity both in the present and in the remote past. The museum's neoclassic building was designed at the turn of the century by the French architect Marcel Dourgnon. By that time, Western Egyptology had completed its conquest of ancient Egypt; the elegant reflecting pool with its lotuses and papyrus stalks and the carefully arranged statues of ancient gods and pharaohs reflected the way European scholars had decided the essence of Egyptian culture should be seen. Even Auguste Mariette himself, the first director of the Egyptian Antiquities Service, found a peaceful, final resting place in that garden. His stone sarcophagus, surmounted by a statue, might—for some tourist without a guidebook—be easily mistaken for the tomb of a late and rather short-lived Egyptian king.

I was surprised to discover that this day at the Cairo Museum was to be one of celebration for the Western archaeological community in Egypt. The normal exhibits in the museum's ground-level entrance hall were being pushed to the sides. As I entered, young curators were directing custodians to position special glass cases and to set up large photomurals of selected ancient sites. The Czechoslovak Institute of Egyptology was celebrating its twenty-fifth anniversary of digging and discovery in Egypt. And since the entire community of archaeologists in Cairo was invited to the opening ceremony for the special exhibition, I waited patiently in the comforting shadows of some towering pharaonic sculpture in hopes of making contact with the scholar whom I had failed to reach by telephone.

Gradually, the guests began to assemble, filtering into the cool shade of the museum from the glare and the traffic outside. Sedate black limousines with diplomatic license plates pulled up at the entrance, delivering their important guests for the ceremony. The arrival of the younger members of the archaeological community was less auspicious, although their three-piece suits and respectable dresses clearly set them, too, apart from the tourists and the museum employees. A film crew from Egyptian Television tested its floodlights when the last displays were put into place. And as white-coated waiters circulated through the crowd with trays of soft drinks, Dr. Muhammed Salah of the Egyptian Antiquities Organization called the assembled guests to attention and began his respectful appreciation of the work of the Czechoslovak Institute of Egyptology.

While the speeches continued, and as the TV crew moved forward to record Salah's warm introduction of the guest of honor, Professor Miroslav Verner, I navigated through the knots of chatting scholars and finally located one of Bietak's colleagues, Dr. Dorner, a heavyset man with a thick mustache. After introducing myself, I explained to Dorner that I hadn't been able to contact Professor Bietak by phone. "Of course," he reassured me, "our phone number was suddenly changed. But anyway, Professor Bietak has been back in Vienna. He's returning to Cairo tomorrow and we'll be leaving for Tell el-Dab'a next week. So if you want to speak with him, you'll have to do it right away." With time an obvious problem, I copied down Dorner's directions to the Austrian Archaeological Institute, which was located in one of Cairo's most fashionable and modern neighborhoods.

"Just tell the taxi driver to take you to Wimpy Zamalek," Dorner told me. "Everybody in Cairo knows where that is."

The taxi left me off outside Wimpy Zamalek, an obviously popular outlet of the British fast-food chain. Egyptian schoolgirls in prim pleated skirts and blouses sat happily munching on hamburgers beneath the garish transparencies of the specialties of the house. All along Khedive Ismail Muhammad Street, the windows of Western-style boutiques and shops displayed products and fashions that perhaps would have made the street's nineteenth-century namesake surprised at where his program of westernization would lead. Just a few steps toward the Nile was the apartment building that served as the home of the Austrian Archaeological Institute in Cairo. Finding that the elevator in the entrance hall wasn't working, I climbed the back stairway to one of the upper stories. I was relieved, yet somewhat surprised, when I finally found a door with a shiny brass plaque that identified the apartment of the Austrian Embassy Scientific Counsellor.

I wasn't aware that Bietak had diplomatic status, yet the fact of governmental support of archaeological work seemed reassuring, an indication that the Austrian government valued the cultural and educational contributions of its Egyptologists. I rang the bell and was politely greeted by a woman who led me through a semidarkened living room with oriental carpets, heavily upholstered furniture, and a grand piano—a touch of Vienna in the Middle East. Then I followed her up an interior staircase to a well-lit office whose small brass plaque identified it as that of the director of the institute. She motioned for me to enter, then closed the door. I waited patiently inside, admiring the detailed excavation plans and topographical maps tacked to bulletin boards on the walls. Bookcases of Egyptological and archaeological journals stood near the windows. Account books and unfinished correspondence covered the director's desk.

In a minute or so, Professor Bietak entered and I introduced myself. We chatted briefly about common archaeological acquaintances as he sat down behind his desk to sign a few of the neatly typed letters that had been set out for him. Bietak apologized for his obvious distraction, explaining that having just returned from Vienna and with the excavation season about to begin, he was in the midst of finalizing the budgets, accounts, and the thousand-and-one other details that had to be attended to before he and the other members of the team could leave Cairo for the field.

Somehow I expected Bietak to look older. As I watched him go over the administrative forms and correspondence, I couldn't help but think of the Egyptologists of an earlier age. With his neatly trimmed beard, plaid tweed jacket, sweater and tie, he reminded me of a young Flinders Petrie—the famous British explorer who had come out to Egypt in the 1880s and who had dealt with some of the same historical problems that now concerned Bietak. But times had changed since Petrie, and Bietak's place in modern Egypt required a dramatically different approach to the same history. He now rose from his desk and took a chair near mine to answer my questions about his work at Tell el-Dab'a. And before long, I began to understand the significance of his discoveries there, as a vivid illustration of ancient economic and cultural change.

According to the accepted chronology of the dynasties of Egypt, the Hyksos domination of Egypt began around 1670 B.C., but Bietak explained that the chain of events that made the Hyksos takeover inevitable began long before that. Pointing to one of the excavation maps on the wall, he started to tell his story, one that began around 2000 B.C. It was then that the earliest settlement at Tell el-Dab'a was founded, but its establishment had nothing to do with foreigners. Its architecture and pottery were thoroughly Egyptian in style, and, according to Bietak, it had the character of a military outpost, probably established by the Egyptian kings of the 11th Dynasty to guard the eastern approaches of the Nile Delta from incursions by the nomads of northern Sinai, who were then the most threatening outside elements.

But two hundred years later, long after that first military garrison had been abandoned, Bietak went on, the natural advantages of the location attracted a new wave of settlers, who practiced a quite different way of life. The Egyptian determination to keep out intruders had apparently lessened, for in the remains of the mud-brick houses of this and the succeeding levels, the Austrian excavation team discovered molds and crucibles for the manufacture of metal tools and weapons of distinctly un-Egyptian types, and, no less important, vast quantities of fragments of distinctively shaped storejars, known from contemporary Egyptian wall paintings to have contained imported oil and wine. The source of these storejars was not Egypt, but the busy trading cities of the eastern Mediterranean coast—in the area of modern Israel and Lebanon—and Bietak believed that they represented the establishment of a foreign trading colony in the Nile Delta, a commercial emporium that was sanctioned and possibly even encouraged by the Egyptians themselves.

Archaeologists working in the ruins of Egypt in the distant future may find that Coca-Cola bottles and rusty spark plugs are far more significant historical evidence than the "official" histories of the late-twentieth-century Egyptian regimes. Bietak was looking for similarly evocative artifacts at Tell el-Dab'a, and he believed that he had found one on the floor of a large public building, which, from its reception halls and storerooms, seemed likely to have been the headquarters of a local Egyptian governor or administrator. This artifact was a tiny cylinder seal, less than one inch in length and only one-half inch in diameter, of a type used in antiquity as an official stamp of ownership or authority when it was rolled across the wet-clay sealings of documents or jars. As Bietak stressed to me, its significance lay in the elaborate design carved into the surface: the striding figure of Baal Zaphon, the storm god of the early Phoenician pantheon, shown protecting a sailing ship.

Statistics are no less important in modern archaeology than in modern business, and Bietak was anxious to reveal some of the big numbers that certainly seemed to cement his case. The characteristic oil and wine jars that had first led him to his identification of the Hyksos as northern traders were found in abundance in the levels of Tell el-Dab'a. Abundance, though, was not a precise enough description of those storejars' significance. Bietak and his team had attempted to calculate their approximate number by sampling the quantity of fragments found in representative excavation areas and extrapolating the quantities that might be found in the entire ancient city. They came up with a round figure of approximately two million for the 250 years of Hyksos occupation at the site. And since these fragments, Bietak believed, represented only those jars that happened to be broken or left at the Nile Delta port of arrival, they represented only a small part of the total volume of trade.

The statistics revealed that for every day between 1800 and 1550 B.C., at least twenty of the large jars filled with the valuable commodities were dropped or lost in transit on their way to the cities, towns, and villages farther up the Nile. And for each one of those days, additional dozens, if not hundreds, successfully passed through the storehouses of Avaris, loaded onto barges or donkey caravans, leaving no visible trace at the site. This enormous volume of trade was in itself surprising, but even more so was Bietak's realization of its original mode of transport. Since virtually no trace of overland commerce in this period had been found in extensive archaeological surveys along the northern coast of Sinai, Bietak was convinced that the millions of storejars filled with oil and wine came to Tell el-Dab'a in the holds of merchant vessels, and that the long-distance maritime trade from the coast of Lebanon—*not* overland migration or warfare—was the key to understanding the Hyksos' spectacular rise.

In the modern Middle East, dramatic changes in the patterns of overseas trade and commerce have become matters of both economic and political significance. Since the mid-1970s, the region has witnessed, for example, a gradual flight of multinational businessmen and their corporate headquarters from their formerly secure haven in Beirut. And a similar phenomenon in the Middle Bronze Age provided Bietak with what he believed was the clinching piece of evidence for his new theory of Hyksos origins. As earlier French excavations on the Lebanese coast had revealed, the ancient port city of Byblos, long a flourishing center of trade with Egypt, entered a period of catastrophic economic decline around 1720 B.C.

The precise reasons for market crashes and economic depressions in antiquity are as uncertain as those of the present, but whether the cause of Byblos's hard times was the territorial expansion of the neighboring kingdom of Yamkhad (on the site of modern Aleppo) and the disruption of Byblos's traditional trade routes, or whether the cause was serious internal unrest, Byblos suddenly entered what Bietak described to me as an "archaeological blackout." Law and order in the rich city crumbled; the elaborate tombs of the nobles of Byblos were plundered and abandoned; ongoing construction projects in the city were suddenly halted; and the embattled population—consisting mainly of those too poor to flee the violence—was increasingly concentrated in the city's slums.

A "Beirut" of the eighteenth century B.C.? Bietak suggested that this was the approximate state of affairs. The sudden appearance of a new wave of immigrants in Avaris at precisely the same time—wealthy personages who established impressive cemeteries and Syro-Phoenician-style temples—seemed to Bietak to be persuasive evidence that the original trading colony was now augmented by the arrival of upper-class merchants and their families who had fled from their homeland and subsequently made Avaris their permanent base.

The groundwork for these wealthy immigrants' rise to power in Egypt had been laid during the previous eighty years of lucrative commerce. The increasing dependence of the Egyptians on the trading services of foreigners had encouraged those foreigners, in a time of economic upheaval, to take advantage of the natural wealth of Egypt—not as a distant, if profitable, foreign market, but as the headquarters of a new and more extensive commercial empire. And here, the written records of the Egyptians seemed finally to match

Bietak's archaeological reconstruction: With the decline and disintegration of the 13th Egyptian Dynasty in the following century, the Hyksos "rulers of foreign countries," whose capital was Avaris, gradually assumed political control of Egypt. But Bietak still believed that the match between archaeology and ancient records needed some reshaping. The Hyksos did not assume political control through a sudden, massive invasion and the brutal massacre of women and children. The pomp and circumstance of pharaonic power was merely a fringe benefit of their having completely taken over the country's economic machinery. As I listened to Bietak's description of the process, the image of the Hyksos suddenly changed. Those conquerors may not have been the shaggy warriors of ancient legend; they now seemed more like ancient multinational corporate executives.

Bietak's work hundreds of miles to the south in Nubia in the early 1960s provided him with an archaeological tool to trace the extent of that Hyksos trading network, for at Avaris he found some characteristic Nubian pottery types. It was clear to him that the riches of Nubia that had once been directed to the coffers and tombs of the native kings of Egypt now fueled overseas commercial enterprises on an unprecedented scale. The discovery of Hyksos artifacts on the island of Cyprus and on the Aegean islands of Crete and Thera had always puzzled scholars who had underestimated the economic basis of Hyksos rule. But Bietak's economic analysis now undermined the violent stereotype and explained the wide distribution of Hyksos products. That distribution, he believed, was the result of the commerce of a group of skillful international merchants whose free hand in Egypt enabled them to piece together a complex trading network that a strong central government in Egypt previously had prevented.

There were, of course, weaknesses implicit in this trading network. For the Hyksos merchant princes to maintain their economic power, they had constantly to elicit and cultivate the cooperation of the local Egyptian population up and down the Nile. The object was to keep the trade routes open all the way from Nubia northward to the Mediterranean Sea. This required the services of local administrators, commercial agents, warehouse clerks, and district officers—and an appropriately massive bureaucracy. The city of Thebes in Upper Egypt was a crucial link in this Hyksos commercial chain, and its local rulers, growing tired of being mere middlemen, may have eventually schemed to become merchant princes themselves. Some suggestive clues in this direction emerged in the course of the Tell el-Dab'a excavations, where Bietak discovered that in the last of the Hyksos levels of the city, the previously common types of Nubian pottery suddenly disappeared. The city of Thebes, soon to become the capital of a resurrected, native Egyptian kingdom, was in a position to sever the connection between the Nile Delta and Africa. And once that economic coup d'état was accomplished, Bietak believed that the leaders of the Theban aristocracy skillfully persuaded the rest of Egypt that the military defeat and expulsion of the Hyksos was nothing less than a patriotic crusade.

The expulsion of the Hyksos and their "insidious" foreign influence was, for centuries, celebrated as a triumph of Egyptian self-determination, but as Bietak now explained to me, the Hyksos' transformation of the Egyptian economy had effects that persisted long after they themselves were driven out of the country to become the bogeymen of Egyptian history. In the hands of the Theban kings of the 18th Dynasty, the trading network established by the "rulers of foreign countries" provided the basis for the unprecedented wealth of the palaces, temples, and royal tombs of New Kingdom times. Much of what modern scholars consider most typically Egyptian in its splendor and opulence may, in fact, have been due to the earlier economic achievements of traders who came from the outside.

The extensive Egyptian trade with Cyprus, the Aegean, and the cities of the eastern Mediterranean was seemingly made possible by the commercial infrastructure established during the Hyksos period. Never again could Egypt be content to separate itself from the outside world, and, from that perspective, the Hyksos were of paramount importance for understanding ancient Egyptian history. What was remembered by later Egyptians as an unpleasant interlude of outside domination, Bietak believed, may actually have been a mechanism of profound—not to say evolutionary—cultural and economic change.

By this time, I had already taken more of Professor Bietak's time than he had apparently expected. In his recounting of the story of the Hyksos, he had forgotten how much he still had to do before departing for the field. His associate, Dr. Dorner, knocked quietly and entered the office with a sheaf of typed pages. I rose and suggested the obvious—that it was probably time for me to leave. But Bietak seemed anxious that I read more of his articles, and he generously pulled a few copies from his files. After leaving the two scholars to continue their preparations, I stopped for lunch at the Wimpy on the corner of Khedive Ismail Muhammad Street.

As I waited for my hamburger, I looked over the articles about Tell el-Dab'a that Bietak had given me. Most were technical discussions of dating systems and pottery analysis published in professional archaeological journals, but one seemed more significant than the rest. Written for a nonacademic audience, it had appeared in a recent issue of *Marhaba*, an Austrian trade journal published by the Verein zur Förderung österreichisch-arabischer Beziehungen, "Society for Fostering Austrian-Arab Relations." Its mission of goodwill was captured even in the journal's name, for *marhaba*, in Arabic, means "hello."

The issue was filled with articles and interviews with Austrian businessmen and diplomats extolling their country's participation in commercial and industrial projects throughout the Middle East. Its message was clearly upbeat and designed to encourage scientific and technological progress—to demonstrate how international trade could be beneficial to all. And, in this respect, it wasn't surprising that the Austrian excavations at Tell el-Dab'a were considered worthy of publicity, as an example of the Austrian contribution to the region's cultural life.

Yet the strange juxtaposition of subjects provided an ironic, modern context for Bietak's study of the ancient Hyksos merchant princes and their corporate history. Wedged between an advertisement for Hitzinger Synchronous Alternators and an article on the growing volume of Austrian exports to Oman was Manfred Bietak's report on his discoveries in the eastern Nile Delta, entitled "Some News about Trade and Trade Warfare in Egypt and the Ancient Near East."

9

EGYPT

An Uneasy Inheritance

🔲 **T**he staff and students at Chicago House at Luxor, living far from the bustle of the town center, with its modern hotels and souvenir hawkers, seemed to relish their isolation. Only the occasional whoosh of an air-conditioned tourist coach headed toward the Temple of Karnak or the clip-clopping of Luxor's ubiquitous *hantours*, or horse-drawn carriages, seemed to disturb their serene if sometimes worried contemplation of ancient Egyptian history. In the elegant stone building described at the time of its construction in the late 1920s as "California-Spanish," an international team of Egyptologists, photographers, and draftsmen employed by the Oriental Institute of the University of Chicago were far more concerned with the past than with the present. They were engaged in the painstaking work of recording and preserving some of the most important details of Luxor's ancient inheritance. Yet in recent years, with the growth of Luxor and the modernization of Egypt, the present had become less easy to ignore. The main objects of their devotion—the impressive temples and tombs of the pharaonic period—were now seriously endangered by the destructive effects of Egypt's changed environment and by the wear and tear caused by the relentless flow of tourist groups.

By the time I arrived at Chicago House to speak with Dr. William Murnane, the assistant director, he had already begun his detailed explanation of the preservation work of the Oriental Institute's Architectural and Epigraphic Survey. In the cool, quiet library of the house, he had spread out large-scale drawings of hieroglyphic inscriptions that his team had carefully copied from the walls of the temples of Luxor and Medinet Habu. A middle-aged couple visiting from Chicago—apparently longtime contributors to the Oriental Institute's fund-raising appeals—seemed impressed with Murnane's explanation of the work of the survey. For, unlike the other foreign expeditions working in Luxor, this archaeological team had not come to dig and discover new relics. Its goal was to preserve and record for future generations the valuable information about ancient Egyptian politics, religion, and culture already visible above the ground.

Off to the side of the library, another staff member was intently making notes and corrections on a recently completed drawing, pausing repeatedly to compare the intricate hieroglyphic symbols with the texts of other ancient inscriptions reproduced on the oversize pages of site reports and Egyptological reference books. Like medieval monks tirelessly hand copying—and occasionally editing—the manuscripts of a sacred tradition, the scholars at Chicago House were the dedicated curators of a hallowed heritage. For more than sixty years, the scholars here had been guided by the faith that they were preserving the precious inheritance not only of Egypt, but of a formative chapter in the cultural development of the Western world.

It was no accident that the spiritual father of Chicago House, Professor James Breasted of the University of Chicago, chose Luxor as the primary focus of his efforts when he initiated the ambitious preservation project in 1923. Few places in the world were as blessed with ancient monuments as this small Upper Egyptian town, located about 450 miles south of Cairo on the eastern bank of the Nile. Close to the center of town rose the enormous ruins of the Temple of Luxor, its façade guarded by a row of obelisks and gigantic seated pharaonic statues and its interior filled with rows of heavy columns surmounted by huge lotus-blossom capitals. To the north of the town center stood the Temple of Karnak, a sprawling, labyrinthine complex of pharaonic statuary and massive architecture covered with acres of finely carved hieroglyphs. And across the river, scattered between the rich floodplain and the desolate desert mountains, were the impressive ruins of royal mortuary temples, the brightly painted tombs of ancient Egyptian aristocrats, queens, and princes, and, most elaborate of all, in a rugged valley snaking its way into the desert, were the deep underground resting places of the pharaohs themselves.

By Breasted's time, Western scholars had already reconstructed the main outlines of Luxor's 4,000-year history, and its influential role in the development of Egyptian civilization was clear. First established as a permanent settlement around 2100 B.C. by the kings of the 11th Dynasty, the cultic and political center they called *Waset* remained for centuries a focus of Upper Egyptian power and prestige. With the rise of the powerful Upper Egyptian dynasties of the New Kingdom around 1600 B.C., and their subsequent expulsion of the shadowy "Hyksos," Waset became a national capital and its local ram-headed god Amun became the divine patron of Egyptian kings.

As the center of an empire that drew its wealth from Africa, Asia, and the lands around the Mediterranean, Waset played both political and spiritual roles. In its magnificent temples were enacted the complex rituals that ensured the continued well-being of the current pharaoh, and on its western bank were the tombs of earlier pharaohs, mummified and laid to rest amid precious offerings and personal possessions for their journey to the afterworld. For hundreds of years, Waset retained its centrality to Egyptian culture, and even after its splendor had faded, its legend endured. To the Greeks, who called this city "Thebes," after a royal city in their own country, the place was one of incomparable beauty and mystery. And to the Romans who came here as conquerors, the magnificent ancient temples of Diospolis Magna—the "Great City of God," as they called it in Greek—provided fitting backdrops for their own imperial dreams.

Yet the long decline of this city added a tragic epilogue to the story. By the first century B.C., at the time of the Roman conquest of Egypt, the priesthood of Amun retained hardly a vestige of its former power. Since the decline and fall of the New Kingdom a thousand years earlier, devotion to Amun and his city had become a venerable tradition rather than a metaphysical necessity. And with Roman emperors now claiming for themselves the prerogatives of the pharaohs, the rituals in the city's temples became little more than gaudy charades. So, during the course of the Roman period, those rituals were slowly abandoned, and as the last faithful priests of Amun died off without heirs to carry on their tradition, the meanings of the hieroglyphs were lost.

With the coming of Christianity in the fourth century A.D. and of Islam three hundred years later, great political changes swept over the country and the ancient city of the pharaohs eventually reverted to just one of dozens of small, self-supporting rural villages of Upper Egypt. The population dwindled and the temples became huge quarries for building materials and convenient shelters within which more modest structures were built. As the centuries passed, the former significance of the place was only vaguely remembered by the local inhabitants, who now called it *al-Uqsur*, "the palaces," a name slurred into "Luxor" by the European explorers of the eighteenth century, whose peculiar fascination with antiquity led them to start digging and resurrecting the splendor of ancient Thebes.

Since that time, Luxor has lived in two uncomfortably simultaneous incarnations: as a modern Egyptian town and as a fairy-tale re-creation of a splendid pharaonic city overrun by tourists from all over the Western world. The tourists, to be sure, were responsible for Luxor's current prosperity; from the time that Thomas Cook and Sons began to bring wealthy visitors here by riverboat in the 1860s, many of Luxor's inhabitants had been drawn into the tourist trade. As Western archaeologists uncovered more and more of the ruins, the tourists came in greater numbers and the monuments themselves began to deteriorate. From the plunder of tombs and inscriptions for the antiquities market to the effects of the elements on exposed temple walls, the same wave of interest that brought the foreign visitors seemed responsible for the slow, yet inevitable, destruction of Luxor's ancient inheritance.

Yet maintaining that inheritance was not easy. Professor James Breasted had an extraordinary talent for conveying both the importance and the endangered state of the antiquities of Egypt to the general public all over the world. He also succeeded in persuading a patron to share his concern. With funds provided by John D. Rockefeller, he established the Oriental Institute in Chicago and built Chicago House in Luxor. Acres and acres of ancient messages had to be copied, and the painstaking work of transcription that had begun when Calvin Coolidge was president of the United States and Ahmad Fuad was king of Egypt was still under way in an era of Ronald Reagan and Hosni Mubarak.

In the years since Breasted's death in 1935, Egypt had gone through both political and environmental revolutions. With the construction of the Aswan High Dam in the early 1960s, even the Nile itself had turned against the pharaonic monuments. No more annual floods washed the natural salt and manmade fertilizers from the soil, so the water table of the region rose dramatically and the earth became increasingly saline. Salt crystals, which would have been absorbed into the earth surrounding the buried monuments, now leached to the stone surface, often forming a crust on the ancient inscriptions that eventually crumbled away. Preservation work was only partially effective; the best hope to save these monuments, under the present conditions, was to copy their texts carefully so that at least a permanent record of their contents would remain.

As I walked with Bill Murnane into his office near the Chicago House Library and he began to describe their painstaking procedure of recording the inscriptions, I began to sense the depth of his dedication to the work. In dealing with an ancient writing system as complex and ambiguous as Egyptian hieroglyphics, he told me, the work simply could not be hurried along. Having been in existence more than sixty years, the University of Chicago's epigraphic survey had still not completed even its first project—the transcription of the reliefs in Ramesses III's Temple of Medinet Habu on the western side of the Nile. For thirteen years, Murnane had been coming to Luxor every winter to participate in the recording of the ancient inscriptions at Medinet Habu and in the Temple of Luxor—and to supervise the training of students to carry on the work. Neither photographs nor artists' sketches could alone meet Professor Breasted's exacting standards of complete, scientific transcription, so over the years the Chicago House's epigraphic survey had developed a time-consuming process that combined photography, drawing, and linguistics in what amounted to an assembly-line production method of "approved" ancient texts.

Murnane took obvious pride in the thoroughness of the process. First, he explained, high-resolution black-and-white photographs were taken of the specific sections of the ancient inscription to be recorded; enlargements of those photographs then were provided to the team of artists and draftsmen, who returned with them to the site. Climbing ladders or crouching in small spaces to get as close as possible to the stone surface, these team members used the photographic enlargements as a basis for further transcription, adding details and nuances that the camera had not detected in the stone and outlining the various hieroglyphic characters and symbols in ink. Yet even this was not the end of the process. With the hand-drawn corrections completed, the prints were bleached to remove the photographic image, leaving only the line drawings visible. Then they were transferred onto blueprint paper and taken to the site once again. Now that the photographer and the artist had combined to give their impressions, the experienced Egyptologists—who knew more about the grammar and syntax of the symbols—made the final comments and corrections before approving the transcription of the ancient text.

I had myself seen the patient team members peering at the walls at the Medinet Habu temple, but I was amazed as Murnane described the lengths to which they went to copy all of the shrine's religious text. In many cases, an involved cleaning operation had to precede the copying. Since the interior chambers of the temple had often been used as dwellings for the people of the nearby village, the thick layers of soot from their cooking fires had blackened the hieroglyphics on the walls. The survey team, finding that a solution of 5 percent nitric acid removed the soot encrustations, began slowly to clean sections of the wall with Q-Tips. By means of this exacting and time-consuming process, they gradually uncovered the original colors and previously overlooked nuances of the hieroglyphic reliefs—discoveries that provided a new understanding of the ancient rituals of the Egyptian god Amun.

Murnane was proud of the new interpretations that his readings had offered the scholarly world. His doctoral dissertation on the concept of co-regency in ancient Egypt (a subject "very much in the Chicago tradition," Murnane proudly emphasized) had provided scholars with a new understanding of the development of Egyptian political thinking, utilizing the sometimes-neglected information from the hieroglyphic inscriptions. He and the other team members were clearly dedicated to preserving the inheritance of ancient Egypt, but in recent years, he admitted, this dedication had not been particularly easy. They now had to contend with a human, as well as an environmental, problem: the conflicting feelings toward ancient Egypt of the modern Egyptians themselves.

"**O**ur relations with the Egyptian Antiquities Organization are good and they appreciate what we're doing," Murnane told me, "but you have to remember that this is an Islamic country." In his words was a tacit acknowledgment of the uneasy relationship between the religion of modern Egypt and Western-style Egyptology. Islam had long taken an uncompromisingly hostile attitude toward the pre-Islamic history of Egypt and, by extension, to the country's pre-Islamic artistic and architectural works. In the Quran, as in the Bible, *Fir'awn*, "the Pharaoh," was the evil oppressor of Musa and Harun— Moses and Aaron—who forced his people to worship him as a god. Hoping to gain access to heaven by means of his riches rather than his righteousness, he ordered his vizier to build him a tower that reached to the sky. Even though he came to accept the wickedness of his ways at the moment of his death by drowning in the waters of the Red Sea, the One True God decreed that his body be left on the land of Egypt as a gruesome example of the ultimate cost of sinfulness.

Later Muslim tradition related the stories of a number of pharaohs—*Fara'in*—both before and after the time of Moses and unfailingly depicted them as archetypal tyrants who terrorized the people of the country throughout the long, murky period of ignorance—the *Jahiliya*—that preceded the coming of Islam. So complete was the association of the pharaohs with wickedness that in the Arabic language, *tafar'ana*—a verb form derived from their name— meant "to be arrogant and tyrannical." So, in the eyes of many fundamentalist Muslims, excessive interest in the remains of the pharaonic period was, at best, the folly of those unschooled in the lessons of the Quran; at worst, it was outright idolatry. Egyptology and Islam were not easy to reconcile in modern Egypt.

"A few months ago," Bill Murnane told me, "I had an experience that really underscored that fact for me." He explained that he had decided to take a field trip to visit the ancient Temple of Denderah, about an hour's drive to the north of Luxor; as luck would have it, he shared the ride in a local "service taxi" with a bearded and turbaned *qadi*, a Muslim religious judge. The *qadi* took an obvious interest in Murnane, whom he could tell was not an ordinary tourist. He was surprised at Murnane's fluent Arabic and asked how long he'd been in Egypt and what his profession was. When Murnane answered that he was an Egyptologist working to record and preserve the ancient monuments of Luxor, their conversation cooled noticeably. The judge remained ominously silent for the rest of the trip, at least until they arrived at Denderah. As Murnane climbed out of the taxi, the *qadi* shook his head and told him sternly: "The pharaohs are all in the fire now, you know. . . ."

That was an extreme example of antagonism toward the country's pre-Islamic heritage; according to Murnane, a more common attitude is ambivalence. In Sadat's time, he explained, the Egyptian government was anxious to promote the glory of the pharaonic past, and when the mummified body of Ramesses II was flown to France for some much-needed preservation work in the laboratories of the Louvre, Sadat insisted that it be treated like an arriving head of state and be greeted at Charles de Gaulle Airport with a twenty-one-gun salute. Yet, at approximately the same time, clerical pressures *within* Egypt forced a dramatically different treatment for the surviving mummies of the other pharaohs. They were withdrawn from their display cases in the Cairo Museum, so the official explanation went, to avoid offending religious sensibilities.

Bill Murnane was diplomatic in his discussion of this delicate matter, for he knew that his good relations with the officials of the Egyptian Antiquities Organization could be quickly shattered by an explicit offense to the local religious authorities. Yet, as I continued my visit to Luxor, I came to realize that religion was only *one* of the reasons for modern Egyptian ambivalence toward remains of the pre-Islamic past. Another source of the tension was more strictly nationalistic. Egyptology had always been, after all, primarily a foreigner's game.

A Frenchman, Jean-Francois Champollion, was the first modern scholar to decipher Egyptian hieroglyphics, and the steadily growing economic and political influence of France in Egypt led to the French creation and domination of the "Service des Antiquités d'Égypte" for almost a hundred years. From the time of Auguste Mariette in the late 1850s to the time of Étienne Drioton in the early 1950s, French citizens were perfunctorily chosen by the khedives and kings of Egypt to administer their ancient heritage. The official French preeminence in Egyptology, though, was not uncontested, for throughout the nineteenth century, German, Austrian, Italian, American, and British scholars competed in the race for Egyptian antiquities. And after the forces of the British Empire conquered the country in 1882, British scholars claimed an official role alongside the French in the administration of ancient Egypt. By the turn of the century, three Englishmen served as provincial "inspectors of monuments"—the most famous of whom was Howard Carter, who would later gain archaeological immortality as the discoverer of the Tomb of Tutankhamun in the Valley of the Kings.

A few short-lived attempts to train and employ native Egyptians were doomed by the hostility and suspicion of the foreign scholars, who feared that locally trained Egyptologists might threaten their preeminent position in the discovery and interpretation of the nation's inheritance. By the end of the nineteenth century, Egyptology had come to possess a respected social function in Europe; to be called an "Egyptologist" was, beyond its academic respectability, a useful means of access to the highest strata of society. No matter how humble his origins, a scholar's expertise in the esoterica of ancient Egypt could attract wealthy and influential patrons. Like the Eastern religions and religious fads of the late twentieth century, pharaonic Egypt, in the Late Victorian period, exerted a mystical fascination for many members of the leisure class. Wintering in Egypt would not be complete without an excavation to visit—or, better yet—an excavation to underwrite. Howard Carter's discovery of the Tomb of Tutankhamun on behalf of Lord Carnarvon was, in that sense, a culmination of early Egyptological tradition. Carter quickly became a worldwide celebrity and Carnarvon gained enormous prestige among his Egyptophile peers for "his" discovery of Egypt's richest unplundered tomb.

The discovery of the Tomb of Tutankhamun, however, changed the tenor of archaeology in Egypt. Lord Carnarvon's triumph occurred at a time when nationalistic sentiments were gaining strength in Egypt; in 1924, only two years after the great discovery, the British cabinet finally bowed to growing agitation and granted the Egyptians limited sovereignty. The nationalist Wafd party rode to victory on a wave of public support in the parliamentary elections, but the restricted nature of their governmental responsibilities forced them to wage their campaign for Egyptian independence over marginal issues—such as the foreign domination of Egyptian antiquities.

The ownership of the riches of Tutankhamun's tomb soon became a nationalistic *cause célèbre*. Sa'ad Zaghlul, the new Egyptian prime minister, exerted pressure on director Pierre Lacau of the Egyptian Antiquities Service to place strict conditions on Carter's ongoing excavations—to prevent the unauthorized export of its treasures. Carter reacted angrily to this intrusion and closed the Tomb of Tutankhamun, intent on regaining his freedom of action through legal action, but Lacau didn't wait for the lawyers. He ordered that the English padlocks be sawed off the tomb entrance and he declared all of its contents to be Egyptian property. The British weren't the only victims of the nationalization of Egyptology; in the same year, Lacau demanded that a painted bust of Nefertiti, discovered by German excavators at Tell el-Amarna and sent to Berlin, be returned to the Cairo Museum. The nationalists' point was made abundantly clear: Henceforth, all antiquities excavated in Egypt would automatically become the property of the Egyptian authorities.

Professor James Breasted had anticipated these changes, and Chicago House—established in this period of archaeological upheaval—reflected his conception of ancient Egypt as an ideal, rather than as a valuable work of art. Many of his colleagues, however, felt differently. Without the incentive of ancient treasure for exhibit and private collections, few Western institutions or philanthropists saw much of an attraction in big-budget Egyptology. Besides, the unpleasantness and turmoil of the "new" Egypt now made it impossible to spend a relaxing winter there. So, through the 1930s, as the scale of Western involvement in Egyptian archaeology steadily declined, the care of the country's antiquities was increasingly shouldered—partially out of nationalistic motives, partly out of necessity—by the Egyptians themselves.

Egyptian institutions of higher learning were now encouraged to train a new generation of local Egyptologists who could, on graduation, assume positions of responsibility. No longer would the history of antiquities of the country be the exclusive cultural province of outsiders; it was felt that the Egyptians themselves must take control of their ancient inheritance. This change in attitude toward archaeology was reflected even in the bureaucratic reshuffling. In 1929, the Egyptian Antiquities Service was officially transferred to the ministry of education—from the ministry of public works. Only the continuing friendship of King Farouk kept a Frenchman in the position of director, and even that was subject to political change. Soon after the 1952 revolution under Nasser, an Egyptian—Mustafa Amer, the president of Alexandria University—finally took over as director of the Service des Antiquités d'Égypte, now renamed *Hai'a al-Athar al-Misriya*, the Egyptian Antiquities Organization.

Egyptians, like other peoples in the region, had at last gained legal title to their past. Even when large foreign archaeological expeditions began to return to Egypt at the time of the Aswan High Dam Rescue Project, their position was changed. They understood that they were now just concession holders, operating at all times under the jurisdiction and supervision of the Egyptian government. Yet for the officers of the Egyptian Antiquities Organization, the legal title to the country's antiquities came with some significant strings attached. Egyptology's institutions, professional jargon, excavation methods—even the popular image of the pith-helmeted Egyptologist—had been born in the social world of nineteenth-century Europe and America, and Egyptian scholars now had to fit in. As it turned out, acculturation to professional identity as Egyptologists proved, in many cases, to be difficult. Howard Carter, the Earl of Carnarvon, and even James Breasted had bequeathed to the new generation of Egyptian archaeologists an elegant tradition of "gentlemanly archaeology" that was as seductive to the general public as it was difficult to achieve—in an era when the profits and prestige of treasure hunting were no longer the main motivations for digging.

At first, when I arrived to visit a new excavation in the village of Sheikh Abd al-Qurnah on the west bank of the Nile opposite Luxor, it seemed that nothing had changed in Carter's old stomping grounds. As I walked past the mud-brick houses and animal pens of the village toward the slope honeycombed with dark tomb openings, I was greeted by a scene reminiscent of a faded turn-of-the-century photograph. A cloud of dust rose from the slope above the village as a gang of workers in long, flowing *galabiyas* and white turbans hacked away at the parched soil partially covering an ancient tomb façade. A young archaeologist sitting nearby in a camp chair was intently writing in a notebook, glancing up every now and then to check on his workers' progress. But as I introduced myself and began to talk with him about his project, I saw that its similarity to an earlier era of archaeology in Egypt was illusory. This archaeologist was not a scholarly stranger to Egypt; he was a twenty-seven-year-old officer of the Egyptian Antiquities Organization named Rady Ali Muhammed.

The ancient tomb that Rady was excavating in collaboration with another young archaeologist—Dr. Karl Syfreed of Heidelberg University—was not likely to grab any headlines. It was one of nearly three hundred rock-cut burial chambers dating from the New Kingdom period (ca. 1567–ca. 1085 B.C.), when the area served as a cemetery for the wealthiest and most influential members of the Theban aristocracy. Throughout the nineteenth and early twentieth centuries, however, all the tombs in this area had been opened, examined, and plundered by a succession of foreign archaeologists and local antiquities thieves. In recent years, the most elaborate of the tombs had been cleared by the Egyptian Antiquities Organization and opened to tourists, even though all the valuable objects originally placed inside them were now scattered in museums and private collections all over the world.

But that wasn't to say that a great deal couldn't still be learned from the "Tombs of the Nobles." Rady explained that up to the time of the renewed excavations, many of the vivid reliefs and hieroglyphic inscriptions painted on the walls of the tomb chambers had never been properly photographed or transcribed. Howard Carter, during his brief tenure as inspector-general of monuments in Upper Egypt and Nubia, spent several years excavating here in the village of Qurnah before moving on to fame and fortune in the nearby Valley of the Kings. But the goal of the digging today, unlike that of the earlier expeditions in Qurnah, was, according to Rady, not a hunt for spectacular museum objects, but a methodical attempt to explore and record the valuable historical information that the early archaeologists had ignored.

This all sounded quite similar to the archaeological philosophy I had heard from Bill Murnane at Chicago House, but here at Qurnah I saw that it was being carried out on a much humbler scale. Rady agreed to show me his latest discovery, and when Karl Syfreed arrived at the site from another tomb in the village, he took Rady's place in the camp chair to oversee the work gang. Rady then led me down a sloping path into the darkness of the underground tomb chamber, which was still designated by the number that the earlier Egyptologists had given it—"Tomb #68."

On the back wall of the entrance chamber, eerie processions of human and divine figures were still clearly visible. To the left of the entrance, the deceased and his family presented offerings to Re-Harakhty, the enthroned, hawk-headed spirit of the rising sun. To the right, an identical procession offered gifts to the pale god Osiris, guardian of the afterworld. Howard Carter and the other British Egyptologists who explored the Tombs of the Nobles from 1903 to 1913 found many such scenes depicting the ancient Egyptian duality of life and death, and they saw this rather uninspired painting as of no particular consequence. But in their more careful examination of the hieroglyphic characters painted on the walls of Tomb #68, Rady and Syfreed had discovered that the earlier Egyptologists had been hasty in their judgment. They had mistaken the identity of the aristocrat for whom the religious scene had been painted and had thereby misunderstood the tomb's true social significance.

Here was a typical case of usurpation, Rady told me, the unabashed reoccupation of a monument that belonged to someone else. The British Egyptologist Alan Gardiner, who published a report on the tomb in 1913, maintained that it had belonged to a chief scribe and prophet of Amun named *Nesu-pa-nefer-hor*, who was buried here around 1085 B.C. In historical terms, that was the last great period of Theban power, when, after the death of the last pharaohs of the 20th Dynasty, the priests of Amun briefly ruled the country themselves. But it now seemed that Nesu-pa-nefer-hor's posthumous prestige was inherited rather than earned. When Rady and Syfreed closely examined Tomb #68's wall paintings, they discovered the traces of an earlier hieroglyphic inscription *beneath* Nesu-pa-nefer-hor's name. Not having the wealth to build his own sepulcher, the prophet and chief scribe of Amun took over the tomb from *Pa-ankh-enamu*, a true nobleman of the 20th Dynasty who had been laid to rest there nearly a century before.

Rady was born and raised a Muslim, but as a graduate of Cairo University's Department of Egyptology, he seemed to have no theological hesitations about making a scholarly contribution to the study of ancient Egyptian history. Unfortunately, his excavation was being carried out on a shoestring; gone were the days when wealthy European aristocrats would lavish their fortunes on digging up ancient aristocrats' tombs. When Alan Gardiner first dug Tomb #68 at the turn of the century, he was supported by the largess of the British industrialist and art lover Sir Robert L. Mond. Syfreed and Rady's limited resources, now just about exhausted, came from what the budget-strained University of Heidelberg Egyptology Department and the Egyptian Antiquities Organization could spare.

As a result, Tomb #68 doubled as their excavation storeroom; at one side of the entrance hall, Syfreed and Rady had stacked boxes of pottery fragments dug up by the workers in the excavation of the outer courtyard. They didn't have the funds to attempt a clearance of the inner chambers, whose floors were littered with modern artifacts—empty cigarette packages, wrappers, and tin cans recently left by the villagers. In a dark corner, near the opening of one of the burial chambers, were the disarticulated remains of an ancient occupant, possibly Nesu-pa-nefer-hor but probably an even later usurper, whose remains patiently awaited detailed anthropological study. His leathery mummified head, torso, and hands lay in a grotesque pile on the beaten earth floor of the tomb. Archaeology in the Tombs of the Nobles just wasn't what it used to be. The excitement, the mystery, and the glamour of an earlier archaeological era were gone.

That transition, though natural enough, was not without its irony. I was surprised to learn that Rady, in his position as the Egyptian Antiquities Organization's inspector for Qurnah, now lived in "Carter's House." That elegant, domed villa on a hill just outside the Valley of the Kings had been built by the Earl of Carnarvon for Carter while he was unpacking the fabulous treasures from the Tomb of King Tutankhamun. In its heyday, Carter's House was an oasis of upper-class British gentility in the Egyptian wilderness, fully equipped for formal dinner parties and staffed with suitably trained Egyptian waiters and maids. Of course, dinner jackets were no longer worn there, and the waiters and maids were long gone. But I expected that Rady, as Carter's professional successor at Qurnah, would at least acknowledge the romantic spirit of the place.

When I told him that I thought Carter's House was a prestigious address for any archaeologist, his response surprised me. Rady apparently couldn't understand my fascination and didn't find the surroundings exotic in the least. His education at the University of Cairo might have trained him to read hieroglyphs and speculate on ancient Egyptian history, but his cultural outlook as a wealthy young man from Cairo had led him to reject the conventional stereotype. The image of the refined scholar living the life of the gentleman-explorer in the wilderness was a concept with which he was uncomfortable.

As we stood in the tomb chamber with its wall paintings of ancient Egyptian gods and mortals frozen in their funerary procession, Rady shook his head sadly and revealed his true feelings with almost painful candor. "My life here is very lonely," he told me, "and I'd like to find a woman to share it with me. I come from a good family in Cairo, but since my work requires me to be out here in the middle of nowhere, I'm afraid that marriage is impossible right now." For Inspector Rady Ali Muhammed of the Egyptian Antiquities Organization, personal dedication to archaeology was tempered by a conflicting social reality. For him, Carter's House and the Tombs of the Nobles possessed no charm, no romance.

By the 1980s, the work of discovery and preservation was now seen for what it was. In an age past, Western Egyptologists could regale their families, friends, and eager public with tales of adventure in exotic and ancient lands. But modern Egyptians could see through the false charm of such alluring, imperial adventures; they were acquainted with the harsh realities. An intelligent young man from a prosperous Cairene family had no natural place in a remote Upper Egyptian village, supervising peasant work gangs and crawling into ancient tombs.

Rady was trapped between two modern, yet very different, cultures. "What kind of parents," he asked me as we walked back out into the harsh sun and the rising dust of the excavation, "would allow their daughter to live in a place like this?"

10

EGYPT

Whose Elephantine?

From the Old Cataract Hotel in Aswan, Elephantine Island looked like a perfect subject for a picture postcard—a looming brown hill of ruins rising peacefully from the blue waters of the Nile. Here and there along its surface, recognizable structures—gates, columns, and walls—stood silhouetted above the mounds of collapsed mud bricks and building stones. The lazy progress of the felucca sailboats gliding back and forth on the Nile made the view even more idyllic. But this scene of ruins, river, and graceful, triangular sails of Egyptian cotton once provided more than a pleasant background for tourists. The island was, in antiquity, the "southern gate" of Egypt, a fortress that guarded the approaches to the country from the desolate valleys and deserts of Nubia. Like Tell el-Dab'a, the capital of the Hyksos in the Nile Delta at the other end of the country, Elephantine Island was an ancient boundary point. And it had attracted my interest as a meeting place for foreigners and Egyptians—in both the present and the past.

The short felucca ride to the island from the dock at the edge of a public park in Aswan revealed the contradictions of the modern identity of this southern gate. Waiting for the boatmen to ferry them across to Elephantine Island was a crowd of tourists dressed in polyester and cameras. Nearby stood a knot of local Nubian women, whose heavy, draped fabrics hid all their features, revealing only the ebony darkness of their skin. Elephantine Island seemed to be part dead and part living; just a few hundred yards north of the mounds of ancient rubble and ruins lay a modern village of mud-brick houses and a grove of date palms. For the villagers of Elephantine, the felucca ferry was the only way to their homes on the island; for the tourists, it was a part of the experience of antiquity in which the quaint, modern customs of Egypt had become mixed.

I stepped off with the others on the sandy bank of the island as some made their way toward the village and some toward the museum and archaeological sites. My interest here was to visit a work in progress—the expedition of the German and Swiss Institutes of Archaeology in Egypt, which had been steadily excavating Elephantine Island's ruins since 1969. In a hollow halfway between the ruins and the modern village stood their headquarters. Its architecture was distinctive: The mud-brick walls and whitewashed domes lay somewhere in a mix of antiquity and nineteenth-century Orientalist romanticism. Inside, the team members were having breakfast, and, armed with an introduction from Bill Murnane at Chicago House in Luxor, I introduced myself to Professor Werner Kaiser, a tall, distinguished-looking scholar who was the director of the dig.

Kaiser's reputation was well known in archaeological circles in Egypt. The main emphasis of his career had been in excavations in the Predynastic and Archaic periods of Egyptian history—the little-known centuries from approximately 3400 to 2700 B.C. when the institutions of pharaonic kingship and governmental authority began to coalesce. Elephantine Island, as a natural fortress controlling movement and trade into Egypt from Africa, was a site of particular interest in this period, and Kaiser and his team members had succeeded in reconstructing the evidence of occupation there by the early dynasties of Egyptian kings. Yet the German-Swiss expedition did not end its work with the mere discovery and publication of detailed excavation reports for the scholarly world. By arrangement with the Egyptian Antiquities Organization, the team members were reconstructing some of the island's ancient temples and improving the facilities for the tourists and archaeological students who came to Elephantine.

That work of restoration had become the expedition's primary objective, and on our first meeting, Professor Kaiser apologized that he didn't have more time to discuss the results and significance of his excavations on the island. A heavy crane and a hired work crew were waiting for him to supervise the repositioning of stone blocks from an ancient temple wall. He suggested that I call in the evening to arrange a more convenient time for a properly guided tour of the dig.

This being my first visit, I had no preconceptions about what I would see on Elephantine; I was only vaguely aware of a century-long controversy connected with the site. I knew that a large and important collection of ancient papyri had been found on the island at the turn of the century, but I assumed that any rivalries or bitterness arising from that discovery had been long forgotten by scholars today. But, as I later discovered, bad feelings sometimes die hard in the world of archaeology, despite the best intentions of the archaeologists themselves. As I learned on a subsequent visit to the island, Kaiser and his team still had to contend with the lingering repercussions of the Elephantine papyri. For in the decades that preceded the German-Swiss excavations, the island's reputation became as noteworthy for the jealousies and mutual suspicions its antiquities aroused as it was admired for its apparent tranquility.

The archaeological controversy on Elephantine Island began, it seemed at the time, innocently enough. In the winter of 1893, a wealthy American expatriate and amateur Egyptologist, Charles Edwin Wilbour of New York City, arrived in Aswan on his private yacht and stumbled onto an incredible find. Wilbour was a familiar figure to the people of Aswan; he had been making annual visits to Egypt for more than a decade, collecting ancient artifacts and pursuing his private passion for Egyptology. At every stop along the Nile, antiquities dealers besieged him with merchandise; on this trip, his luck was extraordinary. When word spread through Aswan that Wilbour had arrived, some women from the village on Elephantine Island sought out the distinguished visitor from America and sold him nine complete papyrus scrolls.

The precise location of the discovery was uncertain, but Wilbour immediately suspected the enormous value of the ancient documents. They were written in Hebrew characters—not Egyptian hieroglyphics—and only a few scraps of similar documents had been discovered previously in Egypt. Wilbour, the model of a Late Victorian gentleman-scholar, was acquainted with the languages of ancient Egypt; he had studied with Professor Gaston Maspero in Paris and was acknowledged to be one of the most accomplished amateur Egyptologists of his day. Just to be sure, though, he sent a single, small fragment of one of the scrolls to Professor Archibald Sayce of Oxford—a fellow Nile traveler and established authority. Sayce quickly recognized the script as Aramaic and urged that, in light of the rarity of this biblical language in Egypt, it be copied carefully. But Wilbour had not revealed the full extent of his acquisition; he apparently intended to make the most of his good fortune by translating and publishing the ancient documents himself. And therein lay the first of the long chain of events that would ultimately lead to an archaeological conflict, for the existence of the nine complete Aramaic scrolls from Elephantine Island was still a closely guarded secret when Charles Edwin Wilbour died suddenly in 1896.

It did not take long for other scrolls acquired by foreigners in Aswan to surface. In 1898, two years after Wilbour's death, an Aramaic document was purchased on the local antiquities market by a German collector; in 1900, Professor Sayce obtained a complete scroll from some villagers on Elephantine Island itself. The greatest discovery, however, came in 1904, when two English aristocrats and patrons of Egyptology, Lady William Cecil and Sir Robert Mond, were wintering in Upper Egypt and bought seven complete Aramaic scrolls. The state of preservation of these documents was remarkable; all of the tightly rolled and folded papyrus manuscripts were still secured with string, and the clay sealings of most were still intact. Yet the remarkable condition of these documents was not the only factor that merited scholarly attention. The historical information they contained created an immediate sensation in European academic circles—a sensation equaled only by the much later discovery of the Dead Sea Scrolls.

The papyri purchased by the foreign visitors to Aswan proved to be legal documents, written in Aramaic, by the members of a garrison of Jewish mercenary soldiers stationed on Elephantine Island in the fifth century B.C. This was the historical era described in the biblical books of Ezra and Nehemiah, from which practically no other Jewish texts had survived. The picture of Jewish life that the scrolls provided was surprising in many of its details. At a time when the authorities in Jerusalem were rebuilding the ruins of Solomon's Temple—and declaring it to be the only legitimate place of Jewish worship—the Jewish soldiers at Elephantine Island apparently had a shrine of their own, an impressive structure they called the "Temple of Yaho."* How those Jewish soldiers got to Upper Egypt was a mystery, as was the nature of their temple and its connection to the Temple in Jerusalem. Only one thing was clear: If more scrolls could be recovered at Aswan, they would be of inestimable value for understanding the Hebrew laws and customs from the late biblical period— a subject of enormous importance in the contentious theological debates then raging about the date and historical authenticity of the biblical text. So it did not take long for scholars from Britain, France, and Germany to begin a mad scramble up the Nile to obtain more of the precious documents.

The key to additional discoveries was knowledge of the provenance of the earlier papyri, but the antiquities dealers of Aswan were understandably protective of the source of their lucrative merchandise. The documents, they said, were discovered by a work gang building a road from the new railroad station in Aswan to the Cataract Hotel. There was no need, they assured the arriving scholars, to look anywhere else. This explanation satisfied the French and the British, who were well aware of the disturbingly rapid modernization that was threatening the antiquities of Aswan. A number of ancient sarcophagi bearing Aramaic inscriptions had recently been uncovered by the road crews, and it seemed possible that the Aramaic papyri could have come from the same cemetery. Yet one German scholar, though aware of those finds, was not deceived. Dr. Otto Rubensohn of the Berlin Museum had taken note of the extensive damage caused to the ruins of Elephantine Island by local inhabitants digging the rich soil for organic fertilizer. It was there, after all, that Sayce had

---

*This divine name is an abbreviation or alternate form of the name of the Israelite God, which is commonly transliterated into English as "Jehovah" or "Yahweh."

acquired a scroll from the hands of some local diggers. And believing that the *island*, not the mainland, was the source of the ancient papyri, Rubensohn applied to the Egyptian Antiquities Service for permission to dig there himself.

Here politics entered the picture. And it was politics that would transform the search for more papyri into a bitter struggle for national prestige. Dr. Gaston Maspero, the French director of the Egyptian Antiquities Service, had already conducted some brief excavations on Elephantine Island and had found only a handful of insignificant papyrus fragments, so he assumed that no harm would be done by indulging Rubensohn's whim. In 1906, Rubensohn was accordingly granted an excavation concession for the southwestern sector of the island, where, it was confidently felt, an expedition of the Berlin Museum would obtain no better results than the earlier French dig. The British and French scholars still believed that the best hope lay in coaxing more papyri from Aswan's canny dealers in antiquities. Yet in spite of his colleagues' skepticism, Rubensohn's subsequent excavations among the tangled and complex mud-brick structures on Elephantine Island provided a surprising confirmation of the true origin of the ancient documents. He recovered a large, new hoard of papyrus scrolls, buried near the foundations of an ancient structure, still contained in their original clay jar.

The information provided by these documents created an immediate sensation among biblical scholars and soon captivated the imagination of the general public as well. The earlier scrolls had revealed the existence of an ancient Jewish place of worship on Elephantine, a temple of the Israelite God Yaho. But Rubensohn's papyri suddenly transformed the earlier, vague references to the temple into a vivid and dramatic story connected directly to a previously known biblical personality.

The newly discovered scrolls revealed that the Jewish colonists at Elephantine, loyal servants of the Persian conquerors of Egypt, had constructed a massive religious edifice built with stone gates and pillars, covered with a roof of cedar beams like that of Solomon's Temple, and equipped with an altar for animal sacrifice. No such sanctuary was known to have existed outside Jerusalem in this period, yet the temple on Elephantine Island was clearly an independent place of worship—a parallel, if not a rival, to the Temple in Jerusalem. Even more unexpected was the fate of this temple, as reported by Rubensohn's newly discovered documents. In the fourteenth year of the reign of Darius II—equivalent to 410 B.C.—when the Persian *satrap*, or governor, was temporarily absent from Egypt, a group of Egyptian priests persuaded the local authorities to order the destruction of the Temple of Yaho. The once-magnificent structure was accordingly looted and burned by Egyptian troops, but the members of the Jewish community were determined not to be driven away. In an emotional letter written by the leaders of the Jewish garrison, they appealed to Bagohi, the governor of Judea, to intercede with the Persian authorities so that they might be granted permission to rebuild their place of worship. An earlier copy of this appeal, addressed to the High Priest Yochanan in Jerusalem—a figure mentioned by name in the Book of Nehemiah—was among the documents in the clay jar found by the German excavation team.

At a time when every archaeological discovery that verified the historical accuracy of the Bible was trumpeted from pulpits and praised by heads of state as a source of national pride, the French, who controlled the Egyptian Antiquities Service, recognized that they had missed a great opportunity and now hastened to make up for their mistake. Since the Germans had been granted only the southwestern part of the island, a French expedition, headed by the renowned Orientalist Charles Clermont-Ganneau, was granted the right to excavate the rest. The two excavations were accordingly separated by a carefully drawn border that ran down the center of the island, across which neither the French nor the German excavators were allowed to encroach. Unfortunately, the remains of the ancient Jewish garrison buildings were not evenly distributed between the two excavation areas, and this fact aroused new and even more intense national rivalry.

The French expedition was, at the start, a papyrus hunt, pure and simple. Clermont-Ganneau instructed his workers to plow through the ruins relentlessly in a single-minded search for documents. If any plans of the ancient structures they uncovered were ever drafted, none have been found. Luck, however, did not favor these frantic French efforts. For all their digging, they found only a single tiny scrap of papyrus, and this disappointing harvest caused Clermont-Ganneau to change the goal of his dig. On the basis of the information contained in the already recovered papyri, he became convinced that he could uncover the ruins of the Temple of Yaho itself.

Clermont-Ganneau had begun his own archaeological career in Jerusalem and had made a number of important discoveries in and around the Temple Mount. He was therefore well aware of the ground plan and structural history of the Jerusalem Temple, which was—at least in its later stages—built on a raised platform supported by massive retaining walls. He now suspected that the temple on Elephantine Island would be similar in form, so he began to search for archaeological clues among the rubble of fallen building blocks and collapsed mud-brick walls. The most promising indications were the remains of a large structure built of granite blocks—more massive than any other ancient building in the vicinity. This structure seemed too large for a private dwelling, but it was just what one would expect for the foundation of an imposing shrine. Unfortunately, the edge of the granite structure lay just across the border, in the area of the German concession. "I can see the Promised Land," wrote Clermont-Ganneau during the excavations. "I can almost touch it with my hand." But, much to Clermont-Ganneau's frustration and consternation, that Promised Land would not be entered—even by his competitors—for the Germans showed absolutely no interest in digging there.

Otto Rubensohn, the German excavation director, was aware of Clermont-Ganneau's frustration, but he stubbornly clung to his own theory about the location of the Temple of Yaho. He believed that it had stood about fifty yards to the south of Clermont-Ganneau's proposed site, and he was also quite certain that the structure had been completely destroyed. Thick layers of ruins from the Roman, Byzantine, and medieval periods covered the entire area of his excavation, and Rubensohn believed that the builders of these later settlements had leveled any remaining traces of the fifth-century B.C. sanctuary. And there was another factor that would have made the search impossible, even if the French and German expeditions had been willing to cooperate. The excavations on both sides of the dividing line, in their feverish search for papyri, had thoroughly ransacked the ruins and hopelessly confused the stratification at the site. With haphazard pits dug throughout the area and piles of discarded earth lying everywhere, any attempt to date and identify the various structures of the ancient Jewish garrison by means of the characteristic pottery of the Persian period would be a failure. The previously distinct archaeological levels had been irredeemably mixed up.

By 1910, Elephantine Island was abandoned by both the French and the German archaeologists, who gave up the search for more papyri—and for the remains of Yaho's temple—with mutual recriminations and disgust. A brief excavation by the Pontifical Biblical Institute in 1918 likewise proved fruitless, and it was only in the late 1940s that a new archaeological hope was born.

The nine complete scrolls purchased by Charles Edwin Wilbour in 1893, long packed away in a trunk in a New York warehouse, were finally brought to light by the staff of the Brooklyn Museum, to which Wilbour's daughter had bequeathed her father's large collection of Egyptian antiquities. These documents provided highly detailed information on the location of the Temple of Yaho on Elephantine Island, indicating possible alternatives in places where the earlier excavations had not dug. But by the time these scrolls were translated and published in the early 1950s, a new expedition was impossible. Egypt was officially at war with the newly established State of Israel and the Egyptian government led by Gamal Abdel Nasser was, to say the least, unsympathetic to the idea of a search for ancient Jewish remains.

By the time of my visit to Elephantine Island, the German-Swiss expedition had succeeded in revealing a new and quite different picture of its past. During more than fifteen years of renewed digging, they had clarified the long history of the island and had finally made some sense of the high mounds of rubble so violently disturbed by the turn-of-the-century digs. But their achievement had nothing to do with papyri or settlement on the island by outsiders; the modern archaeologists working on Elephantine were concerned with more technical questions of urban development and architectural history. That's why I was surprised at Professor Kaiser's reaction when I called him in the evening to arrange a more leisurely tour of the site. When I mentioned that I had just come from Israel, he assumed that I was primarily interested in the question of the Temple of Yaho. I reassured him that my interest was more general; I just wanted to see anything that *he* thought significant. And, strangely enough, the next morning when I arrived at Elephantine and introduced myself to Dr. Horst Jaritz, the expedition architect whom Professor Kaiser had assigned to show me around, I encountered an identical reaction. Jaritz, too, thought I had come in search of the ancient Jewish temple. Once again, I denied any ulterior motives and the subject was quickly dropped from our conversation.

I could see that Jaritz felt at home on Elephantine Island and was understandably protective of its antiquities. His relationship with the Egyptian workers he directed was relaxed and informal, and duing our tour of the excavations, he stopped occasionally to offer them polite words of encouragement and instruction in Arabic. Jaritz was now a senior staff member of the expedition, but he had come to the field of Egyptology in an unconventional way. As an architecture student, he had first worked in Egypt as a volunteer with the expedition of the American Research Center to Gebel Adda in Nubia during the campaign to salvage the ancient monuments of the region from the rising waters of Lake Nasser behind the Aswan High Dam. He also told me that on his return to Germany and completion of his studies, he quickly tired of just "building houses" and eventually returned to Egypt for good.

His was a fascination with both the past and the present of the country, and his position with the Swiss Archaeological Institute allowed him to pursue an architectural career on his own terms. He had designed and supervised the construction of the expedition headquarters on Elephantine Island, had drafted the detailed plans of the various ancient structures that the expedition had uncovered, and had been instrumental in the extensive reconstruction projects now under way. Jaritz's main interest was in tracing the development of the ancient settlement on the island through the form and function of its architectural remains. And as I walked with him through the widely scattered excavation areas, he offered his own perspective on the meaning of Elephantine's history.

We wound our way through the ruins to the southernmost tip of the island, where, Jaritz explained, excavations still in progress were uncovering remains of the earliest occupation at the site. In the hollows and crannies of the bedrock, the excavation team had discovered a number of graves from the Predynastic period with their human remains amazingly well preserved. Jaritz and I stood at the edge of one of the excavation pits as a staff member opened a newly discovered burial pit; inside was a desiccated body in a contracted, fetal position, surrounded by wooden utensils and wrapped in a woven reed mat. The warm, dry conditions of the Aswan area had ensured the preservation of the organic objects that in a rainier climate would have long ago rotted away. This archaeological advantage, Jaritz explained, had additional implications for the Elephantine excavations. Since most of the ancient structures and fortifications on the island were built of mud bricks, and since there was virtually no rain to dissolve them, many were still standing to almost their original height.

Along the southeastern shore of the island, Jaritz showed me the impressive remains of the fortification wall of the settlement built at the end of the Old Kingdom period, around 2200 B.C. By that time, the early settlement had expanded to a city, the important trade and military post controlling river communication between Egypt and Nubia to the south. As the first major strategic position below the First Cataract of the Nile, the early kings of a united Egypt used Elephantine as a fortress and customs center to monitor the rich African trade. As inscriptions from that period indicated, the noblemen of Elephantine bore an honorific title befitting their strategic responsibilities. They were known as the "keepers of the southern gate."

But that strategic function was greatly reduced, Jaritz told me, during the Middle Kingdom (ca. 2000 through ca. 1750 B.C.), when the kings of Egypt conquered Nubia and pushed the "southern gate" hundreds of miles farther south. The city walls were rebuilt and even expanded in this period, and, as the new excavations had discovered, the function of the city became primarily religious—an important pilgrimage shrine. Egyptian mythology identified Elephantine as the abode of Khnum, the ram-headed god of creation who, with the goddesses Satis and Anukis, presided over the annual inundation by the Nile. Beginning in the Old Kingdom, Khnum—the patron of the First Cataract—and Satis—the mistress of Elephantine Island— were honored with temples. As the centuries passed, those structures were expanded to cover most of the island's eastern side. The earlier French excavations under Clermont-Ganneau, Jaritz told me, had uncovered most of the sanctuary of the Temple of Khnum, yet only in recent years, Jaritz explained, with the renewed investigations of the German-Swiss team, had scholars finally been able to understand the various stages in the development of the ancient temple plan.

The huge portal of that temple was still standing, and Jaritz pointed out the fragmented evidence for the temple's repeated renovations and rebuildings. Many rulers of Egypt, from New Kingdom times to the end of the Roman period, added something to this temple, eventually dismantling the original structure and rebuilding it as an even more impressive edifice. Jaritz had himself meticulously documented the structural transformations of the Temple of Khnum in a volume of technical description and architectural drawings published by the Swiss Archaeological Institute.

Like a scrapbook of stone, the temple's remains offered glimpses of many rulers and epochs. In the courtyard were the huge, detached feet of a larger-than-life-size statue of Ramesses II (ca. 1304 through ca. 1237 B.C.)—a fragmentary reminder of the splendor of the temple in New Kingdom times. The standing portal, erected by the pharaoh Nectanebo II (360–343 B.C.), bore traces of subsequent royal patronage. On its unfinished outer relief was the *cartouche*, or royal insignia, of the son of Alexander the Great, also named Alexander (317–304 B.C.), whose flexible Hellenism easily accommodated the worship of a ram-headed god of the Nile. And on a lateral gate, Jaritz pointed out the evidence of the devotion of a later, even more powerful Egyptophile: the cartouche of the Roman Emperor Augustus, who ruled Egypt from 30 B.C. to A.D. 14, memorialized his own contribution to this temple at the First Cataract of the Nile.

Behind the temple rose high mounds of mud-brick ruins. "That's the Aramaic quarter," Jaritz said as he motioned toward the site of the earlier excavations, "but so far we've left it alone." I wanted to ask Jaritz about those earlier excavations, but I didn't. I could see that he was anxious to show me his recent reconstruction of the entrance to the Temple of Khnum, which overlooked the banks of the Nile. But just then, something unexpected happened. As we walked toward the ceremonial platform at the entrance to the temple—where in ancient times Khnum's image was displayed before throngs of eager, supplicant pilgrims—an Israeli tour group passed by. Ever since the signing of the Egypt-Israel peace treaty in 1979, Egypt had become a popular vacation locale for Israelis. Like tourists from the rest of the Western world, they too now flocked to this Promised Land of archaeological attractions, biblical associations, and modern exotica. This group seemed especially excited about visiting Elephantine's ruins, but because the tourist paths in this area were not yet clearly marked, some children of the group wandered dangerously close to a fragile mud-brick wall that Jaritz and his workers had recently restored.

I could see that Jaritz was nervous, so I spoke to the children in Hebrew, asking them not to climb on the wall. One of the adults in the group smiled broadly, surprised to hear Hebrew spoken at the German-Swiss dig. He apparently knew quite a bit about Elephantine's history, but he mistakenly assumed that I was on the excavation staff. He approached me to get some inside information. "Any news about the Temple of Yaho?" he asked.

I had no answer for the tourist, and, after the group had left, I admitted to Jaritz that my curiosity had gotten the better of me. I wanted to know about the issue that had by now become unavoidable. Didn't the current expedition have even a passing interest in solving the mystery of Yaho's temple? Didn't they feel any archaeological obligation to deal, at least briefly, with the confusion and uncertainty left by the destructive and inconclusive earlier digs?

Jaritz shook his head in mild frustration. He had apparently heard similar questions before. As a longtime staff member of the Elephantine excavations, he was well aware of the legacy of the original archaeological controversy and he knew that, even now, so many years later, the earlier excavations had left a lingering suspicion in the minds of the Egyptian authorities. The fifth-century B.C. Jewish garrison and its Temple of Yaho, Jaritz assured me, was just one chapter of many in the long history of Elephantine Island, and he felt that it perhaps didn't deserve all the attention that it still received. For the past sixteen years, the German-Swiss expedition had been concentrating on the full range of Elephantine's archaeological record, and, as a clear demonstration of their unwillingness to become entangled in the turn-of-the-century controversy, they had consciously avoided the area of the earlier digs.

But now, even though they were confident that the Egyptian Antiquities Organization fully supported them in their attempt to place Elephantine in the mainstream of Egyptian history, there was the danger that any renewed interest in the ruins of the ancient Jewish garrison in Upper Egypt might be interpreted the wrong way. Jaritz revealed that some Israeli scholars had visited the island soon after the 1979 peace treaty between Egypt and Israel and had suggested the possibility of new excavations in the area once occupied by the Jewish garrison. After years of archaeological tranquility, their visit seemingly had opened up the old issue again. And that old issue had taken on new political implications that posed a direct threat to their own work.

From Jaritz's perspective, a collaboration with Israeli scholars— in the current political atmosphere of the Middle East—could only endanger his own dig's scientific objectives. The current German-Swiss expedition had survived for so long by avoiding controversy. In the decades since the earlier excavations, scholars had continued to study the papyri and had made considerable progress in reconstructing the political, economic, and religious life of the members of the Jewish garrison. Yet Jaritz believed that present conditions were not favorable for a continuation of the excavations in the Aramaic quarter. From his honest yet slightly annoyed tone, I could see that the mention of the search for the Temple of Yaho, its connection to biblical history and to the Temple in Jerusalem, was unsettling. Jaritz plainly felt trapped by an archaeological and political controversy that was not of his own making, yet one from which there was little hope of escape.

There were, of course, two sides to the story. Always, there seemed to be a Rashomon-like reality lurking beneath the surface of modern versions of the past. So after I left Aswan and returned to Jerusalem, I went to see Professor Bezalel Porten of the Hebrew University, a scholar who had spent the better part of his career studying and writing about the Elephantine papyri. Porten's name had come up during my discussion with Jaritz—as one of the Israeli scholars who had come to Elephantine Island with the uncomfortable suggestion that the search for the Temple of Yaho be resumed. Yet when I spoke with Porten at his home in a quiet southern suburb of modern Jerusalem—a world apart from the idyllic scenery of Upper Egypt—he was clearly discouraged. He surprised me with his deep doubts that the ancient Jewish sanctuary on Elephantine Island would, or ever could, be found.

For years, Elephantine had been an almost dreamlike place for Porten. As a graduate student and visiting scholar at the Hebrew University in the 1960s, he had painstakingly analyzed photographic reproductions of the Aramaic papyri to reconstruct the way of life, the religious and legal customs, and even the layout of the private homes of the various members of the ancient Jewish garrison on Elephantine. He had traced family histories through the juxtapositions of the names of fathers, sons, husbands, wives, and daughters. He had speculated on the community's Temple of Yaho—even suggesting that it was not a rival to the Temple at Jerusalem, since certain geographical indications preserved in the papyri seemed to indicate that it was oriented toward the Holy Land. His book *Archives from Elephantine: The Life of an Ancient Jewish Military Colony* had become a standard for scholars and students. Yet until the late 1970s, he had never been there. Unfortunately, his first visit to the island in 1978, in the period of newfound friendship between the Egyptians and Israelis following the signing of the Camp David Accords, cured him of any lingering illusions about what might be accomplished at Elephantine by a new archaeological dig.

His reception by the members of the German-Swiss expedition, he told me, was cordial. Professor Kaiser was aware of his scholarly background and interest and had arranged a thorough tour of the area of the earlier excavations for him. But the difficulties became apparent immediately. It was impossible to match the specific buildings and landmarks mentioned in the papyri with any of the surviving mud-brick structures, for the levels of the Persian period were jumbled with the remains of other historical eras, and much of the critical archaeological evidence was now gone. Because of the extensive damage to the site caused in the nineteenth century by the villagers digging for fertilizer, it was possible that the remains of the Temple of Yaho had been obliterated even *before* the turn-of-the-century digs.

The substantial granite structure that Clermont-Ganneau had yearned for in the area of the German excavations was clearly *not* Yaho's temple. Dr. Günther Dreyer, one of the senior members of the current German-Swiss expedition, had convincingly identified it as the remains of a step-pyramid dedicated to one of the kings of the 3rd Dynasty, who lived some 2,000 years before the establishment of the Jewish garrison at Elephantine. Of course, there were still a few relatively untouched areas in the Aramaic quarter where excavation was possible, but Porten felt that there was little chance for success in locating the Temple of Yaho. Such a monumental building, even if completely destroyed in antiquity, should have left monumental traces. So his hopes for a great discovery grew dim. And in the years after that first visit, Porten came to understand that political tensions between Israel and Egypt and the cautiousness of the German-Swiss expedition made Israeli participation in the Elephantine excavations highly unlikely.

The situation really should have been different, Porten told me wistfully: "Israel now has full diplomatic relations with Egypt, we have our own research institute in Cairo, and theoretically, we should have the privileges of any other foreign mission working there." But wishes did not create realities, either in the scholarly world or in the archaeological bureaucracies of the Middle East. And in the meantime, Porten had encountered other, even more serious, obstacles to his academic work.

For the previous two years, the trustees of the Cairo Museum had denied him permission to study the Elephantine papyri stored in the museum's vast manuscript collections, despite his repeated appeals. For a linguist and historian such as Porten, those texts were far more important than potsherds and mud bricks. In the tiny details of tightly woven papyrus fibers and ancient scribes' penstrokes lay clues to the decipherment of obscure words, phrases, and even passages of the Elephantine documents. Photographic reproductions, though readily available, were of little value for discovering minute, overlooked details. And although Porten had relatively free access to the documents in the years immediately after the Camp David Accords, his freedom to work in the museum had been progressively restricted after the death of Anwar Sadat, as relations between Egypt and Israel had progressively chilled.

During those years, the authorities of the Egyptian Antiquities Organization had provided various imaginative explanations for their refusal to allow Porten to continue his examination of the Elephantine papyri. According to Porten, Dr. Muhammed Salah, the director of the organization, went so far as to ask him if there weren't papyri closer at hand in Jerusalem that he could study instead. And the official response to his repeated applications was even less encouraging. A formal letter from the Egyptian Antiquities Organization stated that since they had helped Porten so much in previous years, the imbalance would have to be corrected by reserving the Elephantine papyri for their *own* scholars to examine and study from then on.

"These things tend to go with political events," Porten told me pessimistically, describing how he intended to go to Egypt again that spring. The trustees of the museum were scheduled to meet and once again to weigh foreign scholars' requests for access to items in their collections, and Porten intended to press his application in person. Yet, as I later learned, his presence in Cairo didn't alter his scholarly chances; his application to study the Elephantine papyri was rejected once again.

So that spring, as the archaeological work went on at Elephantine Island, Bezalel Porten had traveled to Cairo to await an answer from the museum authorities. His situation was markedly different from that of the earlier explorers of Elephantine Island. And it was different from that of the current German-Swiss expedition team. Yet I realized that he had something in common with all of them. All scholars involved in the historical problems of Elephantine Island were participants, willingly or unwillingly, in a painful and politically sensitive archaeological controversy. For beneath the apparent tranquility of Elephantine Island lay the remains of a turn-of-the-century European rivalry that had been compounded and transformed by the politics and shifting currents of modern Middle Eastern diplomacy.

11

SOUTH ARABIA

Lost Kingdoms and Caravan Routes

🔳**I** had high hopes of seeing some history-making discoveries in Wadi al-Jubah, a remote valley in the Yemen Arab Republic* that was being explored by an American archaeological team. Wadi al-Jubah is located in what is today a sparsely inhabited borderland on the edge of Arabia's vast Empty Quarter, yet by the time of my visit, the American expedition had already uncovered finds of great importance for the study of the little-known civilization of ancient South Arabia: the remains of ancient cities, villages, burial monuments, and sophisticated irrigation systems throughout the valley's entire twelve-mile length. The Wadi al-Jubah Project, the first foreign expedition granted permission to excavate in North Yemen in more than three decades, marked a dramatic turning point in the rise and development of Yemeni archaeology.

This project, sponsored by the Washington-based American Foundation for the Study of Man (AFSM), was intended as the first stage in a modern, systematic reconstruction of ancient South Arabian

*Commonly called North Yemen, to differentiate it from South Yemen, or the People's Democratic Republic of Yemen, formerly the British Protectorate of Aden.

history, and that scientific challenge, I learned, was especially difficult. In a country as relatively unexplored as North Yemen, every facet of archaeological analysis—from the dating of pottery to the study of architectural development to the interpretation of settlement patterns—had to be started from scratch. The archaeological situation was roughly comparable to that of Greece, Egypt, and Palestine more than a century ago. In few other areas of the modern Middle East were the archaeological finds so plentiful and the archaeological background so thin.

The willingness of the Yemeni government to sanction the expedition was, in itself, something of an achievement. In the early 1950s, a previous expedition of the American Foundation for the Study of Man, led by the organization's founder, Wendell Phillips, encountered such intense hostility from the local authorities that they eventually had to abandon their finds and excavation equipment and flee from the country in fear of their lives. Their goal had been the excavation of the ancient city of Marib—only twenty miles north of Wadi al-Jubah—the legendary home of the Queen of Sheba and capital of the most powerful kingdom on the ancient Arabian spice and incense route, along which frankincense and myrrh had been shipped northward throughout antiquity. After gaining initial permission for this exploration from Imam Ahmad, the king of Yemen, Phillips and the other members of his expedition found themselves harassed, isolated, and eventually threatened at the instigation of some distinctly xenophobic members of the Yemeni court. To those officials, "archaeology" seemed to be just a pretext for Western entanglement in their country's affairs. The antiquities of Marib were "the window through which the world would have looked at us," the Yemeni chief *qadi* reportedly proclaimed after Phillips's hasty departure. And it was a dangerously transparent window for a country trying to keep itself secluded. "Now we have closed it," the chief *qadi* said.

But much had changed in North Yemen since 1952. The country was no longer ruled by a medieval-style monarchy but by the bureaucrats of a development-minded revolutionary republic, eager to expand North Yemen's contacts with the outside world. The earlier distrust of foreign archaeologists had been replaced by a determination to uncover and display the country's archaeological heritage. The window of Yemeni antiquities was therefore no longer shut so tightly, and when I accompanied an eight-member archaeological delegation of the American Schools of Oriental Research on a visit to Wadi al-Jubah, I was interested to see what the new era in Yemeni archaeology could reveal about Yemeni society today.

As it turned out, I found myself better prepared for the antiquities of Yemen than for the country's modern realities. Our guide and group leader, Dr. James Sauer, current president of the American Schools of Oriental Research and chief archaeologist of the Wadi al-Jubah Project, was out at the dig when we arrived on an afternoon flight from Cairo, but he had arranged that we would spend the first part of our visit traveling around the country to get a better idea of its present-day culture and geography. Sauer later put it well when he expressed the feeling that the Yemen Arab Republic was experiencing "a head-on collision with the twentieth century," for during our travels I was made constantly aware of the fragmentation of traditional Yemeni culture under the tractor treads and steamrollers of rapid industrialization.

In an earlier era, the country's rulers could keep their people secluded, but in a world of superpower conflict and petroleum dependence, seclusion was no longer a possibility. North Yemen's strategic geographical position at the narrow straits between the Red Sea and the Indian Ocean and its sensitive political position between the conservative kingdom of Saudi Arabia and the radical Marxist People's Democratic Republic of Yemen were factors that policy planners in Moscow and Washington could hardly overlook. As a result, foreign aid and foreign involvement in the country had risen steadily through the 1980s. And, as I later realized, the massive economic and cultural transformation that North Yemen is now experiencing may be one of the important factors behind its newfound interest in archaeology.

The National Museum in the capital city of Sana'a provided me with a clear demonstration of the eagerness of the present government to display the grandeur of the country's heritage without a fully crystallized conception of that heritage. The top floors of the building, which once served as a royal palace, were filled with some of the knickknacks and luxury goods acquired by the last of the Yemeni kings. But the glass cases filled with ashtrays, cigarette lighters, watches, firearms, and ceremonial robes lacked a focus of presentation. From the vaguely written descriptions, I wasn't quite sure whether the objects were meant to be viewed with revolutionary contempt or national pride. And on the lower floors, which contained North Yemen's more ancient artifacts, the same ideological uncertainty prevailed. The ancient statues, inscriptions, and pottery gathered from archaeological sites during the last hundred years were labeled haphazardly and followed a vague chronological order. Like the royal knickknacks on the floors above them, they seemed to be objects of interest, yet they too lacked a coherent thematic context.

That presentational problem reflected the current state of the study of ancient South Arabian culture, not only in the Yemen Arab Republic, but also by scholars all over the world. Although thousands of individual artifacts had been discovered and studied, the character of the society that produced them was still largely unknown. The reason was at least partly historical: The most important surviving ancient descriptions of South Arabian civilization were written by outsiders who had only a superficial knowledge of the distant kingdoms from which the famous incense caravans set out. To the ancient Israelites, the Greeks, and the Romans, South Arabia was a mysterious region on the outer edge of the known world. Mystery was one of its most intriguing attributes, so it is not always easy to disentangle fact from fantasy in the ancient accounts.

Chapter 10 of the first biblical book of Kings, for instance, described the journey of the Queen of Sheba to visit King Solomon in Jerusalem. It is a record of somewhat questionable historical value, but it nevertheless conveys the impression made by the ancient South Arabians on the people living around the Mediterranean rim. According to the biblical account of the visit, which presumably took place around 950 B.C., the queen came "with a very great retinue, with camels bearing spices, and very much gold, and precious stones." The object of this visit was the queen's desire to learn more about Solomon's kingdom; the result was a lucrative commercial exchange. The Israelite king offered the Queen of Sheba the products of his kingdom, and she, in turn, presented him with the gold, spices, and precious stones that she had brought in her caravan. According to the biblical narrative, this was an event to be remembered, for "never again came such an abundance of spices as these which the Queen of Sheba gave to King Solomon."

The Bible offered no sequel to this business transaction, but the writings of certain Greek and Roman authors did. From the time of Herodotus in the fifth century B.C. to that of Pliny the Elder in the first century A.D., South Arabia was known as the source of the precious frankincense and myrrh, so highly esteemed as perfumes and pungent incense in the temples and palaces of the Mediterranean world. Because of a quirk of climate and geology no less capricious than that which laid down the petroleum fields, the trees bearing the fragrant resins grew only along the southern coast of the Arabian peninsula and along the opposite Horn of Africa. The Greeks and the Romans, like the Israelites before them, knew of the Kingdom of Sheba and its incense. But because the people of Sheba—the Sabaeans—wanted to maintain their monopoly, they carefully guarded themselves from the prying eyes of the outside world. As a result, the ancient legends and accounts about southern Arabia that have come down to us vividly described the incense and the prosperity of the region's kingdoms, but not a great deal more than that.

In the fourth century A.D., with the triumph of Christianity and its relatively smokeless ceremonies, the Mediterranean cities no longer had a need for great quantities of Arabian incense, and so the kingdoms of South Arabia slowly sank into oblivion. All that remained of their former glory were the legends, and when the forces of Islam conquered Yemen in 633 A.D., those legends were given a decidedly negative twist. The Queen of Sheba, known in the Quran as "Bilqis," became a figure of diabolical power, and the fall of her kingdom was attributed not to economic factors but to its inhabitants' sinfulness. The achievements of the ancient civilization of South Arabia were at first disparaged and then, for the most part, forgotten. After all, they belonged to the dark days before the rise of Islam, which the Quran called the *Jahiliya*, "the time of ignorance."

Except for the erudite works of medieval scholars such as Wahb ibn-Munnabih and al-Hasan ibn-Ahmad al-Hamdani, it was only in the nineteenth century that the ancient history of South Arabia began to be studied intensively again. At the same time that many European antiquarians were relentlessly ransacking the ruins of Egypt, Palestine, and Mesopotamia in their quest for biblical confirmation, a few of their colleagues made their way to Yemen and had their first glimpses of the civilization that had once flourished there. These early explorers found no direct evidence of the Queen of Sheba, but their drawings and photographs of inscriptions and city ruins substantiated a biblical link. The language of the ancient South Arabian inscriptions was found to be a previously unknown ancient Semitic dialect, distantly related to Phoenician and biblical Hebrew. And the imposing remains of the ancient city of Marib (whose most impressive ruins were known locally as the "throne" and "sanctuary" of Bilqis) testified to the importance and wealth of the Sabaean kingdom.

Unfortunately, the remoteness of Yemen and its inhabitants' religious conservatism discouraged what might otherwise have been extensive archaeological research. Restricted to the universities and museums of Europe, Western scholars therefore had only limited material with which to work. Poring over the few recovered inscriptions, they pieced together a rough chronology of ancient Sabaean priests and kings. But large-scale excavations at Marib—or any other South Arabian city—that might have broadened the picture of ancient South Arabian civilization were a practical impossibility. Throughout most of the twentieth century, when the country was ruled by autonomous kings (who also held the title *imam*, or "prayer leader," of the Zaydi sect of Islam), most Yemenis saw no need for an investigation of what the Quran had already made clear. Wendell Phillips's brief 1951–52 excavation at the "Sanctuary of Bilqis" in Marib was an exception, but its untimely end proved the rule.

I was surprised to see a few of Phillips's finds from Marib on display in the National Museum in Sana'a. The bronze statues and inscriptions left behind by the fleeing AFSM expedition, once considererd evidence of Western perfidy, were now among the cornerstones of a new national history. That history was still under construction, but like the modern schools, factories, water systems, and highways being built by foreign experts, advisers, and construction crews throughout the country, the new archaeological interest of the Yemeni government seemed to be an element of its ambitious development plans. In sanctioning the return of Western archaeological exploration, Yemen's leaders now seemed to be seeking a "modern," archaeology-based past with which to survive their country's head-on collision with the twentieth century.

The scenery on the ride out to Wadi al-Jubah was spectacular. From the high central plateau of Sana'a, we wound our way down through the eastern mountains, or *mashriq*, toward Marib, where deep ravines pour out the flash floods onto the gentle plain that gradually merges with the arid sands of the Empty Quarter to the east. Jim Sauer, back from the dig with the enthusiasm of a true believer, excitedly described the region's archaeological background and underlined the special significance of the team's selection of Wadi al-Jubah as its first exploratory site.

It was there along the desert fringe that the ancient cities of South Arabia had flourished. Only after that early civilization had crumbled did the bulk of the people move up to the rugged hilly regions of the country, where its main population centers are now. The desert fringe was able to support thriving centers only when the capricious rainfall and the violent floods were controlled and used for irrigation. And that agricultural self-sufficiency made the ancient South Arabian cities natural caravan stages, convenient ports of call along the edge of an uninhabitable sea.

The caravan, of course, was one of the central images of Arabia in the mind of the West, and an important challenge facing the nineteenth-century explorers of Yemen was to reconstruct the precise line of the caravan route by comparing the ancient descriptions with actual topography. According to Pliny the Elder, there were two other kingdoms, to the south and east of Sheba, through which the incense caravans passed. Every autumn, the camels were loaded and set off from the city of Shabwa, capital of the kingdom of Hadhramaut, now within the modern state of South Yemen. The next major stopping place, about ninety miles to the west, was the city of Timna, capital of the kingdom of Qataban. From there, the route led northwestward to Marib, in the kingdom of Sheba, but Pliny did not describe its exact path. The most direct way was straight across the desert, but a number of scholars suggested that the fully laden caravans would not have attempted this waterless crossing. A more practical route would have stayed close to the mountain slopes, with their shelter and freshwater springs.

This passage between Qataban and Sheba was therefore of particular interest to the members of the Wadi al-Jubah expedition, for it had a direct bearing on the valley's historical significance. Pliny mentioned a Qatabanian city called "Nagia" between Timna and Marib, but its location was uncertain until the Austrian scholar Eduard Glaser visited Wadi al-Jubah in the course of his wide-ranging explorations in the 1880s. There, roughly halfway between Timna and Marib on the indirect route, he found a modern village called "Najja"—a name too suspiciously close to "Nagia" in both geography and spelling not to suppose that Wadi al-Jubah lay on the path of the ancient caravan route.

Even before the current Wadi al-Jubah Project began its work, there were some additional clues. In a preliminary reconnaissance of the area, Dr. Albert Jamme, a member of the original AFSM expedition to Marib and now the new expedition's epigrapher, found several ancient inscriptions, among which were two dedications to the Qatabanian moon god *'Amm*. Those finds seemed to substantiate the identification of the valley as an important region on the northern boundary of the kingdom of Qataban. Now, after several years of exploration, few questions had been answered conclusively, but the AFSM expedition had already begun to transform the accepted archaeological understanding of ancient South Arabian culture and its legendary highway.

We approached Wadi al-Jubah from the direction of Sheba, precisely the opposite direction that the incense caravans would have taken on their journey to the north. After leaving the asphalt road where it ended near Marib, we headed south into the stretch of sand dunes that led to the kingdom of Qataban. In the distance rose towering granite mountains, and, as we neared them, we could make out the narrow gap beyond which lay Wadi al-Jubah. Within a half hour, our Toyota Landcruiser had made it through the pass and onto the hard-packed washboard surface of the valley, along the path once taken by the caravans of camels loaded down with precious incense.

Wadi al-Jubah was much larger than I expected—not a narrow valley, convenient for archaeological exploration, but a self-contained world. Although we were far from the last asphalt surface, we drove through several villages, with schools, shops, and gas stations, nestled beneath the valley's steep granite walls. And some things had apparently not changed in the centuries since the incense caravans stopped coming this way. Sauer explained that the nearby borders with Saudi Arabia and South Yemen were not marked precisely and remained mostly unguarded, and I soon got the impression that Wadi al-Jubah was—even today—a smuggler's paradise.

As we drove farther into the valley, we began to see some of the merchandise brought across the border under the cover of night. A pickup truck roared past us, loaded with open barrels of cut-rate Saudi gasoline. Not long after, when we stopped for gas in the village of Jubah al-Jadidah, we found the gas station piled high with cases of canned peach halves in heavy syrup marked "Product of the USA." One of our guides, a native of the area, proudly described some of the ways an ambitious man could become rich and respected here. He told us, for instance, about all-night drives he and his friends had made up through the canyons to the Saudi border to bring back new cars for resale in Sana'a without paying the high Yemeni customs fee. I now realized that the ancient caravan route might still have a cultural impact; we had entered a world that strangely mimicked its archaeological image—a world of modern-day caravaners.

Continuing past a side valley called al-Faraah, we spotted one of the Jeeps of the expedition team. Although it was already late in the afternoon, Sauer couldn't resist the temptation to see what they were doing there. Leaving our Landcruiser at the foot of the rocky slope, we climbed up to meet two members of the expedition who were standing beside a huge pile of stones. Sauer introduced us to Barbara Hartmann, a field assistant, and Mike Toplyn, a graduate student from Harvard who, with his drawing board and authoritative manner, was obviously directing the work here. As I later learned, Toplyn had previously worked on archaeological projects in the Iranian highlands, Saudi Arabia, and the eastern Jordan Valley, and his main interest in Wadi al-Jubah was not its caravan routes. His experience and academic training as a scientist had equipped him to assess the settlement patterns and culture of early human societies, and he hoped to establish the date and character of the earliest human civilization here.

Toplyn explained that the "feature" before us was a cairn, or burial monument, and since they hoped to begin its excavation the following day, he and Hartmann had remained at the site to complete the scale drawing of its surface details before the digging began. This cairn was not chosen for excavation because it was the most impressive of its kind in Wadi al-Jubah, Toplyn told us. There were at least twenty more around the edges of the valley, each containing a stone-lined chamber in its center for the burial of a single body and the deposit of grave goods. But all the others so far discovered had been dismantled by the local inhabitants for building stones, or damaged by erosion down the slopes. This cairn alone held out the possibility of recovering the skeleton and offerings intact. And if those finds could be dated by carbon-14 analysis, one of the most intriguing mysteries in the study of South Arabian archaeology might finally be solved.

Similar cairns had been found throughout the Arabian peninsula, Toplyn informed us, but the date of their construction and the nature of the society that built them had eluded scholars thus far. In other parts of the Middle East, such structures were dated to the Neolithic period (ca. 8000 through ca. 4000 B.C.), the era when mankind here began to emerge from its dependence on hunting and gathering for survival, during which a number of early communities settled down to an agricultural life. The possibility that this cairn might reflect the beginnings of settled civilization in southern Arabia was of more interest to Toplyn than the substantiation of the legends of the caravan routes. And even though the carbon-14 date of this particular cairn later proved to be unexpectedly recent—late sixth century A.D.—there were other such monuments throughout the valley of possibly far earlier dates.

Whatever the subsequent findings, Toplyn believed that only by detaching Wadi al-Jubah's history from its romantic and legendary background would a clear evaluation of its cultural development emerge. And only through the careful recording and analysis of its ancient ruins and burial places would the isolated world of Wadi al-

Jubah be closely linked—at least in remote antiquity—with human civilization in the rest of the world.

Wendell Phillips, founder of the American Foundation for the Study of Man, didn't live to see the return of his organization to Yemen. It's a question, though, how he would have gotten along with the staff of the new expedition, for he was an old-fashioned professional explorer who eagerly played the role of Indiana Jones decades before *Raiders of the Lost Ark* ever hit America's movie screens. Although Phillips's academic credentials were modest (a B.A. in paleontology from the University of California), he contributed more to the modern knowledge of South Arabia than any other Westerner of his generation. A life of adventure, not conventional academics, was the focus of his career. At age twenty-six, he organized and led a large University of California expedition to Africa, and three years later, after having established the AFSM, he assembled an even more impressive staff of archaeologists and scientific specialists for his head-on assault on the antiquities of South Arabia.

Phillips was not a tradition-bound scholar. His personal interests far transcended the technical and often tedious archaeological fieldwork that he both initiated and led. The fact that no one had ever excavated an ancient South Arabian city attracted him as much as the specific historical information that could be gained. For those who knew him, his brash self-confidence and love of the exotic was unforgettable. And his characteristic costume—an Arab *keffiyeh* on his head and a pearl-handled Colt .45 in a tooled leather holster slung low around his waist—made him, as well as his quixotic foray into the Land of Sheba, not only a Saturday afternoon serial come to life, but also a modern archaeological legend. Before digging at Marib, he directed excavations at Timna, then in British-controlled Aden, and he uncovered a breathtaking array of ancient statues, jewelry, inscriptions, and architecture that testified to the city's prosperity from the caravan trade. But the image of the Queen of Sheba and her legendary capital attracted him so strongly that he took the unprecedented step of appealing directly to the king of Yemen, Imam Ahmad, seeking permission for his expedition to enter North Yemen and dig.

While South Yemen—then under British colonial rule as the Protectorate of Aden—was a relatively accessible country, North Yemen was not. All the more miraculous, then, that Phillips received word from Prince Abdullah, one of Imam Ahmad's brothers, that he would be granted an audience with the king. Leaving the work in progress at Timna, Phillips lost no time making his way across the border to the royal residence in the mountain city of Taiz. Phillips thoughtfully took along a cornucopia of American consumer products that he hoped would demonstrate good intentions to Imam Ahmad. The cases of Colgate toothpaste and Coca-Cola, Colt pistols, Western ammunition, General Electric fan, Hallicrafters radio, Royal typewriter, and Polaroid camera, once gratefully accepted, were cause for a gift in return. Royal permission was granted for Phillips's expedition to the Queen of Sheba's capital of Marib, jewel of the ancient caravan route.

Unfortunately, Phillips was unaware that his expedition had become an object of bitterly contentious infighting within the Yemeni court. His chief supporter was Prince Abdullah, who, a few years later, would be executed for his leadership of an unsuccessful palace coup. His chief opponent was Prince Seif al-Islam Hassan Mohammed Ahmad al-Badr, favorite son of Imam Ahmad, who would ultimately become North Yemen's last, embattled king. And although this prince was designated to be the official signatory of the royal document that granted Phillips permission to dig at Marib, he was determined from the beginning to make the Americans' position within his country both difficult and dangerous.

Prince Badr began by appointing an official Yemeni supervisor for the excavations at Marib, a *qadi* named Zeid Inan, whose chief personal assets were loyalty to Badr and a deep-seated suspicion of Western archaeology. Zeid Inan began his own campaign of obstructionism by placing severe restrictions on the AFSM work schedules and methods, prohibiting any explorations of the area around Marib and demanding a latex cast of every ancient inscription uncovered by the expedition team. His secret dispatches back to the palace, not surprisingly, succeeded in sowing resentment toward the American archaeologists. He accused them of destroying the ruins at Marib; he even hinted at espionage. Dr. Albert Jamme, the team's

Belgian epigrapher, was summarily imprisoned on Zeid Inan's orders—on charges of incorrectly deciphering the ancient Sabaean inscriptions. But this was all just a prelude. When Phillips sent a message to the palace bitterly protesting the unfair behavior of the *qadi*, his support in royal circles collapsed completely.

The imam himself became enraged at this breach of protocol, and Phillips's situation at Marib quickly deteriorated further. The work was now frequently suspended by openly hostile local guards. The finds and the recorded inscriptions were confiscated and the expedition's supply and communications links to the outside world were cut off. When their only supporter at Marib, the local governor, was suddenly summoned to the palace, Phillips and the other team members quite rightly began to fear for their lives. Escape was the only remaining possibility. So, pretending one morning to go to work as usual, they surprised their supervisors-turned-captors by jumping onto their expedition vehicles at a prearranged signal and making a desperate break for freedom across the Aden border to the south.

The members of the AFSM expedition did escape with their lives, although they left behind all their finds and more than $200,000 worth of excavation equipment. Phillips never returned to dig in North Yemen, yet he kept alive the dream of excavating the Queen of Sheba's city. His later popular books and vivid lectures on the lure of the ancient incense route and his own daring escape from Marib might be frowned on by today's generation of archaeologists, but it was the memory of Wendell Phillips that they had to thank for being in Yemen again. After his death in 1975, his younger sister, Merilyn Phillips Hodgson, committed herself to the cause of American exploration in South Arabia, and her fund-raising efforts resulted in the rebirth of the American Foundation for the Study of Man.

My first glimpse of most of the staff members of the Wadi al-Jubah Project was a sight reminiscent of Wendell Phillips's heyday. As we waited under the full moon outside the expedition headquarters in the village of al-Wasit, a convoy of pickup trucks roared into the village, each with two or three rifle-toting guards standing in the truck beds and clinging to the roofs of the cabs. This was no ordinary convoy, but the entourage of the governor of the province, al-Bahri bin Hishlah Abdullah Bahri, who was bringing the American archaeologists back to their headquarters after a day of feasting and celebrating as his personal guests. The team members tumbled out of the trucks in a whirlwind of laughter and high spirits. Jim Sauer introduced us to Jeff Blakely, the project's field director; Bob Stewart, the expedition's botanist; Maurice Grolier and Bill Overstreet, the team geologists; and Abdu Othman Ghaleb, a doctoral candidate in South Arabian archaeology at the University of Pennsylvania and the current liaison with the YAR Organization for Antiquities.

Close behind was the guest of honor, Merilyn Phillips Hodgson, the moving spirit behind the renewed activity of the AFSM. She had visited her brother's excavations at Timna as a teenager and was obviously enjoying her triumphant return. After telling each of us how happy she was that we were able to visit the expedition, she proudly introduced us to a gnarled old *qabili*, or tribesman, who claimed—according to her—that he had "taken Wendell all around."

As the members of al-Bahri's convoy returned to their pickups and drove off into the darkness, we followed Jeff Blakely and the rest of the expedition members into the team's compound. Here, my romantic illusions about Wendell Phillips's adventures ended, for this was a scene of pioneering that was long on difficult living conditions and decidedly short on romance. Just inside the entrance to the low stone building was the largest room in the complex, a fifteen-by-thirty-foot living space, its beaten earth floor covered with mats and sleeping bags and its rough stone walls illuminated by a single, glaring, generator-powered light bulb. Beyond was the expedition's social center, an unpaved dirt courtyard surrounded by high stone walls, with some live chickens pecking around the legs of the field cots and camp stools. Most of the group found places to sit and listen to Merilyn Hodgson's enthusiastic description of her visit with the women of the governor's family, but since I was anxious to talk with Jeff Blakely, I followed him into the expedition's kitchen, a small, dark room quickly made unbearably hot by the hissing gas jet of a portable camp stove.

"Want some hot Tang?" Blakely asked me, offering the specialty of the house. I took tea instead and sat down on a low rush stool as Blakely mixed up his own steaming orange drink. I had met him several years earlier in Jerusalem when he was working at Tell el-Hesi, an important and well-known ancient city mound near the Mediterraneaen coast. At that time, he was just one of several younger staff members on a large excavation, but since then, his status had changed. As the field director of the Wadi al-Jubah Project, and as the archaeological heir of Wendell Phillips, he was not only in a position to determine the day-to-day course of this important new expedition, but he was also—I assumed—in a perfect position to make the future exploration of Yemen the focus of a successful archaeological career.

It wasn't really that simple, Blakely quickly countered. Compared to the kind of archaeological work he was used to, this project had a long way to go before it could be the basis of anyone's career. It might have been enough for Wendell Phillips to lead his expeditions into unexplored regions, but Jeff Blakely was the product of a more sophisticated and technical archaeological milieu. Around the rim of the Mediterranean, where Jeff had gained his training, the historical sources were abundant, the most important sites were identified with famous cities of antiquity, and the study of pottery and architecture was based on an enormous body of comparative material from dozens, even hundreds, of previous digs.

Here, though, the ancient descriptions of South Arabia were of questionable accuracy, only two or three cities had been securely identified, and the study of the local pottery hadn't really begun. Blakely's doctoral dissertation, on the Late Iron Age pottery of southern Palestine, traced the progressive changes in shape and form of various vessels, in intervals of a decade or less. The situation he faced in Wadi al-Jubah was entirely different; no archaeologist had yet been able to distinguish potsherds dating to King Solomon in the tenth century B.C. from potsherds made in the time of Pliny the Elder, more than a thousand years after that. Blakely hoped that someday ancient South Arabian pottery might be dated with equal precision, and the two ends of the caravan route might again be linked. Times had changed since Wendell Phillips's earlier expedition to the Land of Sheba, both in Yemen and in the world of archaeology. Jeff Blakely and the other members of the new AFSM expedition may have been following in Phillips's footsteps, but as I learned the following morning, their goals and methods had little to do with romantic caravan dreams.

It was hard to be enthusiastic at five A.M. in Wadi al-Jubah, but everyone was trying his or her best. Over steaming mugs of Tang, Jeff Blakely and Mike Toplyn huddled to plan the strategy of the excavation of the cairn, with Jim Sauer offering his own methodical advice. Bob Stewart quietly went through his botanical field notes, and Maurice Grolier and Bill Overstreet conferred about the areas still remaining to be explored for the geological survey. On everyone's mind was the limited time remaining in the expedition's season. With the ominous possibility of blinding sandstorms unexpectedly rising at this time of the year, all were anxious to accomplish as much as possible as quickly as possible. But before leaving for the day's exploration, Bill Overstreet modestly surrendered to Sauer's prodding and agreed to share with us some of his preliminary findings about Wadi al-Jubah's geology.

Taping two brilliantly colored satellite photographs to the stone wall of the expedition courtyard, Overstreet pointed to a tiny dark patch that he identified as Wadi al-Jubah and explained that his main challenge was to help the archaeologists understand the physical setting and to suggest some environmental reasons why ancient people might have come to settle and build a culture in this particular place. According to Overstreet, the story began about 570 million years ago with the formation of an isolated mass of granite, which he described in his Maryland drawl as "something like a knot in a wooden plank." Over the next 550 million years, atmospheric conditions altered that initial formation; wind and rain gradually weathered the "knot's" surface, and its center crumbled away. Then came the more recent developments—from a geologist's perspective at least. During the Pleistocene period (ca. 700,000 through ca. 10,000 B.C.), the hollow in the granite crater was filled with fine, windblown silt. With the dramatic increase in rainfall that the entire region experienced at the end of the last Ice Age, Overstreet concluded, the silt floor of the valley became rich farming land.

What happened after that was of only marginal interest to Bill Overstreet; his specialty was natural processes, not history. He had devoted his career to analyzing the structure and possible usefulness of geological resources, and because of that expertise, he was no stranger to the Middle East. Now retired from the U.S. Geological Survey, Overstreet and Maurice Grolier, who had previously worked in Saudi Arabia, had been called to the Yemen Arab Republic at the beginning of the massive aid programs in the mid-1970s to carry out a geological survey of the entire country. The map they constructed at that time for the installation of USAID rural water projects in North Yemen had become the basis—practical and philosophical—for their work in Wadi al-Jubah.

It was clear to me that the geological survey was an essential element of the Wadi al-Jubah Project; it provided a firm environmental framework on which the hazier historical conjectures could finally assume a definite shape. But the new picture provided a striking, if unintentional, contrast with Wendell Phillips's faith that the romance and mystery of the ancient caravan cities of South Arabia could be brought to life again. By concentrating on the environmental factors *within* the valley, the current expedition was constructing a version of history molded by forces beyond the vagaries of human emotions, beyond the specific greed, wealth, or ambition of ancient kings and queens. They were forces whose traces could be photographed, measured, and chemically analyzed through modern technology. Like the technical-assistance programs of the other foreign experts in North Yemen, the Wadi al-Jubah Project dealt with questions of the country's development. No matter that those developments lay at the dawn of human history in the region; at their core lay a basic faith in human manipulation of the environment.

A new day of exploration in Wadi al-Jubah was now beginning. As the expedition team gathered together their equipment and left the headquarters and we began our own tour of the valley with Jim Sauer, I finally began to realize how deeply the environmental approach had already colored the archaeological understanding of the ultimate impact of South Arabia's ancient caravan trade.

Had there been no legends or ancient descriptions to rely on, I might have been inclined to think that the ancient civilization in Wadi al-Jubah was a purely agricultural one. As we bumped along the wadi bed, Sauer pointed out the remains of dams, water channels, wells, and agricultural terraces that the expedition had discovered and mapped. Here and there were mounds of light brownish soil with steep sides sharply carved by the rushing waters of the winter flash floods. Those mounds of silt, Sauer explained, were the remains of ancient agricultural fields, whose cultivation was based on the intensive and efficient use of the same natural factor that destroyed them: the seasonal runoff of rainwater from the surrounding mountainsides.

Less than a mile south of al-Wasit, we stopped at the foot of a small settlement mound, locally known as Hajar at-Tamrah, a site that could easily be mistaken for another heap of ancient agricultural soil were it not for the dark layers of building stones and ashy deposits extending horizontally through the mud. The site numbers recorded on the expedition's maps were chosen according to geographic sector and time of discovery, but if they had been assigned in terms of relative importance, this site, HT12, might have been number one. In its slope was a neatly cut vertical section, which the team had excavated to test the nature of the occupation layers and to determine, if possible, the site's initial and final occupation dates.

The finds from this small dig were certainly not worthy of exhibition in the National Museum, but they clearly suggested the nature of Hajar at-Tamrah's ancient settlement. In addition to a scatter of crude potsherds, carbonized seeds, and cooking hearths were the skeletal remains of goats. There was little question that this was once a small farming village, not a caravan city. Although the lack of any evidence of trade might have been explained away as due to the small size of the site, the dates of its occupation were not so easy to explain. Hajar at-Tamrah's lowest layer yielded a carbon-14 date of 1330 B.C. ± 110 years, which, because of a standard inaccuracy of all dates before 1200 B.C., has been "calibrated," or adjusted, to ca. 1600–1500 B.C.

That new date suddenly placed the rise of towns in Wadi al-Jubah in a completely different context than previously thought. The accepted ideaes about the beginnings of urban settlement in South Arabia were based roughly on the assumed date of the Queen of Sheba's visit to Jerusalem—that is to say, in the early Iron Age, not more than a century or so before 950 B.C. But according to the carbon-14 evidence, the settlement at Hajar at-Tamrah would have been established in the Bronze Age, more than half a millennium earlier. Most important, its origins would probably not have been linked to a northern demand for incense, but to the first efficient harnessing of rainwater for agriculture—an indigenous technological development.

That finding was not the only surprise to come from the carbon-14 samples of Hajar at-Tamrah; the date of its abandonment, even more than that of its origins, threatened to upset the conventional theories about the valley's prosperity in the era of the incense trade. The samples from the uppermost levels indicated that the last occupation and final abandonment of the village took place between 500 and 400 B.C.—more than 500 years before Pliny the Elder wrote so glowingly of the power, wealth, and trade of the Qatabanians.

And what of the Qatabanian city of Nagia, tentatively identified with the modern village of Najja on Wadi al-Jubah's western side? Another complicating factor for seekers-after-caravan-routes, it seemed. The expedition's initial explorations in and around Najja failed to uncover any evidence of ancient occupation; the earliest artifacts and structures found in the village seemed not to be more than two or three centuries old. All was not lost, though, for as the explorations moved eastward, the team located and mapped a site that seemed to fit the ancient descriptions: a huge city mound, with fortification walls still standing, which the local inhabitants called Hajar ar-Rayhani and which the archaeologists called HR3.

HR3 was certainly impressive; the remains of its ancient city wall still stood in some places to a height of thirteen feet, pierced by a massive city gate on its northern side. Off toward the east was a gap in the mountains through which many scholars believed that the ancient caravans passed on their way from Timna to Marib. If any site fit the description of the caravan city of Nagia, between the Qatabanian capital of Timna and the border of the kingdom of Sheba, HR3 seemed to be it. But as we arrived at the site and walked over its eighteen-acre surface, winding our way through the litter of ancient building stones and modern trash from the nearby town of Jubah al-Jadidah, Sauer's description of the results of the recent excavations here provoked some unsettling questions in my mind about the nature and impact of the ancient caravan route.

Sauer explained that as the team dug through the superimposed levels of the city, they uncovered a pattern of development similar to that of Hajar at-Tamrah, except on a much larger scale. Surrounding the site were vast stretches of agricultural silt—testimony to extensive ancient farming activity. And although the mound itself yielded remains of an urban character, and its carbon-14 dates indicated that it was occupied as late as the Roman period, nowhere among the many artifacts recovered from its layers was there any evidence for the legendary caravan trade. At both Timna and Marib, Wendell Phillips's excavations discovered characteristic Roman pottery and Greek-inspired sculpture that were apparently brought southward from the centers of the Mediterranean civilization where the Arabian incense was sold. But Wadi al-Jubah apparently did not share fully in this prosperity; the layers of HR3, the largest city in the valley, did not contain a single sherd of readily identifiable Greek or Roman pottery.

The identification of the site with the caravan city of Nagia—thriving in the first century A.D.—was at least chronologically possible, but the preliminary archaeological finds suggested that it was a somewhat different kind of city than previously believed. HR3, Hajar ar-Rayhani, Nagia, or whatever its ancient name might have been, served as a central point of redistribution for a rich agricultural region. In other words, it was, throughout most of its history, a provincial market town. Beginning some time in the Bronze Age, the ancient inhabitants of Wadi al-Jubah established an efficient system of flash-flood irrigation, which, from all archaeological indications so far, was their primary means of subsistence. Yet around 450 B.C., something altered this enclosed economic system. Outlying farming villages such as Hajar at-Tamrah were abandoned, and the central city at Hajar ar-Rayhani grew. Something changed the traditional way of life of the valley's inhabitants. Could that "something" have been the caravan trade itself?

At the time that the kingdoms of Qataban and Sheba began rising in power, shipping their incense northward, South Arabia became linked—willingly or unwillingly—to the economies of the Mediterranean world. The caravans loaded with incense may indeed have passed through the valley, but few signs remained of any prosperity they might have brought. Jim Sauer and the other members of the expedition tended to see the cause of Wadi al-Jubah's decline in a territorial conflict between Qataban and Sheba, but there may have been another explanation. The rise of the caravan trade, with its reliance on an international economy and on massive infusions of foreign capital, might simply have made the small-scale subsistence system of Wadi al-Jubah irrelevant. And when the caravan trade ended, the remaining settlements of the valley were abandoned, not to be occupied again until relatively recent times. The price of economic and cultural change is often paid by marginal areas, and what might have been true of Wadi al-Jubah in the remote past might be equally true today. In fact, the breakup of traditional culture as a result of massive foreign influence is one of the most serious threats facing the people of Wadi al-Jubah and the rest of the Yemen Arab Republic today.

As we left Hajar ar-Rayhani and headed back across the sand dunes toward Marib, Sauer explained how the traditional village culture of Wadi al-Jubah was about to change dramatically. The government had recently approved plans for the construction of a highway from Marib to the town of Jubah al-Jadidah, and the local inhabitants feared that prospect. The geographical isolation that had preserved the essential character of the valley since the time of its modern resettlement would quickly vanish. The young people would leave in ever greater numbers for Sana'a and the cities of the Gulf States and Saudi Arabia for the lucrative, hard-cash-paying jobs that were obtainable there. And with the highway would come closer government supervision and stepped-up police patrols against smuggling. Those fears proved justified. In 1987, the paved road extending to the border with South Yemen was finally completed, and the strengthened presence of officials of the central government in this once-isolated region made it increasingly difficult to supplement meager agricultural incomes with trade in illegally imported goods.

That was also the last year of the AFSM's five-year concession, so the expedition team would not be there to see how the coming economic and cultural changes affected day-to-day life in Wadi al-Jubah. With the first archaeological project successfully completed, Merilyn Hodgson could now finally contemplate the fulfillment of her late brother's dream. The American Foundation for the Study of Man had received a new concession from the Yemeni Organization for Antiquities to excavate the site from which Wendell Phillips and his team members once fled. Their new goal would be uncovering the "Sanctuary of Bilqis" at Marib, the imposing temple built by the ancient Sabaeans with the revenues from their lucrative incense trade.

The staff of the new expedition, though, would be different. Both Jim Sauer and Jeff Blakely chose not to continue work with the AFSM in North Yemen, for the time being at least. Both felt that the new project at the temple site should be led by scholars with slightly different archaeological sensibilities, and both were determined to complete the time-consuming scientific publication of the findings of the Wadi al-Jubah survey. In Wadi al-Jubah, the work had concentrated mainly on environmental and anthropological questions, but the "Sanctuary of Bilqis" could not easily be studied the same way. There, precious museum pieces, monumental inscriptions, and complex architectural structures could be expected; this was the work of an archaeological team more suited to an older, more classically oriented archaeology. Like the temples of Greece, Italy, and Egypt, the Sabaean temple at Marib might someday become a major tourist attraction. What was needed there was a competent reconstruction—not questioning—of Wendell Phillips's alluring caravan dreams.

The terms and length of the new concession for Marib were, of course, determined by the Yemeni government and dictated by the country's perceived needs. The Yemen Arab Republic was a country filled with expectation, fearfully confident that its development dreams would come true. The pace of that development might soon be significantly enhanced by the recent discovery of petroleum reserves in the desert to the east of Marib. The initially optimistic cost/profit projections of the Hunt Oil Company had led to the construction of a pipeline from the province of Marib across the country to a new oil port on the Red Sea coast. By the 1990s, they hoped, tankers filled with Yemeni crude would begin chugging northward.

If and when that happened, the YAR would be more connected than ever with the industrialized world. And the myth of the Queen of Sheba and her rich caravans of incense—so long the obsession of foreigners—might finally seduce the Yemenis themselves.

In the meantime, the archaeological activity continued, and the new era in the history of Yemeni archaeology had progressed too far to turn back. The Wadi al-Jubah Project was just a beginning; even more spectacular discoveries at Marib certainly lay ahead. In 1987, the new National Museum was opened in Sana'a; the glass cases of gifts to the imam and the haphazardly displayed relics were replaced by an up-to-date—if still not final—presentation of the country's ancient history. The former presentational ambiguity was finally on its way to being resolved. Yet somehow I felt that the real significance of the ambitious archaeological activity remained unnoticed, or at least unspoken by all. The fact that potsherds, carbon-14 dates, and geological analyses had become the building blocks of North Yemen's national history was, in itself, a symptom of profound cultural change.

12

ISRAEL

Back to the Stone Age

▣ **T**here were clearly many pasts being resurrected by archaeologists in the Middle East and the eastern Mediterranean, and there were, it seemed, almost as many techniques. The scene at Kebara Cave, for instance—a prehistoric site on Israel's coastal plain near Haifa—could have come from a science-fiction film. For me, having returned to Israel after visiting Egypt and North Yemen, the excavations there seemed alien and unfamiliar, strangely lacking in the large-scale earthmoving operations, the noise, and the clouds of dust that I'd come to identify as characteristic of Near Eastern archaeology. But the goal of these excavations was different. Off the old Tel Aviv–Haifa highway, in a side row of a steamy banana plantation, the team's cars and vans were parked tightly together. There was no trace of human life here—at least not at first. The steady hum of a generator drowned out the high-pitched whine of the cicadas; the heavy electric cables attached to it snaked through the thick banana plants toward the towering ridge of limestone cliffs to the east. The path upward was steep and rocky, and I followed the cables toward the huge, jagged opening of Kebara Cave. On the natural terrace in front of its dark entrance, I could make out piles of sifted earth, sifting screens, and wooden trunks of excavation equipment. And I could hear the muffled sounds of voices from within the cave itself.

The view from the terrace was panoramic. Stretched below were the thick banana groves, and beyond them, the brilliant blue of the Mediterranean Sea. Inside the cave, the scene was not nearly so idyllic. Suspended beneath the mossy, fissured dome of the cavern was a large aluminum grid frame, tightly strung with wire, dividing the amorphous cave surface into precise one-meter squares. From each corner of the grid network, a plumb line established the vertical dimension, reaching down to the soft, ashy cave floor. Narrow wooden walkways crisscrossed the sharply defined excavation areas; to the side, a wooden floor, worktables, and shelves had been installed as a field laboratory. The effect was of artificial order imposed on an irregular natural formation, a primeval dankness overlaid by antiseptic high technology.

The coolness of the cave, the glare of the electric light bulbs strung along the stone walls, and the steady whir of the electric fans in the deepest of the excavation areas set this scene apart from all the other digs I'd seen recently. Different, too, was the pace at which the work was progressing. The dozen or so team members, crouching in their individual digging areas at various depths beneath the surrounding cave surface, slowly scraped away the soil with undersized trowels, stopping to measure and record each artifact uncovered, never digging down more than two inches at a time.

Painstaking excavation and precise recording were, of course, not ends in themselves. The challenge that faced the Israeli, French, and American members of the Kebara Cave expedition was, by any standard, difficult. They were not attempting to uncover the impressive, readily recognizable remains of an ancient fortress or city whose name was known and whose rise and fall could be fitted into the familiar epochs of Israel's political, economic, and religious history. They were, instead, hunting for far more elusive quarry: the ephemeral traces of a unique animal species that survived by hunting and foraging in the nearby hills and along the coastal plain approximately 50,000 years ago.

Propped up against the cave wall—near the high metal shelves filled with excavated flint implements—was a mounted, life-sized replica of the skeleton that had made Kebara one of the most important prehistoric sites in the world. Found in 1983, this skeleton had already called into question some neat assumptions about the course of human evolution and had raised new doubts about our species's early cultural and biological history. The Kebara skeleton was that of a stocky young man, found lying on his back, with his right hand resting on his chest and his left hand lying on his abdomen. Most of the skull, the right leg, and much of the left leg were missing. But despite the fragmentary nature of the remains, this young man's physical type—at least to the team's physical anthropologists—was clear.

In 1965, the skeleton of an infant with many of the same physical characteristics was discovered in a parallel layer at Kebara, a first indication of the character of the cave's occupants from about 60,000 to about 40,000 years ago. Throughout that entire period—about four times longer than all of recorded human history—Kebara Cave apparently was inhabited, at least intermittently, by individuals of the species *Homo sapiens neanderthalensis*—in other words, by Neanderthal men, babies, and presumably Neanderthal women as well.

I had come to Kebara Cave to talk with Professor Ofer Bar-Yosef of the Hebrew University about the significance of the team's latest discoveries—about the mysterious origins and disappearance of Israel's Neanderthals. But when I entered the cave, he was busy with another visitor, a staff photographer sent by the National Geographic Society to bring the sights and discoveries of Kebara Cave to the attention of armchair readers all over the world. So as Bar-Yosef and the photographer discussed the logistics of the planned photo session, I chatted for a few minutes with Dr. Anna Belfer-Cohen, another member of the expedition. She answered my questions about the Neanderthals politely, showed me some of the flint implements and chipped stone debris recovered from Kebara's deep levels of accumulation, and pointed out details of the mounted skeleton replica. Before long, I came to realize that despite its unfamiliar appearance, this excavation was neither science fiction nor completely different from the other Near Eastern archaeological projects that I had seen. I sensed that the controversy over the Neanderthals' place in human evolution was—like disputes over later historical epochs—based on a modern philosophical controversy.

It took a trained eye to distinguish the Kebara skeleton from that of a modern human. The anatomy of arms, legs, rib cage, spinal cord, and pelvis seemed normal enough to me. But cartoons, rather than excavated skeletal material, had colored my preconception of the Neanderthals of Israel and everywhere else. There's no denying that they have been saddled with a bad reputation in popular culture. They usually are depicted as dim-witted cave dwellers whose courtship rituals are seen to involve heavy clubs, loud animal-like grunts, and the bridegroom's firm grasp of his fiancée's hair. Their characteristically heavy, overhanging brows, thick body hair, and stooped posture don't suggest great intelligence or grace of movement. They hardly seem a part of the human race. But, as I learned at Kebara, that apelike caricature may not be justified; it's an inheritance from an earlier stage of prehistoric research in Europe, from a time when European scholars, statesmen, and philosophers classified human groups by their outward physical characteristics and accorded each an unchanging place on an ascending ladder of moral and cultural ability that led from the higher apes on the lowest rungs, through the "colored" races of Asia and Africa in the middle, to the lily-white Europeans at the top.

In our world of the late twentieth century, with development and upward mobility our watchwords, it's difficult to conceive of a world so static, but it is precisely that hierarchical ranking, the "Great Chain of Being," that is at the core of the current Neanderthal dispute. Naturally, the terms are now different from those used in the early nineteenth century, when it was firmly believed that everything on earth—from the simplest rock crystal to the Archbishop of Canterbury—had been placed by God at the moment of Creation in its appropriate position of power and respect. In an era of rank and domination, that concept sanctioned the "natural" order of things. Human races were no different than other life forms, at least in being ranked hierarchically. The continuing discoveries of the exotic and unusual peoples of Asia, America, and Africa added abundant material for the classification process, providing the necessary links between Europeans and the rest of the animal world. And this scheme's stability was its most endearing quality, especially for those at the top of the scale. No Hottentot should—or ever could—become a businessman, a politician, an accountant, or an anthropologist. The message of the Great Chain of Being was clear and laden with modern social meaning: Colored races should remain in their places, especially at a time when the Great Powers of Europe were beginning to piece together empires all over the world.

Just slightly more than a century before the current Kebara Cave excavations got underway—a microsecond of time on the paleontological scale—few respectable scholars even suspected that any different human types had ever existed. That's why the discovery of a strange skeleton in August 1856 in the Neander Gorge, or *Neanderthal*, near Düsseldorf, Germany, caused such an uproar. The physical transformation of the modern world was at that time just gathering momentum; the once-secluded section of the valley then resounded with the sledgehammer blows of the quarry gangs mining the hard limestone for the construction of factories, railroad bridges, and office buildings for a "new" Germany. High on a cliff face above the Düssel River, one of the work gangs, in the course of digging out the muddy layers in a natural cave, unexpectedly discovered a group of ancient bones whose significance is still a matter of bitter debate.

Those quarry workers thought they knew what they had found—the thick bones of a modern cave bear that had crawled into the cave to die—and they threw away most of the bones. That could very well have been the end of the matter, and the name *Neanderthal* might today be familiar only to the residents of the nearby town of Elberfeld as a place for Sunday afternoon walks. But Dr. Johann Fuhlrott, a local schoolmaster and amateur naturalist, heard of the discovery and made his way to the cave in the Neanderthal. By the time he arrived, all that remained were some of the long bones and the broken top of the skull. They were sufficient, however, to convince him that this was no bear, but a human—and a very strange one at that. The limb bones, though familiar in shape, were unusually thick and heavy. The equally thick skull fragment bore an unmistakably prominent overhanging browridge just above the eyes. This discovery, Fuhlrott realized, was far too important merely to add to his private collection. He believed that the Neanderthal bones did, in fact, represent an earlier stage in human biological development, and he knew a professor of anatomy at the University of Bonn who might be sympathetic to that idea.

Just three years earlier, in 1853, that professor, Hermann Schaaff-hausen, had published an article suggesting that extinct species had changed over time to modern life forms by "continued reproduction" rather than by divinely ordained catastrophes and instantaneous creation—a daring, not to say dangerous, idea for those pious and tradition-bound times. On examining the heavy bones and skull fragment from the Neander Valley, Schaaffhausen agreed with the schoolmaster from Elberfeld that the human species, like all the others, had very likely evolved. In February 1857, at a meeting of the Lower Rhine Medical and Natural History Society, Schaaffhausen made his findings public, concluding that Neanderthal man was a type "hitherto not known to exist, even in the most barbarous races"; that it antedated the era of the ancient Celts and Germans; and that it lived at a time when "the latest animals of the Diluvium still existed." In other words, the bones found in the cave above the Düssel River represented a different kind of man who lived in the age before the great biblical flood.

On every count, this was an outrageous theory. It challenged the biblical story of Creation and the fixity of animal species and human races. And, not unexpectedly, bitter criticism of Schaaffhausen's theory was forthcoming almost immediately. Since the Neanderthal bones were found without any other archaeological finds—bones of extinct animals or prehistoric flint implements—his dating was immediately suspect. Some of the most prominent scholars in Europe tried their best to make the "Neanderthal man" a modern laughingstock. Among the first to respond was C. Carter Blake, honorary secretary of the Anthropological Society of London, who suggested that the unique characteristics of the specimen were hardly evidence of great antiquity, but rather "compatible with the Neanderthal skeleton having belonged to some poor idiot or hermit who died in the cave where his remains have been found."

One of Schaaffhausen's colleagues at the university went even further, spicing his argument with a unique mix of derision and fanciful modern history. According to Professor Friedrich Mayer, the strangeness of the skeleton's features could be explained easily by the specimen's life history and race. This was no antediluvian man, Mayer contended, just a Mongolian Cossack who had ridden westward in pursuit of Napoleon's retreating armies in 1814, and, suffering from a serious case of rickets (caused by horseback riding since childhood), had crawled into the Neanderthal cave to die. The president of the Société d'Anthropologie in Paris, Franz Prunner-Bey, who had spent several years as a personal physician to the Khedives of Egypt and had gained a reputation for his classification of racial types through cranial measurement, maintained that the specimen's stupidity and strength were obvious. He suggested, on the basis of his own anthropological expertise, that the Neanderthal bones were of "a powerfully organized Celt somewhat resembling the modern Irish with low mental organization."

There were, however, a few dissenting scholars who came to Fuhlrott's and Schaaffhausen's aid. In the wake of the publication of Darwin's *On the Origin of Species*, a new consensus was forming that would ultimately enshrine evolutionary progress—not divine Creation—as the motive force in biological history. The British geologist Charles Lyell and the British anatomist Thomas Huxley included a description of the skeleton from Neanderthal in Lyell's epoch-making book, *Geological Evidences for the Antiquity of Man* (1863). Not only did they conclude that this unusual physical type was of extreme antiquity, they also suggested that it lay on the evolutionary path between the higher apes and modern man. William King, professor of anatomy at Queen's College in Galway—a scholar who certainly possessed an above-average "mental organization"— argued even more strenuously for the evolutionary distinctiveness of Neanderthal man by classifying it as a separate human species: *Homo neanderthalensis.*

As the years passed and additional Neanderthal fossils were discovered throughout Europe, it became increasingly difficult for even the most conservative scholars to deny their antiquity. The find of two skeletons in a cave near Spy, Belgium, in 1886 marked the end of the "modern idiot" theory; they were found with the remains of extinct animal species that had roamed Europe before the last Ice Age. And soon after the chronological horizon of the Neanderthals was established, scholars noted apparent evidence of the Neanderthals' cultural capacity. A distinctive class of chipped flint tools was eventually associated with the Neanderthals, taking its name from the prehistoric site of Le Moustier, France, where this class of tools was first recognized. The Mousterian industry included dozens of tool types—specialized scrapers, borers, and spearheads—that were manufactured by deftly striking flakes from a solid flint core. And there were other aspects of Neanderthal culture that merited attention; there seemed among Neanderthals to be intentional burial rituals, and presumably some sort of religious consciousness as well.

The problem was that despite their admirable proficiency with flint and concern for their dear departed, the Neanderthals still seemed quite primitive when compared with modern mankind. Their distinctive physical type—the pronounced browridges, receding forehead, heavy jaw, and squat, heavily muscled body—superficially evoked images of crudeness and limited intelligence, even though the thick Neanderthal skulls contained a slightly larger brain than did the skulls of modern man. And despite the theories of some evolutionists that all humanity had passed through a "Neanderthal stage" of development before assuming its modern form, the picture of the Neanderthals became progressively more disparaging as prehistoric research in Europe went on.

In turn-of-the-century excavations at Krapina near Zagreb, Yugoslavia, and in the Grimaldi Caves on the French Riviera, fossil discoveries seemed to indicate that the Neanderthals were not the only inhabitants of Europe in the Late Ice Age. Along with the Neanderthal skeletons were remains of a more modern human type: *Homo sapiens* ("man the wise," to emphasize its intellectual superiority). The earliest-known skeletons of *Homo sapiens* in Europe were associated with distinctive flint industries—slender blades (in place of the flakes of the Mousterian) that provided lighter, more efficient cutting edges and were easier to attach to the ends of bone- or wood-handled tools.

Add to that the sudden appearance of elaborate cave wall paintings and fertility figurines associated with *Homo sapiens* in Europe, and it's fairly easy to see why many early twentieth-century scholars began to return to a far more static view of human origins. The closeness in date between the last of the Neanderthals and the first of the *Homo sapiens* seemed too short for the physical and cultural differences to be bridged evolutionarily. It seemed almost as if the

Neanderthals were physically incapable of progress and it therefore took the arrival of a new human type—entering Europe from the *outside*—to push human history along.

That comparative IQ assessment led, in turn, to a neat and convenient explanation for the disappearance of the Neanderthals at more or less the time when modern men first appeared in Europe during the last Ice Age. Assuming that intelligent *Homo sapiens* and the less-gifted Neanderthals belonged to two quite distinct evolutionary lines, many European prehistorians suspected that a genocidal conflict had taken place between the two groups. They theorized that the first of the *Homo sapiens*, arriving from somewhere in Central Asia—that vague and often-suggested homeland for mysterious ancient peoples—skillfully hunted down and exterminated the dumber and clumsier Neanderthals, who stood in the way of their complete possession of the land.

In retrospect, that early-twentieth-century archaeological theory was hardly less symptomatic of the era's dominant philosophical approach than the Great Chain of Being it replaced. At a time when the sun never set on the British Empire and almost never on those of the French and the Germans, history was seen as the continuing succession of triumphs of the more talented races over less talented ones. Hadn't it happened with the sweeping conquests of the Aryans, the Israelites, the Greeks, the Romans, and, in modern times, with the Europeans themselves? Why should the dawn of human history have been any different? So the dumb and clumsy Neanderthals were effectively stripped of their humanity, branded as an evolutionary dead end, and banished to the world of cartoons.

As it turned out—as it always turns out—this archaeological verdict was not final. Subsequent discoveries of both Neanderthal and *Homo sapiens* fossils continued to complicate that neat archaeological reconstruction. And the nature of the relationship between the two human types has remained an issue of scholarly debate throughout the twentieth century.

Israel is today the scene of one of the world's most intense debates about the connection between Neanderthals and *Homo sapiens*, but it's a debate in which very few of the archaeologists working in the country care to participate. Like the Great Chain of Being of the days before Darwin, the structure of archaeological species in Israel is quite static. Positioned, as if by God, at the time of the discipline's creation, prehistorians are seen as distinct and somewhat limited in their capacities, experts in bones and flint tools but not really involved in the more meaningful questions of human history. History in Israel is, after all, distinguished by its unique biblical inspiration, famous wars, and ancient cities, and the poetry of the resurrection of a people who came back to their land again. The idea of prehistory—of understanding universal human phenomena—is, at best, irrelevant to the main social function of Israeli archaeology.

Academic specialization, of course, is not unique to Israel, but in respect to the status of prehistoric archaeology, a long historical development made its present isolation inevitable. Throughout the nineteenth century, the European archaeologists working in Palestine were almost entirely preoccupied with biblical relics and biblical history. The fierce debates over the antiquity of man in Europe held little allure in the land where the Book of Genesis was written, and where every ancient site uncovered and every artifact claimed by the museums of the Great Powers was seen as a validation of the Bible's historical accuracy. The crux of the Western competition for the Holy Land (beyond its obvious geopolitical advantages) was the right to claim the biblical heritage as one's own.

Calling the Bible into question, even writing a new story of the Garden of Eden, merely undermined one's religio-territorial claims. So, as the evolutionists and antievolutionists did battle over the bones of Europe, Palestine was left to the side. The question of Neanderthals and *Homo sapiens* was seen as irrelevant to the biblical archaeologists. But, as in Europe, progress in archaeology was eventually brought about by progress in other fields. In the late 1920s, a time of rapid modernization in the country during the early British Mandate period, a few European and American scholars began to recognize that Palestine, lying on the natural route of overland animal migration from Africa to Asia and Europe, might provide the missing link in the fossil record of the relationship between *Homo sapiens* and Neanderthals.

The circumstances of the first great discovery of human fossil remains in Palestine seemed to be an ironic replay of the discovery of Neanderthal Man more than a half-century before. Development and modernization again played a major role; quarrying operations for limestone for a new breakwater in Haifa harbor unexpectedly led to the discovery of some unique human remains. The site of the quarrying was a group of natural caves about twelve miles south of Haifa, at the outlet of one of the ravines running down toward the sea through the Carmel Range. Until the 1920s, those caves had been of no interest to anyone but bats and bedouin shepherds, but when the depths of their rich prehistoric levels were made known to the British officials of the newly established Palestine Department of Antiquities, the quarrying operations were halted and the digging began. And while biblical excavations went on at the famous ancient cities in other parts of the country, a different story of human heritage began to be pieced together from the archaeological remains in the caves of Mount Carmel. A joint expedition of the British School of Archaeology in Jerusalem and the American School of Prehistoric Research—headed by a British prehistorian named Dorothy Garrod—uncovered an unprecedented diversity of fossil human types in three adjoining caves.

In comparison with the earlier finds in Europe (where Neanderthal and *Homo sapiens* fossils were scattered among many sites and never found together), the archaeological picture in the Carmel Caves was both rich and puzzling. In the easternmost of the caves, called by the shepherds *Mugharet el-Wad*, or "The Cave of the Valley," there were fossils of *Homo sapiens*. Only a few yards away, in *Mugharet et-Tabun*, or "The Cave of the Oven," were remains of "classic" Neanderthals. And, most surprising, in the third of the caves, *Mugharet es-Skhul*, or "The Cave of the Kids," the excavators found the fragmentary skeletons of ten individuals ranging in age from infancy to around fifty, of a physical type that seemed to be halfway between Neanderthals and modern humans—a unique hybrid type that became popularly known as "Carmel Man."

Those discoveries obviously called for a revision of the earlier theories of invasion and genocide, for the existence of an intermediate type between Neanderthals and *Homo sapiens* suggested that all the human variants might, after all, be part of a single evolutionary continuum. Not unexpectedly, the Carmel cave finds reopened a bitter scholarly debate, and in the decades that followed, the position of the Neanderthals in human evolution underwent a far-reaching reassessment. In reaction to the earlier assumptions that the Neanderthals were hopelessly apelike in comparison to modern humans, a new generation of European and American scholars now tended to see them as nothing more than a distinctive—if not particularly beautiful—human type. In 1957, for instance, American prehistorians William Straus and A.J.E. Cave went so far as to suggest that a typical Neanderthal, "if bathed, shaved, and dressed in modern clothing," wouldn't attract even a second glance during rush hour in the New York subways. And in 1964, Professor Bernard Campbell of UCLA suggested that the Neanderthals should unquestionably be regarded as members in good standing of the human species, under the revised scientific classification *Homo sapiens neanderthalensis.*

Once more, the Neanderthals came to be seen as a stage of human evolution rather than an evolutionary dead end. The pendulum of scholarly consensus had swung back to the idea of progress rather than conquest, and the modern understanding of human genetic inheritance hung in that pendulum swing. The turn-of-the-century cartoons of dim-witted cave dwellers now seemed distinctly old-fashioned as explanations were put forth in scholarly journals and public lectures about how—with the refinement of tool types and less need for strong jaws and strong bodies—the Neanderthals gradually changed into *Homo sapiens sapiens*, now considered "twice wise" to emphasize the type's acquired intellectual gains. The nineteenth-century faith in unchanging racial characteristics and cranial capacities had become an unacceptable position in the late twentieth century. And so, whereas earlier scholars had banished the Neanderthals from any share in the human historical drama, the Neanderthals were now seen—at least theoretically—hanging from the lower branches of all of our family trees.

The Carmel Caves of Israel, with their deep deposits of artifacts and fossils, once again came to the fore in the discussion of the emergence of modern mankind, for they were now seen as sites where the evolutionary sequence could be definitively proved. In the decades since Garrod's pioneering discoveries, the techniques of prehistoric excavation had become far more precise, and from 1967 to 1972, Professor Arthur Jelinek of the University of Arizona, a strong advocate of the evolutionary hypothesis, returned to Mugharet et-Tabun, "The Cave of the Oven," in an effort to discover a clear pattern of transition from Neanderthal to *Homo sapiens sapiens*. And where Garrod had distinguished ten successive layers in the cave accumulations, Jelinek and his team identified no fewer than eighty-five superimposed levels of geological action and human activity in the thick sediments of the cave. Even more important, they collected and studied more than 44,000 flint artifacts that offered a dramatically new insight into the development of the various tool types.

Conventional, antievolutionary wisdom maintained that the earlier flakes (associated with Neanderthals) and the later blades (associated with *Homo sapiens sapiens*) reflected those two human types' differing manual dexterity. But Jelinek observed what he believed to be a gradual transformation in the shape of the earlier flakes that seemed to foreshadow the technology of the blades. In fact, the finds from the renewed Tabun Cave excavations led him to support the conclusion that the technical ability of the Neanderthals was not static, but had clearly improved.

By measuring the width and the thickness of the flint flakes associated with the distinct human types in the Carmel Caves and comparing them with finds from other prehistoric sites in Israel, Jelinek recognized what he believed to be a clear pattern of change. According to him, a progressive thinning of the flakes began with the "classic" Neanderthals of Tabun Cave; the flakes associated with the transitional human types in nearby es-Skhul Cave were thinner; and the flakes found with the *Homo sapiens sapiens of* Qafzeh Cave near Nazareth were the thinnest of all.

So, by the late 1970s, a new version of the Book of Genesis was written, based on the finds in the Holy Land. Jelinek and his supporters felt confident that the evolutionary hypothesis had been confirmed by indisputable scientific analysis—and that the Neanderthals of Israel (and presumably elsewhere) were an evolutionary bridge, not a dead end. According to his version, the disappearance of the Neanderthals was not due to an invasion and prehistoric genocidal conflict, but rather to an evolutionary transformation. The evidence, as Jelinek himself noted in an article in the prestigious *Science* magazine in 1982, suggested "an orderly and continuous progression of [flint] industries in the southern Levant, paralleled by a morphological progression from Neanderthal to modern man."

It would have been nice if Jelinek's theory had been the last word on the matter, for his theory fit the tenor of our times so well. The replacement of brutal colonial conquest by steady technological improvement—with all peoples and races potential contributors to world progress—was in neat accord with the policy papers of many Western governments and international development agencies. Unfortunately, archaeological conclusions, however reassuring, are more like restored mosaics than inscriptions carved into stone. The many fragments from which they have been pieced together can be arranged and rearranged in an uncomfortably wide range of ways. In regard to the Neanderthals, the debate had not ended with Jelinek, but had continued—and even intensified—in the light of the emerging discoveries from Kebara Cave. Professor Ofer Bar-Yosef, one of the directors of the expedition, was convinced that the neat Neanderthal-to-modern-man hypothesis was little more than wishful thinking, and he and his colleagues had come to Kebara to prove beyond a reasonable doubt that even in the theories of the neo-evolutionists, the Neanderthals of Israel had still not received a fair shake.

Bar-Yosef had gained the reputation of an iconoclast in Israeli archaeological circles, and even as I asked him some naïvely serious questions about his excavations, he took obvious delight in playing the devil's advocate. "Sometimes the early archaeologists were right—but for the wrong reasons," he told me as we climbed down into the excavation area and he pointed out the level on which the Neanderthal skeleton had been found in 1983. The physical differences between Neanderthals and modern humans, he contended, were difficult to ignore. And the suddenness of the Neanderthals' disappearance from the archaeological record seemed to indicate—to him—that they did not represent an evolutionary stage that all mankind had passed through, but were a distinct human population that had passed on without heirs. On *that* score, Bar-Yosef sided with the European scholars of the turn of the century, but on another he lumped them together in their mistaken presumptions with the onward-and-upward ideas of the late-twentieth-century evolutionists.

The Neanderthal concept that Bar-Yosef was attacking was of "primitiveness" itself. Both the earlier prehistorians and their latter-day successors felt confident that the Neanderthals were decidedly inferior to *Homo sapiens sapiens*. Whether as victims of efficient colonial conquest or as the subjects of a long process of technological improvement, the Neanderthals were seen as obsolescent biological machinery that had to be removed from the scene before the real work of human history could begin. For Bar-Yosef, the idea of such uniform stages of prehistory confused a complex reality with the optimism of modern development plans. His own archaeological work seemed dedicated to proving that physiological differences between human groups—in the Stone Age or in the present—had nothing whatsoever to do with innate technological or intellectual ability.

Bar-Yosef had come to that conclusion partly as the result of his earlier work at Qafzeh Cave, near Nazareth, in collaboration with Dr. Bernard Vandermeersch of the University of Bordeaux. There, Vandermeersch had discovered a large group of fossil human skeletons that clearly threatened to undermine Jelinek's basic evolutionary timetable. At Qafzeh, the skeletons were quite modern in form, and Vandermeersch confidently described them as *Homo sapiens sapiens*. The flint types found on the same level were the thin flakes that Jelinek had suggested were the products of fully modern humans emerging from a Neanderthal stage of development. Yet Bar-Yosef and Vandermeersch's dating of those levels told a dramatically different story. Paleontological analysis of the various animal species found on the *Homo sapiens sapiens* level at Qafzeh by their colleagues Eitan Tchernov and Georg Haas revealed the presence of two archaic rodents—*Mastomys batei* and *Arvicanthus ectos*—that were only found in the lowest, pre-Neanderthal levels at Tabun Cave. And subsequent chemical tests of the sediments of the same level confirmed this initial finding, dating the *Homo sapiens sapiens* fossils of Qafzeh Cave to approximately 90,000 years ago.

This early date would therefore mean that *Homo sapiens sapiens* existed in Israel long before the appearance of the first Neanderthals, and the evolutionary transition between the two types would have been impossible. These finds and the ongoing excavations at Kebara led Bar-Yosef and Vandermeersch to believe that a revision of even the most time-honored ideas of the comparative intelligence and manual dexterity of *Homo sapiens sapiens* and Neanderthals was necessary. Since 1982, Kebara Cave had been the scene of yearly excavations undertaken by an international team of specialists whose professional prominence and shared directorship of the project was evidence of the importance of the site.

In addition to Bar-Yosef, the Israeli team included Anna Belfer-Cohen, a specialist in Upper Paleolithic archaeology, geologist Paul Goldberg, and zoologist Eitan Tchernov of the Hebrew University, as well as physical anthropologist Baruch Arensburg of Tel Aviv University—all of whom had previously cooperated in the excavation of some of Israel's most significant prehistoric remains. And the French contingent, including Bernard Vandermeersch and geologist Henri Laville of the University of Bordeaux, and physical anthropologists A.M. Tillier of the University of Paris and Liliane Meignen of the Centre de Recherches Archéologiques of Valbonne, were among the most well-known scholars of the problem of the European Neanderthals.

The results of the Kebara excavation had already justified their hopes that new light might be shed on the Neanderthal question. The superimposed levels of Kebara proved to be unusually rich in the remains of human activity: ash layers, hearths, and such a large quantity of worked flints and flint chips that the team had concluded that the cave served not only as a place of habitation but also as a tool workshop for thousands of years. And the flint tools did, in fact, provide a pattern that seemed to contradict the idea of steady technological progress throughout the Stone Age. The tools in the *upper* levels were predominantly flakes of the supposedly earlier and more "primitive" type, while those in the lower, and therefore *earlier*, levels contained an unexpectedly large proportion of the supposedly advanced blade types.

What's more, even the human fossil evidence from Kebara had contradicted the neat Neanderthal-to-modern-man progression of intelligence and manual dexterity. Bar-Yosef obviously enjoyed pointing out the fact that the stocky, young Neanderthal—of supposed limited dexterity—who lived and died at Kebara about 50,000 years ago was buried on a level that contained a large quantity of the "advanced" thin flint blades. There was no legitimate reason to doubt that this Neanderthal and his cavemates had fashioned those tools; according to Bar-Yosef and his colleagues, the Neanderthals were apparently as capable of producing them as the *Homo sapiens sapiens*. And in view of this presumed lack of difference in technical ability between Neanderthals and modern humans, Bar-Yosef had returned to the earlier theories of prehistoric migrations to explain Israel's surprising Stone Age human diversity.

It was getting toward noon and the team members began to lay aside their digging equipment, make some final notes in their excavation registers, and get ready to break for lunch. I joined them in the long climb down from the cave to the banana plantation, and gratefully accepted an invitation to join them for lunch at the nearby kibbutz, Maagan Michael. Down in the rows of thick banana plants, Bar-Yosef and the others piled into their vans and cars, whose interiors had become oppressively hot from the midday sun. I followed behind them in my own car—in caravan—out onto the asphalt road, across the overpass above the six-lane highway that had replaced it, and then through the main gate of the kibbutz.

The dining hall was a modern glass-and-concrete structure, a piece of late-twentieth-century suburban architecture that signified the material success achieved by the community. We entered the large dining room that was already crowded with kibbutz members, guests, and the young volunteers who had come from Europe and America to lend a hand in the settlement's agricultural and industrial work. The small group of prehistorians easily merged into the lunchtime crowd, finding some available places at long Formica tables near the large plate-glass windows overlooking the sea. The fare of breaded soybean patties and cauliflower was unappetizing, but the relaxed conversation—away from the cave and its painstaking excavations—allowed me to get a more general reading of Bar-Yosef's ideas about the significance of Israel's Neanderthals.

He was a hard man to pin down to a sweeping statement, but I was persistent, so he offered his thoughts on some basic historical and philosophical questions between bites of a hurried lunch. The real story of human evolution, he contended, was not one of uniform stages, but of the gradual spread of humanity in its earlier form, *Homo erectus*, from its African homeland all over the world. Facing different environmental conditions and differing practical challenges, mankind blossomed into a wide spectrum of forms. As many scholars had long ago noted, the main concentration of "classic" Neanderthals was in Europe, and their distinctive physical type might have merely been a regional adaptation to the conditions they encountered there for tens of thousands of years. Their characteristic stockiness, for example, might have enabled them to maintain body heat more efficiently in Europe's periglacial environment.

Homo sapiens sapiens populations were different but not necessarily "superior"; it wasn't necessarily the struggle for the "survival of the fittest" they won. Bar-Yosef suggested that this type might have been just another regional adaptation that evolved at the same time or even earlier than the Neanderthals. The human fossil finds at Qafzeh and at North African sites such as Jebel Ighoud in Morocco seemed to indicate that the distinctive physiology of *Homo sapiens sapiens* may have begun to emerge as early as 150,000 years ago. But with the onset of the bitterly cold glacial climate of the last Ice Age (beginning around 75,000 years ago), the previously distinct types may have been forced to mingle. As conditions grew colder and large areas of their former hunting and foraging grounds in Europe were covered with the advancing ice sheet—so Bar-Yosef explained—scattered groups of Neanderthals apparently began migrations southeastward, some of them arriving in the area of modern Syria, Lebanon, and Israel and settling among a preexisting population of *Homo sapiens sapiens*.

Bar-Yosef wouldn't even try to speculate on the nature of their social relations, or on the reason for the final disappearance of those Neanderthal "colonies." He refused to tell a tale of heroic Stone Age conquests, tragic massacres, or even of the genetic outcome of passionate Neanderthal–*Homo sapiens sapiens* trysts. But Bar-Yosef was convinced that whatever the day-to-day reality of the Late Stone Age, the extinction of the Neanderthals in the Middle East and, later, in Europe was almost certainly not a reflection of their intelligence relative to *Homo sapiens sapiens*. The modern experience of hostile ethnic interaction in the region had shown the reality to be too complex to be described simply by sweeping racial generalities. Maybe the Neanderthals disappeared because their bodies had grown too specialized in Europe to survive a long period of dramatic climatic fluctuations. Maybe the course of events—of opportunities, decisions, and actions—just didn't flow in their favor, as it didn't flow in the favor of countless doomed groups throughout the millennia of recorded human history.

This was all, of course, just lunchtime speculation, and with the midday break almost over, we rose from the tables with our trays of dirty dishes as a new wave of kibbutz members coming in from their work in the fields and factories arrived to take our places. Bar-Yosef and the other team members made their way through the doors of the dining hall and out to the parking lot. Their workday at Kebara Cave was far from over; several more hours of digging, registration of artifacts, and recording lay ahead.

Even after this excavation season was concluded, the search would go on for the conclusive answer to the Neanderthal mystery. But whether the Neanderthals ultimately proved to be our own ancestors, or whether they proved to be a specialized population doomed by forces beyond their control, the image of the Neanderthals was in the midst of a dramatic transformation. The controversies of prehistory—like those of the archaeology of the later periods of Israel's history—seemed to conceal a more deeply felt modern debate about the basic issues of culture and race. But in the often vague and ambiguous evidence of cave sediments, flint chips, and human bone, the past somehow seemed slightly more resistant to fossilized conceptions of historical destiny.

13

ISRAEL

Tobacco Pipes, Cotton Prices, and Progress

📵**T**here had never been any excavations in the palace at Deir Hanna, even though its archaeological remains were among the most impressive I had seen in the Galilee. Few ancient sites in the region were so suggestive of the vast gulf between the past and the present, between an era of political power and an era of powerlessness. Situated at the top of a steep hill overlooking the green Sakhnin Valley with the modern village houses clustered in and around, the ruins of the once-ornate palace were surrounded by crumbling gates and fortification walls. Its main courtyard, though now used as a common backyard by the residents of the adjoining houses, still bore unmistakable evidence of the luxurious tastes of its builders—men who had suddenly gained enormous fortunes and sought to legitimate their newfound political power by clothing it in the trappings of royalty.

Today, Deir Hanna is one of many small Arab villages nestled on the hilltops of the central Galilee. Since 1948, with the establishment of the State of Israel, the Muslim and Christian inhabitants of this remote, rural area had lived in quiet, if sometimes tense, coexistence with the neighboring Israeli towns and agricultural settlements. Like the people of the other Arab villages of the region, the people of Deir Hanna made their living by farming the fields at the foot of the village and by working at nearby construction sites and factory jobs. The cars and pickups parked along the main street of the village and the television aerials bristling from the roofs of its houses bespoke at least a certain measure of prosperity. But few tourists ever stopped at Deir Hanna, for it was situated on a winding back road far from the popular biblical attractions of the Jezreel Valley, Nazareth, Mount Tabor, and the Sea of Galilee. This was a part of Israel that few foreign visitors even knew existed, despite the apparent impressiveness of its archaeological remains.

For a few decades in the eighteenth century, the situation was quite different. The village of Deir Hanna became one of the main foci of dramatic economic and political changes in the life of the country, changes felt as far away as the commercial counting houses of Europe and the Topkapi Palace in Istanbul. Beginning in the 1720s, the Zaydani family of the Galilee made Deir Hanna one of its most important strongholds in a nearly successful attempt to establish the economic and political independence of the Galilee—and, eventually, much of the territory that would later become the State of Israel—from the country's Ottoman overlords. Taking advantage of new economic opportunities and skillfully adapting themselves to new social influences and technological innovations, the various members of the Zaydani clan amassed tremendous personal fortunes and began to change the face of the country before the combined land and sea forces of a newly appointed Ottoman governor put a premature end to their plans.

In July 1776, just a few weeks after other imperial subjects—in faraway North America—had officially begun their own struggle for independence, the autonomy of the Zaydani leaders of the Galilee was finally crushed. An army led by the new governor of the province, Ahmad al-Jazzar Pasha, accompanied by a contingent of two hundred sailors and a heavy cannon removed from an Ottoman warship, made its way overland from the Mediterranean coast into the Galilee and laid siege to the palace at Deir Hanna. The village was surrounded and the palace fortifications were slowly shattered by the pounding; on July 22, Deir Hanna's defenders surrendered and the Ottoman forces razed its buildings. Local farmers later returned to reoccupy the ruins, but their small village was never again a threat to the ruling powers. Only those ruins stood as a memorial to the vanished splendor of Deir Hanna, a short-lived splendor recalled in vague local legends and folktales about the power and prestige of the Zaydani family.

After more than two hundred years, a sense of sad, faded glory clung to the crumbling ruins at the summit of the village's main hill. Just beyond a covered arch that was once part of a fortified entrance to the palace, an eighteenth-century mosque still served as a spiritual center for the community. As I entered and stood at the back of the prayer hall, a few elderly men knelt in their afternoon devotions on thin rugs laid over the cold stone floor; the original, ornate stonework of its walls had been painted over and repaired here and there with cement.

Leaving the mosque, I followed a path over large, weed-covered mounds of dirt and fallen masonry into the roofless palace ruins. In an area once occupied by the main courtyard and reception area, goats now grazed and chickens pecked for seeds. Above them rose the heavy, square columns of a once-elegant colonnade, whose alternating courses of grey and orange limestone were mirrored in the smooth masonry of the enclosing walls. A neat perforation of small, rectangular holes extended around the main hall—above a line of intricately carved windows and niches—and marked the positions of the now-vanished beams of the palace's second floor. Another covered entrance to the palace, spanned by a pointed arch, was now blocked by lines of drying laundry, but its onetime magnificence was evident. The palace at Deir Hanna was similar in style and design to the famous Mamluk mosques and fortresses of Egypt, and even as a crumbling ruin, it evoked vivid images of mounted warriors, rising twists of smoke from Turkish pipes, and the romance of medieval Middle Eastern chivalry.

Excavations here would certainly yield a wealth of finds from the era of Deir Hanna's short-lived glory. They would shed light on the economics and political life of the country during an important historical period. The standing walls and colonnades of the palace were substantial enough to serve as the foundation of a detailed architectural restoration—perhaps even as a tourist attraction and a memorial to the village's heritage. It would be hard to ask more of a potential site for excavation. Unfortunately, no excavation at Deir Hanna was imminent or even likely. For despite the occasional interest of historians and geographers in the surviving monuments of the Galilee's Ottoman history, the remains of the palace at Deir Hanna—and dozens of ruins from the same period—lay well beyond the expertise and even the professional interest of Israel's archaeologists.

In Israel, as in every country of the Middle East and the eastern Mediterranean that I had visited, archaeology was, in strict accordance with its dictionary definition, the study of *ancient* peoples and cultures; the historical development of the modern people and cultures of the region had never been seen as an appropriate subject for archaeological research. From its beginnings in the eighteenth century, Near Eastern archaeology's raison d'être was, after all, the exploration of those remote historical periods seen as the "foundations" of a particular national history or chapter in Western cultural development: the early empires of Egypt and Mesopotamia, the biblical periods, and the later empires of the Romans and the Greeks.

There had, of course, been occasional excavations of sites from the Early Islamic and Crusader periods, where impressive architecture or elaborate decorative work could be found. But the Ottoman period—except in its most lavish expression in the mosques, palaces, and bazaars of Istanbul and northwestern Turkey—attracted virtually no archaeological attention, either as an important chapter in the history of Western civilization or as a source of national pride. The centuries of Ottoman domination were, to the people of virtually every modern nation in the region, regarded as one of the low points in an otherwise glorious past. Even in Turkey, the modernizing, republican tendencies of the Atatürk era had looked to the ancient Hittites as a national example and had discouraged excessive interest in the corrupt and decadent regime of sultans and viziers overthrown in 1909 by the "Young Turks."

In the countries that were the less favored, outlying provinces of the Ottoman Empire, the memories were even more bitter. In Greece, Cyprus, and in other nations of the modern Middle East where the sultans' governors, tax collectors, and soldiers exerted their unchecked authority over the local populations for centuries, the Ottoman period evoked disturbing memories of oppression and poverty—in sharp contrast to the various "golden ages" of their more remote history. So it was not hard to understand why the remains of the Ottoman period attracted little romantic attention. They represented an historical period that was antithetical to the political independence of the twentieth century.

Antiquities laws in the various countries of the region helped to maintain a legal boundary between the historical periods most highly valued and those that could be safely ignored. In Israel, as in virtually every country of the region, the jurisdiction of the Department of Antiquities did not, except in the most unusual of circumstances, apply to architecture or artifacts that postdated A.D. 1700. Archaeology was, according to the conventional wisdom, not needed in the study of the Ottoman period, for its historical records were abundant and its main political events well known. As a result, the remains of the Ottoman period were seen by most archaeologists as being of little or no archaeological value. And all too often—at sites throughout the region—excavators regularly took advantage of loopholes in the antiquities legislation, using bulldozers or unsupervised work crews to clear away the uppermost levels in order to get to the more intellectually interesting layers below.

The result—however justified by popular feeling, governmental regulation, or conventional wisdom—was a glaring gap in archaeological knowledge, strangely severing the modern cultures and peoples of the region from their roots in the immediate past. No other period in the long history of the eastern Mediterranean and the Middle East was as poorly understood as the Ottoman one—from an archaeological standpoint at least. Extensive, continuing surveys and excavations had enabled archaeologists to trace alternating rhythms of prosperity and decline in the region from the appearance of the earliest *Homo sapiens sapiens*, through the rise of agriculture and the Bronze Age and Iron Age cities, through the spread of Hellenistic culture in the region, to the pagan, then Christian, splendor of the Roman and Byzantine periods. But the massive medieval fortifications and ornate religious structures of the early Muslim caliphs and the European Crusaders were the last major points of interest. Just as the story was beginning to get interesting—when the modern cultures of the region were in the process of formation—the archaeological picture went blank.

In recent years, the developing techniques of "historical archaeology" in Europe and America had underlined the potential importance of *all* archaeological remains—even in places and historical periods that were extensively documented by contemporary records and official histories. Excavations such as those undertaken at the sites of seventeenth-century city dwellings in London, eighteenth-century iron foundries in Sweden, nineteenth-century slave quarters in Mississippi, and early twentieth-century workers' tenements in Paterson, New Jersey, had demonstrated that the official records of an era did not necessarily tell the whole story. Even in the most familiar of historical periods, the discarded debris of daily life and regional culture often revealed surprising insights into demographic and economic trends.

While aspects of the material culture of earlier eras had been detailed in hundreds of doctoral dissertations, while there were hundreds of specialists in the pottery of the Bronze Age who could accurately date an excavated structure to within a half-century from the characteristic pottery types found in it, there was only a handful of archaeologists who had even the most basic knowledge of Ottoman pottery. Few experts could, with absolute confidence, distinguish a simple cooking pot or flask made in the time of Sultan Suleiman the Magnificent in the sixteenth century from a cooking pot or flask made in the last days of Sultan Abdul Hamid, at the beginning of the twentieth century. And as long as the material culture of the Ottoman period lay beyond the interest and expertise of most archaeologists working in the Middle East and the eastern Mediterranean, its ruins would remain shrouded in painful memories.

On the counter in the gift shop in the Jerusalem Citadel, a basket of broken clay pipes immediately caught my attention. Placed conveniently close to the cash register in the midst of the more usual posters and postcards at this popular tourist attraction, the shiny red and dull grey pottery fragments were offered for sale to visitors with specially printed display cards that read: "Smoking pipe sherd found in the Citadel excavations—Turkish period."

These broken pipe fragments offered tourists a chance to take home an authentic piece of history from a place where archaeologists had uncovered the superimposed ruins of the fortresses and fortifications of Jerusalem's many conquerors throughout its long history. Yet unlike the characteristic pottery sherds from the biblical, Hellenistic, Roman, and Crusader levels of the Jerusalem Citadel—which the excavators had registered and studied carefully—the pipe bowls had become a clever merchandising gimmick. One might even doubt that these artifacts had any archaeological value at all.

They certainly weren't rare or uncommon. In the uppermost rubble of many ancient sites throughout the Middle East and the eastern Mediterranean, archaeologists had found tens of thousands of similar red and grey smoking-pipe bowls that had been mass-produced and sold all over the region during the last few centuries. Useful only as providing evidence of late, and therefore rather unimportant, occupation levels, they had been routinely discarded, rarely photographed, and almost never studied seriously. It seemed impossible to date them with any precision; at the excavated sites of Hama in Syria and Baalbek in Lebanon—where the excavators *had*, in fact, paid them some attention—they were dated to the Mamluk period, around A.D. 1400. But since similar pipes were depicted as late as the nineteenth century in drawings and portraits of Ottoman notables, their period of use seemed far too long for archaeologists to utilize them as effective chronological tools.

In a region like the Middle East, where impressive archaeological remains of the Bronze and Iron ages and the classical periods were plentiful, excavators had little hesitation in ignoring or discarding late smoking-pipe fragments. But in other parts of the world, where more recent periods were the main focus of interest, archaeologists could not afford such a luxury. As early as the 1930s, in the excavations of the first permanent British colony in North America at Jamestown, Virginia, the archaeological value of smoking pipes was clear. In examining the thousands of fragments of white clay pipes found at the site, one of the excavators, J. Summerfield Day, had suggested that the gradual transformation of the bowl size and shape—from small and narrow to large and rounded—might reflect the growing popularity and affordability of tobacco at Jamestown and provide a means of dating the levels in which certain bowl forms were found.

Archaeologists working along the banks of the Thames in London soon recognized a similar phenomenon in the thousands of pipe fragments that they found. And as analysis of seventeenth-, eighteenth-, and nineteenth-century pipes continued at excavations on both sides of the Atlantic, other factors such as stem length and the diameter of the stem holes were found to have sufficient dependable chronological significance to make pipes one of the most important classes of artifacts in "historical" archaeology. It was only a matter of time until this understanding spread eastward—although as it turned out, it took nearly fifty years. The heavy red and grey Middle Eastern pipe bowls were, after all, quite different from the long-stemmed white clay pipes found in England and America. But if a pioneering American scholar is correct, they may possess the same degree of cultural and chronological significance.

In a 1984 article in *Hesperia*, the journal of the American School of Classical Studies in Athens, Rebecca Robinson published one of the first detailed studies of this class of artifacts, based on the hundreds of examples found by the American excavators at Corinth and at the Athenian agora. Because both these sites were occupied at least as late as the nineteenth century, and the uppermost layers could be dated, at least approximately, by coins and historical records, Robinson found that she could arrange the pipe-bowl fragments chronologically. On the basis of their form, decoration, and size, she concluded that the pipes of Athens and Corinth—like the similar examples from Turkey, Syria, Lebanon, Egypt, and Israel—underwent a continuous process of development from the early seventeenth to the nineteenth centuries, and—more important—they could be used to trace the diffusion of new cultural ideas from the West to the Middle East.

Those ideas were carried on the smoke of burning tobacco, the various species of the plant genus *Nicotiana*, native to North America and, as archaeologists there had determined, widely smoked by the inhabitants of that continent from around 500 B.C. Although the seeds of *Nicotiana rustica* were first carried to Europe in 1558 by the Spanish explorer Francisco Fernandez, and were subsequently popularized as a wonder cure for migraine headaches by the French ambassador to Portugal, Jean Nicot (in whose honor the genus was named), it apparently was not until a few years later, around 1562, that the early French explorers of Florida took their first drag. Although the precise place and date of that momentous event is uncertain, tobacco's addictive attractions soon became well known. Not long afterward, the British and Dutch explorers farther up the eastern seaboard were also contentedly puffing, and the popularity of tobacco then spread through Europe like wildfire. Quickly becoming the latest word in modern fashion, the habit rapidly gained acceptance in the taverns and drawing rooms of Europe—reaching, by around 1600, the divans, garrisons, and caravanserais of the Ottoman Empire.

The forms of the pipes in which the tobacco was smoked, Robinson suggested, may reveal the routes of diffusion. As earlier scholars had noted, two distinct types of pipes crossed the Atlantic with the dried tobacco leaves. The familiar, one-piece, white clay pipe of the Dutch and the English was adapted from the pipes used by the Indians of Virginia and the Middle Atlantic coastline, with whom the English and the Dutch came into closest contact. And the *chibouk*, or small clay bowl, attached to a separate reed or wooden stem—the type that was to become so common throughout the Ottoman Empire—was derived from the traditional types of the native American tribes of Florida and the lower Mississippi Valley, and spread through the agency of French and Portuguese traders to Africa and ultimately to the Near East.

The uncanny similarity of the polished red pipes of the tribes of southeastern North America to the pipes found in the Middle East and the eastern Mediterranean provided a convincing disproof of their Mamluk (and pre-Columbian) date. It seemed clear that they could not have been dropped or discarded at sites such as Athens, Corinth, Hama, Baalbek, or Jerusalem before the tobacco habit reached the Middle East from its birthplace in the New World sometime in the early seventeenth century. And Robinson noted that the pipes might have an additional chronological significance in the tracing of subsequent developments. She observed, just as American and English excavators had discovered in their own areas, that the Turkish version of the "southern" American pipe gradually became larger as tobacco became cheaper and more readily available. And in the examples from Corinth and Athens that she studied, there seemed to be specific decorative patterns characteristic of the seventeenth, eighteenth, and nineteenth centuries.

Serious archaeological study of Ottoman-period pipes was just beginning, but Robinson's initial theories about the date of their appearance and the development of their decoration seemed already to have been confirmed by the study of additional pipes at ongoing excavations of Ottoman sites in Turkey and on the Balkan peninsula. Pipes could, in fact, soon prove to be the key to an archaeological breakthrough. For once the chronological ranges of specific types are established, it might be possible to date the pottery and other artifacts found with them, and the Ottoman period might become a proper field for archaeological research at last. The appearance—or absence—of the dated pipes of the late seventeenth, eighteenth, and nineteenth centuries would provide an indication of the speed with which the new fashion of smoking spread throughout the region. And the study of the distribution throughout the Ottoman Empire of the products from various pipe-making centers might provide an indication of previously unsuspected cultural connections and economic ties.

If the excavators at the Jerusalem Citadel had taken the time to analyze their samples, they might have been able to date many of the pipes they uncovered and might even have used this evidence to break up the "Turkish period" into a more sophisticated chronology—one more in line with their understanding of far more remote historical periods. But the tobacco pipes tossed in the basket at the Citadel gift shop—and in the dumps of far too many excavations in the region—were yet to be generally recognized as true archaeological artifacts. And every time a pipe was either sold as a souvenir to tourists or thrown away without being studied seriously, its potential significance was lost forever. Only the image of the Ottoman period as a long, monotonous period of desolation remained.

Tobacco pipes were not the only tools that could be used to begin an archaeological exploration of the Ottoman period in Israel. The records of taxation, warfare, and political rivalry preserved in archives at the Topkapi Palace and various government offices in Istanbul offered a story as stirring as those of any of its earlier periods. Although there was virtually no archaeological interest in remains of this period, several Israeli and Palestinian historians had examined the *daftars*, or detailed Ottoman tax records, which provided indirect testimony to the country's settlement patterns, population, and economy. And other sources of information—the account books, journals, and correspondence of the French commercial agents resident in the country in this period—were still preserved in the Chambre de Commerce in Marseilles. They suggest that far from being a neglected backwater in which little of note happened, the Palestinian provinces of the Ottoman Empire were profoundly affected by the changes in lifestyle and economic patterns that were, by the early eighteenth century, sweeping over the entire Western world.

Tobacco was, as the evidence of the pipes seemed to suggest, one of the changes. Another was more directly linked to Europe's Industrial Revolution, just then picking up steam. With innovations such as John Kay's "flying shuttle" (1733) and James Hargreaves's "spinning jenny" (1764), European spinning and weaving were transformed from handicrafts to mass production, and with the greatly increased potential for output came a corresponding rise in the European demand for raw materials. Wool could be obtained from the herders of Europe, but cotton—needing a drier climate and plenty of sunshine—could not. And since European traders discovered that in all of the Ottoman Empire, the best-quality cotton for spinning and weaving was raised in the foothills of the Galilee and southern Lebanon, it was not long before they took full advantage of that natural resource.

In the early eighteenth century, when the Industrial Revolution was just beginning in Europe, the cotton-growing areas of the Galilee and Lebanon fell under the jurisdiction of the Ottoman governor of Sidon, whose main preoccupation was personal profit, not economic development. In accordance with the elaborate system of "tax-farming" that had developed throughout the Ottoman Empire, he had gained his position by submitting a high estimate of the taxes he thought *could* be collected from the province. Any sum he collected above that estimate was his to keep. The result was predictably destructive; the Ottoman administration in the province of Sidon, as elsewhere, concentrated on exacting the greatest possible amount of taxes from the region's farmers, whose yearly payments often were in arrears.

But in this system of tax-farming lay the seeds of its own destruction, since high-quality cotton was becoming such a valuable commodity in Europe. The French traders permanently stationed in the coastal towns of Sidon and Acre quickly recognized the value of Galilee cotton, and their growing profits encouraged the commercial representatives of other European nations to challenge the French monopoly. And in 1704, a Dutch trader named Paul Maashook came up with an ingenious strategy. Directly contacting the sheikhs of the villages in the cotton-growing regions, he agreed to advance funds for the yearly tax payments of the region's farmers—in exchange for the right to purchase their entire cotton crops at an attractive, predetermined price.

The French traders soon joined in the bidding, raising the going price of cotton, and this unofficial "futures market" effected some far-reaching changes in the economic life of the Galilee. Larger crops brought advances that exceeded even the exorbitant tax levies, and before long, the extent of cotton cultivation in the region was dramatically increased. The European demand was increasing even faster, however, and the prices for cotton steadily rose. And since the local farmers were not only fulfilling their tax obligations but also making greater profits, the forces of economic self-interest slowly transformed the agricultural pattern of the province of Sidon from its traditional mix of crops for subsistence to dependence on cotton as a major cash crop.

In the earliest stages of this process, the European traders had established separate arrangements with the sheikhs of each of the Galilee villages, but it did not take long for the highly profitable economic system to become centralized. And that development came as the result of Galilean, rather than European, initiative: Dahir al-Umar, the ambitious younger son of the prominent Zaydani family, gradually extended his power over the entire region to become the unofficial ruler of a cotton principality. And here the story takes on an ominous modern aspect, for Dahir al-Umar knew how to make the most of the Europeans' demand for cotton of the Galilee. He had the foresight to demand that at least a part of his advance payments from the traders be made in the form of European ammunition and guns.

If the worried tone of the Ottoman dispatches of the period is any indication, Dahir's control of the entire Galilee and his contempt for the authority of the governor of Sidon were seen by the sultan and his ministers as a serious threat to the empire's integrity. The influences from the West, once assimilated and manipulated by a local leader, had effects that were hard to anticipate. With firm control over the region's cotton crop and its export, Dahir changed the face of the land. The ancient port of Acre was rebuilt and a new port at Haifa was established, making the links between the Galilee and the Mediterranean closer than ever before. And throughout the villages of the hill country, Dahir's relatives and allies ensured efficient internal administration and security by the construction of palaces, fortresses, warehouses, watchtowers, and caravanserais.

This chapter in the history of Israel is largely forgotten; the most recent biography of Dahir al-Umar was published in 1942. Although many of the public buildings that he and his family erected during their period of power in the eighteenth century are still standing, they are like the palace at Deir Hanna, crumbling, beyond the protection of the country's antiquities laws. Of course, archaeology and archaeological legislation don't have to be static; the sharp differentiation between the periods that are considered interesting and the periods that are not could be erased.

The architecture, artifacts, and settlement patterns of the country in the eighteenth century could be used to trace the initial stages of a process that is still going on throughout the Middle East today. For even after Dahir's death in 1775, the country's economic connection with the West grew stronger and its economic centralization continued to intensify. And in that perspective, a serious examination of the Ottoman period would do more than fill a glaring gap in our knowledge of Israel's history. It might be possible to recognize in the buried remains of the last few centuries the first signs of modernity.

There's an unhappy ending to Dahir al-Umar's story. In 1775, the Ottoman government, which for decades had been displeased with the independence and wealth of this upstart Galilean leader, finally succeeded in destroying his power once and for all. After encouraging the governor of Egypt to launch a direct attack on Dahir's territory, Sultan Abdul Hamid dispatched his fleet to the port town of Acre, one of the main centers of the Galilean export trade. Dahir's army proved helpless in the face of combined Ottoman land and sea forces, and in August 1775, the port of Acre was conquered and Dahir was killed. His neatly severed head, proudly sent back to Istanbul by the Ottoman admiral, was displayed briefly at the gates of the Topkapi Palace as a grim warning to other would-be rebels.

Dahir's sons managed to hold out for a while in their Galilean fortresses, but with the successful siege of the family stronghold at Deir Hanna, the new Ottoman governor, Ahmad al-Jazzar Pasha— a Bosnian by birth and a tyrant by disposition—quickly consolidated his control over Dahir's cotton principality. Yet even though the Galilee and the rest of the province of Sidon were now safely returned to the Ottoman administration, the economic changes initiated there by Dahir al-Umar remained. Jazzar soon reestablished the long-standing commercial agreements with the European traders, and even after Jazzar's death in 1804, the Ottoman governors of Sidon remained dependent on cotton as one of their primary economic supports. And therein lay the danger. With the European demand for Palestinian cotton continuing for more than a century, the region's economy had become increasingly inflexible. When the European demand for Galilean cotton suddenly dropped a few decades later, a painless economic reorientation was impossible.

An end to the Galilean cotton trade came, finally, from the same part of North America in which the pipes and tobacco of the Ottoman Empire originated. The expansion of cotton cultivation throughout the American South in the early nineteenth century eventually created a glut on the world commodities markets, driving down prices to a point where the farmers of the Galilee simply couldn't compete. By 1852, the exports of Palestinian cotton had dropped by more than 90 percent both in total quantity and in price per pound, and, except for a brief rise in prices during the American Civil War and the resulting world "cotton famine," the era of profitable trade that had begun in the era of Dahir al-Umar was over. A new age was about to begin.

The farmers of the Galilee, now having no guaranteed, steady source of income, gradually returned to subsistence farming. New crops, such as sesame and sorghum, were sold to European traders but only on a limited scale. Many villages in the Galilee were abandoned, and fields formerly planted with cotton now lay uncultivated, often presenting a grim and desolate landscape to the increasing numbers of Europeans who came to the country in the later nineteenth century. But because those Western explorers, archaeologists, and travelers were interested primarily in the remains of the biblical and classical periods—and had only passing interest in the recent history of the region—they ascribed this sad state of affairs to *centuries* of Mamluk and Ottoman misrule. And an archaeological tradition was firmly established, as scholars delineated a long period in the history of the country that could safely be ignored.

The situation was, of course, far more complex. The Ottoman period, like all the others in the country's history, witnessed eras of *both* prosperity and decline. And the end of that last era of prosperity paved the way for the next stage of development. The depopulation of certain agricultural regions of the north of the country and the willingness of large landowners to sell off large tracts of the once highly productive farmland were two of the factors that made possible the settlement of a new population in the region—a mass movement that would ultimately result in the establishment of the State of Israel.

So the archaeological remains of the rise and fall of Dahir al-Umar's cotton kingdom could provide not only a fruitful field of study, they might also provide the final link between the country's present and its past. There seemed to be no reason to maintain a scholarly separation between "ancient times" and the "modern era," when the abundant archaeological remains revealed the fact of their continuum. If projects of a regional nature could discern long-range patterns of settlement and economy from the Stone Age to the time of the Crusaders, there was no apparent reason to stop at an arbitrary date such as 1700—and to fail to examine the modern economic and social roots of this part of the Middle East.

That change seemed, in fact, to be coming. A small group of archaeologists born and educated in the country was beginning to investigate the remains of this forgotten period in order to establish a new link to the land. At the village of Ta'annek on the West Bank, about twenty-five miles southwest of Deir Hanna, an expedition of the Department of Archaeology of Bir Zeit University—the most prominent Palestinian university—was digging. From several rows of neat excavation squares in and around the modern village, the archaeological team of students and teachers was carefully uncovering a latticework of pavements, mud ovens, and foundations of ruined walls. Like the Austrian and American archaeologists who had previously excavated the ruins of the biblical city of Taanach, whose high mound loomed above the village, they carefully recorded and analyzed every artifact uncovered and struggled to understand the site's complex stratigraphy. But in their use of other clues—such as the fragments of clay tobacco pipes, detailed Ottoman tax records, and extensive interviews with elderly village residents—this attempt to trace the history of the modern village of Ta'annek was unlike any archaeological project undertaken in the country before.

It wasn't going to be easy to begin a new field of study, especially if the old field—as if planted with cotton—had always produced a standard yield. But to understand the Ottoman period was an essential archaeological challenge. For while the cultural changes in other, more remote periods of the country's history were certainly no less significant, the economic and social developments that took place during the Ottoman period had continuing effects today. The archaeology of the Ottoman period would not miraculously transform the historical image of the last few centuries from a period of desolation into a new "golden age," but in the systematic examination of the remains of that period, *both* Palestinian and Israeli archaeologists might someday come to recognize a shared heritage in that era of dramatic social change.

EPILOGUE

Looking Ahead

It was a perfect night for a party. For weeks, almost everyone in the Israeli archaeological community had been looking forward to the Albright Institute's summer reception, one of the social highlights of the archaeological year. Several hundred invitations had been sent out by the American institute to the major Israeli universities, to the other foreign archaeological institutions, and to the two dozen or so excavation camps scattered across the countryside. The few regrets received indicated that there would be a large turnout and confirmed the Americans' high standing among Jerusalem's foreign archaeological schools.

Within the open, wrought-iron gates facing Salah ed-Din Street, a line of low, candle-lit lanterns illuminated a path down the driveway toward the entrance of the stone mansion that had been the headquarters of American archaeological activity in the country since 1924. And inside, past the high-ceilinged corridor of offices, mailboxes, and library, the open doors to the inner courtyard revealed more candles and bright, colored lights. The dignitaries of the American School stood there in a loose cluster, drinks in hand, ready to greet their professional colleagues.

The American School receptions were justly famous for their abundance in a city that was usually more concerned with religion and politics than with gracious hospitality. This year's party would be no exception; a full bar stocked with the best vodka, gin, bourbon, and scotch was set up in the courtyard and staffed with white-coated bartenders—a lavish contrast to the customary paper cups of orange and grapefruit juice served at most of Jerusalem's professional and social gatherings.

The bar, though, was not the main attraction. The current director of the American School, Professor Sy Gitin, was determined to make this year's party memorable. A standard buffet seemed to him to be drably unimaginative, and earlier in the summer, he had come up with several alternatives. Mexican food was rejected as being too complicated. Chinese food brought in from a local restaurant would probably be too expensive. But the idea that he finally settled on had a true all-American flavor: huge cartons of chocolate, vanilla, chocolate chip, and pistachio ice cream, and a selection of homemade fudge, butterscotch, strawberry, and plum sauces—the ingredients for some of the most elaborate do-it-yourself sundaes Jerusalem had ever seen.

The W.F. Albright Institute of Archaeological Research was not only the center of American archaeological activity in Israel, it was also a part of that country's archaeological history. Established in 1900 as "The American School of Oriental Research in Jerusalem," it was initially just one of several competing Western archaeological institutions dedicated to staking a national claim on the Holy Land's antiquities in the waning days of Ottoman rule. Slowly, however, it gained ascendancy over all the others. In the 1920s, its first long-term director, William Foxwell Albright of Johns Hopkins University (in whose honor the school is now officially named), transformed the school from a modest hostel for visiting American theology students and biblical scholars into an international archaeological landmark.

The building itself, its enclosed courtyard, and the surrounding gardens were vivid reminders of that earlier period of the American School's history. It was there in the shade of the cypress and Aleppo pine trees that the great British explorer W.M.F. Petrie—regarded by many as the father of Middle Eastern archaeology—found quiet refuge in the years before his death in 1942. And it was up the front steps of the school, in 1948, that the first of the Dead Sea Scrolls was secretly brought by Father Butros Sowmy of the Syrian Orthodox

Church soon after it had been obtained by a church official from the Ta'amireh bedouin.

The American School had established its reputation during the turbulent period of the British Mandate by being a comfortable and open meeting place for scholars of *all* nationalities. Not burdened by a semiofficial status such as that held by the British School of Archaeology in Jerusalem (many of whose members filled governmental positions with the Mandatory Department of Antiquities), the American School was able to remain aloof from the academic jealousies and controversies that a privileged position can sometimes bring. And now, in the 1980s, it had little competition among the other foreign archaeological institutions that had maintained a presence in Jerusalem over the previous half-century.

The Centre de Recherche Français, though active in excavation, was a relatively small establishment. The Pontifical Biblical Institute, the Deutsches Evangelisches Institut, the French Dominican École Biblique et Archéologique, the Italian Franciscan Studium Biblicum, and the Swedish Theological Institute were now primarily centers for sectarian religious training rather than for archaeology. And even the staff and students of the British School of Archaeology in Jerusalem, once so dominant in the archaeology of Palestine, now kept largely to themselves. Times had changed, and in their own way those changes reflected the larger developments in the political and economic life of the Middle East.

Among the first guests to enter the courtyard were Thomas Pickering, the American ambassador to Israel, and Morris Draper, the American consul in Jerusalem. The next day, the two diplomats would join the entourage of visiting Vice President George Bush in a whirlwind of high-level meetings with Israeli and Palestinian leaders in an attempt to breathe some life into the moribund peace process. Throughout the city, American flags had been hung along the main streets and in public places. American diplomats—and American archaeologists—obviously were enjoying a position of prestige. But unexpected changes were coming; within two years, the American administration would once again give up the hope of peacemaking by gentle persuasion, and the American School would be shrouded in a burning haze of tear gas fired by Israeli troops at the Palestinian demonstrators burning tires and throwing rocks out on Salah ed-Din Street.

For the time being, though, a more welcome change was already evident in the guest list of the American School's annual reception. Gone were the days when foreign scholars—the Americans as well as all the rest—had only limited professional contact with the peoples of the region. Here in Israel, as in Jordan, Cyprus, Syria, and Egypt, the distribution of archaeological personnel, if not of money, had been altered. Most foreign expeditions now included a significant number of locally trained specialists and field supervisors. And they were supervised and prodded by local antiquities officers—some of whom were now present in the American School's courtyard, happily sharing the latest archaeological gossip, greeting their American colleagues, and enjoying the ice cream.

Only the older, more established scholars seemed to maintain the former lines of national origin and allegiance, keeping their distance and displaying their social caution—remembering the days when this courtyard, this institution, and archaeology in the Middle East in general had a different, colonial character. But the younger generation—American, British, French, German, and Israeli—expressed no such reservations. For them—and for me, in the years I had lived in Jerusalem—the American School had always been a reassuring rather than a forbidding presence: a student-faculty club from some quiet American campus transplanted to the heart of the Middle East.

It was, of course, only in relatively peaceful times like this that true archaeological cooperation seemed possible, and perhaps that's why they all flocked here from the scattered excavation camps, from the more modest foreign institutions, and from the archaeology departments of Israel's universities. An invitation to the American School's annual reception was a membership card in a select and privileged fraternity, a society of scholars dedicated to studying the past without reference to specific religious or national claims. The American School still *did*, after all, stand apart from governmental authority and the sometimes coercive power that government antiquities departments—Ottoman, British, Jordanian, and Israeli—had the prerogative to exercise. The stone mansion and the legends that clung to it like ivy represented the ideal of a single universal archaeology, one in which participants of many nations joined their efforts to construct a coherent, international history.

I had seen other manifestations of that ideal at foreign archaeological institutions in Athens, Istanbul, Nicosia, Cairo, and Luxor, and at archaeological congresses and symposia all over the world. But I had also seen an opposing archaeological tendency in the nationalistic resurrection of specific ancient peoples and golden ages in the various countries of the eastern Mediterranean and the Middle East. Today's archaeologists, like their nineteenth-century predecessors, could not help but be products of their times and national traditions. And their archaeological interests could not help but reflect the challenges, fears, and problems faced by their contemporary societies.

Willingly or unconsciously, the region's archaeologists had become the authors of a modern Creation myth. Broken potsherds, soil layers, crumbled buildings, and fragmentary inscriptions had been fitted together to produce powerful social metaphors and moral lessons convincingly draped in period costume. Nations have always drawn a picture of their infancy in glittering colors, and those vivid self-portraits have always had an undeniable impact on modern national identities. A new generation of local and foreign archaeologists working today in the Middle East and the eastern Mediterranean was beginning to create a new past for the peoples of that region. And the shape that this past would assume in the coming decades—with its potentially enormous political and ideological implications—was now up to the region's archaeologists to choose.

Bibliographic Notes

Introduction: The Power of the Past

Benjamin Thorpe's quotation on the romantic memory of nations can be found in the introduction to his three-volume compilation of European myths and legends, *Northern Mythology* (London, 1851), Vol. I, pp. 1–2.

For the early history of archaeology in Western Europe in general, see Glyn Daniel, *A Hundred Years of Archaeology* (London, 1950). For the history of British archaeology in particular, see Bruce G. Trigger, "Anglo-American Archaeology," *World Archaeology* 13 (1981), pp. 138–55; Barbara D. Lynch and Thomas F. Lynch, "The Beginnings of a Scientific Approach to Prehistoric Archaeology in 17th and 18th Century Britain," *Southwestern Journal of Anthropology* 24 (1968), pp. 33–65; John Michell, *Megalithomania* (Ithaca, NY, 1982); Philippa Levine, *The Amateur and the Professional: Antiquarians, Historians, and Archaeologists in Victorian England, 1838–1886* (Cambridge, 1986); and Kenneth Hudson, *A Social History of Archaeology: The British Experience* (London, 1980).

On the English fascination with Celts, Druids, and Anglo-Saxons, see Hugh A. MacDougall, *Racial Myth in English History* (Montreal, 1982); Asa Briggs, *Saxons, Normans, and Victorians* (Sussex, 1966). On archaeology and nationalism in nineteenth-century Europe, see Don D.

A56

El,

Fowler, "Uses of the Past: Archaeology in the Service of the State," *American Antiquity* 52 (1987), pp. 229–48; Bruce G. Trigger, "Alternative Archaeologies: Nationalist, Colonialist, Imperialist," *Man* 19 (1984), pp. 355–70; K. Sklenar, *Archaeology in Central Europe: The First 500 Years* (New York, 1983); and David Lowenthal, *The Past Is a Foreign Country* (Cambridge, England, 1985).

John Kemble's quote appears in George P. Gooch, *History and Historians of the Nineteenth Century* (London, 1913), p. 289. See also Kemble's *The Saxons in England* (London, 1849).

Background on early European exploration in the eastern Mediterranean and the Middle East can be found in Glyn Daniel, *A Hundred Years of Archaeology* (London, 1950); Richard Stoneman, *Land of Lost Gods* (Normal, OK, 1987); John Rowe, "The Renaissance Foundations of Anthropology," *American Anthropologist* 67 (1965), pp. 1–20; John David Wortham, *The Genesis of British Egyptology* (Norman, OK, 1971); Frederick Bliss, *The Development of Palestine Exploration* (New York, 1906).

Newton's quote comes from his article in *Archaeological Journal* 8 (1851), p. 1. For general accounts of European antiquarian activities, see, for example, Richard Stoneman, *Land of Lost Gods* (Norman, OK, 1987); Fani-Maria Tsigakou, *The Rediscovery of Greece* (New Rochelle, NY, 1981); William St. Clair, *Lord Elgin and the Marbles* (Oxford, 1964); Brian Fagan, *The Rape of the Nile* (New York, 1975), and *Return to Babylon* (Boston, 1979); Yehoshua Ben-Arieh, *The Rediscovery of the Holy Land in the 19th Century* (Jerusalem, 1979); and Neil Asher Silberman, *Digging for God and Country* (New York, 1982).

On the transformation of Greece in the European historical imagination, the most ambitious and revealing study is Martin Bernal, *Black Athena*, Volume I: *The Fabrication of Ancient Greece 1785–1985* (New Brunswick, NJ, 1987). Other sources include Frank M. Turner, *The Greek Heritage in Victorian Britain* (New Haven, 1981); Richard Jenkyns, *The Victorians and Ancient Greece* (Oxford, 1980); E. M. Butler, *The Tyranny of Greece over Germany* (Cambridge, 1935); Michael Vickers, "Value and Simplicity: Eighteenth-Century Taste and the Study of Greek Vases," *Past and Present* 116 (1987), pp. 98–137; and John L. Bintliff, "Structuralism and Myth in Minoan Studies," *Antiquity* 58 (1984), pp. 33–38.

On the European theories of Indo-European origins, see J. P. Mallory, "A History of the Indo-European Problem," *Journal of Indo-European Studies* 1 (1973), pp. 21–65; Leon Poliakov, *The Aryan Myth* (New York, 1974); and Colin Renfrew, *Archaeology and Language* (London, 1987).

For the development of Egyptology, see John A. Wilson, *Signs and Wonders Upon Pharaoh* (Chicago, 1964); Brian Fagan, *The Rape of the Nile* (New York, 1975); Margaret S. Drower, *Flinders Petrie: A Life in Archaeology* (London, 1985); Michael A. Hoffman, *Egypt Before the Pharaohs* (New York, 1979); and T.G.H. James, *Excavating in Egypt: The Egypt Exploration Society 1882–1982* (London, 1982). Regarding the various nineteenth-century European theories on the racial origins of the ancient Egyptians, see Wyatt MacGaffey, "Concepts of Race in the Historiography of Northeast Africa," *Journal of African History* 7 (1966), pp. 1–17.

The history and development of archaeology in the lands of the Bible are reviewed in Neil Asher Silberman, *Digging for God and Country* (New York, 1982); Philip King, *American Archaeology in the Mideast: A History of the American Schools of Oriental Research* (Philadelphia, 1983); William G. Dever, "Archaeological Method in Israel: A Continuing Revolution," *Biblical Archaeologist* (Winter 1980), pp. 41–48; William G. Dever, "Syro-Palestinian and Biblical Archaeology," in *The Hebrew Bible and Its Modern Interpreters*, Douglas A. Knight and Gene M. Tucker, eds. (Philadelphia, 1985), pp. 31–74; Albert E. Glock, "Tradition and Change in Two Archaeologies," *American Antiquity* 50 (1985), pp. 464–77; and Seymour Gitin, "Stratigraphy and Its Application to Chronology and Terminology," in *Biblical Archaeology Today*, Avraham Biran, ed. (Jerusalem, 1985).

The extensive literature on the philosophy and social context of European historical research in the nineteenth and early twentieth centuries includes Glyn Daniel, *The Idea of Prehistory* (London, 1962); J. H. Plumb, *The Death of the Past* (New York, 1969); and Bruce G. Trigger, *Time and Traditions: Essays in Archaeological Interpretation* (New York, 1978), and "Major Concepts of Archaeology in Historical Perspective," *Man* 3 (1968), pp. 527–43.

For related anthropological ideas, see George W. Stocking, *Victorian Anthropology* (New York, 1987); Marvin Harris, *The Rise of Anthropological Theory* (New York, 1968); Mark A. Gordon, "The Social History of Evolution in Britain," *American Antiquity* 39 (1974), pp. 194–

204); Edmund S. Carpenter, "The Role of Archaeology in the 19th Century Controversy Between Developmentalism and Degeneration," *Pennsylvania Archeologist* 20 (1950), pp. 5–18; and Misia Landau, "Human Evolution as Narrative," *American Scientist* 72 (1984), pp. 262–68.

Some examples of the use of history and archaeology for modern political purposes are examined in Bernard Lewis, *History Remembered, Recovered, Invented* (Princeton, 1975); David C. Gordon, *Self-Determination and History in the Third World* (Princeton, 1971); Don D. Fowler, "Uses of the Past: Archaeology in the Service of the State," *American Antiquity* 52 (1987), pp. 229–48; and Bruce G. Trigger, "Alternative Archaeologies: Nationalist, Colonialist, Imperialist," *Man* 19 (1984), pp. 355–70. The cultural and economic impact of modern archaeology in the Third World is examined in Daniel Miller, "Archaeology and Development," *Current Anthropology* 21 (1980), pp. 709–26.

On the patriotic importance of archaeology in Greece, see Fani-Maria Tsigakou, *The Rediscovery of Greece* (New Rochelle, NY, 1981); and Demetrios Loukatos, "Tourist Archeofolklore in Greece," in *Folklore in the Modern World*, Richard M. Dawson, ed. (The Hague, 1978). For Turkey, see Tekin Alp, "The Restoration of Turkish History," in *Nationalism in Asia and Africa*, Elie Kedourie, ed. (London, 1971), pp. 207–24. For Egypt, Donald M. Reid, "Indigenous Egyptology: The Decolonization of a Profession?", *Journal of the American Oriental Society* 105 (1985), pp. 233–46.

For Israel, see Charles S. Liebman and Eliezer Don-Yehiya, *Civil Religion in Israel* (Berkeley, 1983); Amos Elon, *The Israelis: Fathers and Sons* (New York, 1971); and Jacob Shavit, "Hebrews and Phoenicians: A Case of an Ancient Historical Image and Its Use in the Radical Ideology of the Zionist and Anti-Zionist Right," *Cathedra* 29 (1983), pp. 173–91 (in Hebrew), and "Truth Shall Spring Out of the Earth: The Development of Jewish Popular Interest in Archaeology in Eretz-Israel," *Cathedra* 44 (1987), pp. 27–54 (in Hebrew).

For the emerging trends in archaeological research and interpretation, see Bruce G. Trigger, "Prospects for a World Archaeology," *World Archaeology* 18 (1986), pp. 1–20; Michael Shanks and Christopher Tilley, *Re-Constructing Archaeology* (Cambridge, England, 1987), and *Social Theory and Archaeology* (Albuquerque, 1987); Ian Hodder,

Reading the Past (Cambridge, England, 1986); and Mark P. Leone, "Some Opinions About Recovering Mind," *American Antiquity* 47 (1982), pp. 742–60, and "Toward a Critical Archaeology," *Current Anthropology* 28 (1987), pp. 283–302.

1: Yugoslavia and Greece: Who Were the Macedonians?

For general background on the rise of the ancient Macedonian kingdom and the careers of Philip II and Alexander the Great, see Robin Lane Fox, *The Search for Alexander* (Boston, 1980); W. L. Adams and E. N. Borza, *Philip II, Alexander the Great, and the Macedonian Heritage* (Washington, 1982); M. B. Hatzopoulos and L. D. Loukopoulos, eds., *Philip of Macedon* (Athens, 1980); N.G.L. Hammond, *A History of Macedonia* (Oxford, 1972); John R. Ellis, *Philip II and Macedonian Imperialism* (London, 1976); Donald W. Engels, *Alexander the Great and the Logistics of the Macedonian Army* (Berkeley, 1978). For an admiring portrait of a king and his myth, see Mary Renault, *The Nature of Alexander* (New York, 1975).

On the ethnic history of the modern Macedonians, see, for example, Stoyan Pribichevich, *Macedonia: Its People and Its History* (University Park, PA, 1982), and Branko Panov, "Toward the Ethnogenesis of the Macedonian People," *Macedonian Review* (1982), pp. 125–34. For a vivid portrait of Macedonian nationalism in the late nineteenth and early twentieth centuries, see Laura Beth Sherman, *Fire on the Mountain: The Macedonian Revolutionary Movement and the Kidnapping of Ellen Stone* (New York, 1980).

The best general survey of the history of the excavations at Stobi and the development of the ancient city is James R. Wiseman, "Archaeology and History at Stobi, Macedonia," in *Rome and the Provinces: Studies in the Transformation of Art and Architecture in the Mediterranean World*, Charles B. McClendon, ed. (New Haven, 1986), pp. 37–50. Three volumes of the final report of the American-Yugoslav excavations have so far been published: James R. Wiseman, ed., *Studies in the Antiquities of Stobi I* (Belgrade, 1973); James R. Wiseman, ed., *Studies in the Antiquities of Stobi II* (Belgrade, 1975); and Blaga Aleksova and James R. Wiseman, eds., *Studies in the Antiquities of Stobi III* (Skopje, 1981).

For briefer summaries of the excavations, see James R. Wiseman and Djordje Mano-Zissi, "Stobi: A City of Ancient Macedonia," *Journal of Field Archaeology* 3 (1976), pp. 269–302; James R. Wiseman, "Stobi in Yugoslavian Macedonia: Archaeological Excavations and Research 1977–78," *Journal of Field Archaeology* 5 (1978), pp. 391–429; and James R. Wiseman, "Multidisciplinary Research in Classical Archaeology: An Example from the Balkans," in *Contributions to Aegean Archaeology: Studies in Honor of W. A. MacDonald*, N. C. Wilkie and W.D.E. Coulson, eds. (Minneapolis, 1985), pp. 259–81.

For the history and importance of Stobi in the Byzantine period, see James R. Wiseman, "The City in Macedonia Secunda," in *Villes et peuplement dans l'Illyricum protobyzantin. Actes du Colloque organisé par l'École française de Rome* (Paris, 1984), pp. 289–314. Among the published works on the Episcopal Basilica at Stobi are Ruth Kolarik, "Mosaics of the Early Church at Stobi," *Dumbarton Oaks Papers* 41 (1987), pp. 295–306, and "The Episcopal Basilica at Stobi: The Phases of Mosaic Decoration," in *Studies in the Antiquities of Stobi III*, Blaga Aleksova and James R. Wiseman, eds. (Skopje, 1981), pp. 61–80; Blaga Aleksova, "The Episcopal Basilica in Stobi," *Macedonian Review* 11 (1981), pp. 130–36, "Episcopal Basilica at Stobi, Excavations and Researches 1970–1981," *Jahrbuch der Österreichischen Byzantinistik* 32 (1982), pp. 481–90, and "The Old Episcopal Basilica at Stobi," *Archaeologia Iugoslavica* 22–23 (1982–83), pp. 55–67. For a recent Yugoslav interpretation of the meaning of the Stobi excavations, see Ivan Mikulchich, "Some New Factors in the History of Stobi," *Macedonian Review* 15 (1985), pp. 97–104.

For a personal perspective on the politics of Greek Macedonia and its role in the political life of Greece, see Christopher Woodhouse, *Karamanlis: Restorer of Greek Democracy* (Oxford, 1982).

The most complete published accounts of the Vergina excavations, in English, are Manolis Andronicos, "Regal Treasures from a Macedonian Tomb," *National Geographic* 154 (July 1978), pp. 54–77; "The Royal Tomb of Philip II," *Archaeology* 31 (1978), pp. 33–41; "The Finds from the Royal Tombs at Vergina," *Proceedings of the British Academy* 65 (1981), pp. 355–67, and "The Royal Tombs at Aigai (Vergina)," in *Philip of Macedon*, M. B. Hatzopoulos and L. D. Loukopoulos, eds. (Athens, 1980), pp. 188–94. On the identification of the physical remains as those of Philip II of Macedon, see A. J. Prag, J. H. Musgrave, R.A.H. Neave,

"The Skull from Tomb II at Vergina: King Philip II of Macedon," *Journal of Hellenic Studies* 104 (1984), pp. 60–78.

Despite the archaeological evidence presented by Andronicos and his colleagues, the identification of the tomb remains a matter of some controversy. For a supportive view, see N.G.L. Hammond, " 'Philip's Tomb' in Historical Context," *Greek, Roman, and Byzantine Studies* 19 (1978), pp. 331–50. For alternative, critical views, see, for example, Phyllis Williams Lehmann, "The So-Called Tomb of Philip II: A Different Interpretation," *American Journal of Archaeology* 84 (1980), pp. 527–31, and W. L. Adams, "The Royal Macedonian Tomb at Vergina: An Historical Interpretation," *Ancient World* 3 (1980), pp. 67–72.

Two elaborate defenses of the ethnic "Greekness" of the ancient Macedonians were published by the Institute of Balkan Studies in Thessaloniki. See Apostolos Daskalakis, *The Hellenism of the Ancient Macedonians* (Thessaloniki, 1965), and *Alexander the Great and Hellenism* (Thessaloniki, 1966).

2: *Turkey: Searching for Troy*

Michael Wood's *In Search of the Trojan War* (New York, 1985) provides a useful survey of the Trojan legends, the archaeological finds, and an up-to-date interpretation of their possible historical context. See also Frank M. Turner, *The Greek Heritage in Victorian Britain* (New Haven, 1981), chapter 4; Carl Diehl, *Americans and German Scholarship, 1770–1870* (New Haven, 1978), chapter 2; and Martin Bernal, *Black Athena* (New Brunswick, NJ, 1987), chapter 6, for the importance of Homeric interpretation in nineteenth-century Europe.

On the colorful events of Schliemann's earlier career, see his own account in "Autobiography of the Author and Narrative of His Work at Troy," in *Ilios: The City and Country of the Trojans* (London, 1880), pp. 1–66. For a critical survey of the many admiring biographies of Schliemann, see William M. Calder III, "A New Picture of Heinrich Schliemann," in *Myth, Scandal, and History*, William M. Calder and David A. Traill, eds. (Detroit, 1986), pp. 17–47. Schliemann recounted the moment of the discovery of the "Treasure of Priam" in *Ilios*, p. 41. On the negotiations for the final disposition of the finds from Troy, see Karl J. R. Arndt, "Schliemann's Excavation of Troy and American Politics, or Why the Smithsonian Institution Lost Schliemann's Great Troy

Collection to Berlin," *Yearbook of German-American Studies* 16 (1981), pp. 1–8.

For the first openly critical study of Schliemann's psychological motivations, see William G. Niederland, "An Analytic Inquiry into the Life and Work of Heinrich Schliemann," in *Drives, Affects, Behavior*, Vol. 2, Max Schur, ed. (New York, 1965), pp. 369–96.

An expanded and annotated version of Calder's lecture at Schliemann's childhood home at Neubukow was published by him under the title "Schliemann on Schliemann: A Study in the Use of Sources," *Greek, Roman, and Byzantine Studies* 13 (1972), pp. 335–53.

David A. Traill's damning works on Schliemann include "Schliemann's Mendacity: Fire and Fever in California," *Classical Journal* 74 (1979), pp. 348–45; "Schliemann's American Citizenship and Divorce," *Classical Journal* 77 (1982), pp. 336–42; "Schliemann's 'Dream of Troy': The Making of a Legend," *Classical Journal* 81 (1985), pp. 13–24. His reasons for doubting the authenticity and reported circumstances of the discovery of the Treasure of Priam were first set out in his articles "Schliemann's 'Discovery' of Priam's Treasure," *Antiquity* 57 (1983), pp. 181–86, and "Schliemann's Discovery of Priam's Treasure: A Reexamination of the Evidence," *Journal of Hellenic Studies* 104 (1984), pp. 96–115. He added some further documentation in "Schliemann's Mendacity: A Question of Methodology," *Anatolian Studies* 36 (1986), pp. 91–98.

Adolf Furtwängler's comments on Schliemann's character are quoted by William M. Calder III in *Myth, Scandal, and History*, William M. Calder and David A. Traill, eds. (Detroit, 1986), p. 34.

In defense of Schliemann, see a brief, reverential note by Machteld Mellink in *American Journal of Archaeology* 86 (1982), p. 561; and Donald Easton's far more energetic and well-documented articles, "Schliemann's Discovery of 'Priam's Treasure': Two Enigmas," *Antiquity* 55 (1981), pp. 179–83; "Schliemann's Mendacity—A False Trail?", *Antiquity* 58 (1984), pp. 197–204; and "Priam's Treasure," *Anatolian Studies* 34 (1984), pp. 141–69.

For the history of archaeological excavations at Hissarlik, see Michael Wood, *In Search of the Trojan War* (New York, 1985), and for the question of the identification of the Homeric city, see M. I. Finley, "Schliemann's Troy—One Hundred Years After," *Proceedings of the British Academy* 60 (1974), pp. 393–412. Carl Blegen's quote on the significance of Settlement VIIa comes from his *Troy and the Trojans* (London, 1963), p. 164.

For Michael Wood's quotes on Blegen's image of Bronze Age war as a reflection of the conditions of the London Blitz, see *In Search of the Trojan War* (New York, 1985), p. 115; for his "Plausible Hypothesis No. 1," p. 167; for "Plausible Hypothesis No. 2," p. 207; for "Plausible Hypothesis No. 3," pp. 244–45.

Calvert Watkins's article, "The Language of the Trojans," appeared in *Troy and the Trojan War*, Machteld Mellink, ed. (Bryn Mawr, PA, 1986), pp. 58–62. This book is a compilation of articles presented at a 1984 symposium at Bryn Mawr College. See also Lin Foxhall and John K. Davies, eds., *The Trojan War: Its Historicity and Context* (Bristol, 1984), for selected subjects discussed at the Greenbank Colloquium at Liverpool in 1981.

3: Cyprus: Patterns in a Mosaic

For a survey of the antiquities of Cyprus, see Vassos Karageorghis, *Cyprus: From the Stone Age to the Romans* (London, 1982). For more general works on the island's ancient and modern history, see G. F. Hill, *A History of Cyprus* (Cambridge, 1940); Franz Georg Maier, *Cyprus, From the Earliest Time to the Present Day* (London, 1964); Costas P. Kyrris, *History of Cyprus* (Nicosia, 1985); and H. W. Catling, "Reflections Upon the Interpretation of the Archaeological Evidence for the History of Cyprus," in *Studies Presented in Memory of Porphyrios Dikaios*, Vassos Karageorghis, ed. (Nicosia, 1979), pp. 194–205.

On the history of Paphos in the Hellenistic period and the activities of King Nikokles, see, among others, Franz Georg Maier and Vassos Karageorghis, *Paphos: History and Archaeology* (Nicosia, 1984); Kyriakos Nicolaou, "The Topography of New Paphos," in *Mélanges Offerts á Kazimierz Michalowski* (Warsaw, 1966), pp. 561–601; T. B. Mitford, "Nikokles King of Paphos," in *Anatolian Studies Presented to W. H. Buckler* (London, 1939), pp. 197–99; also by T. B. Mitford, "Unpublished Syllabic Inscriptions of the Cyprus Museum," *Opuscula Athenensis* 3 (1960), pp. 198–210; and Jolanta Mlynarczyk, "The Paphian Sanctuary of Apollo Hylates," *Report of the Department of Antiquities, Cyprus* (1980), pp. 239–51.

For contemporary accounts of the discovery and excavation of the

House of Dionysos, see Kyriakos Nicolaou, "Mosaics at Kato Paphos—The House of Dionysos," *Report of the Department of Antiquities, Cyprus* (1963), pp. 56–72, "Mosaics at Kato Paphos—The House of Dionysos, Outline of the Campaigns of 1964 and 1965," *Report of the Department of Antiquities, Cyprus* (1967), pp. 100–125. For the results of the Polish excavations, see the preliminary reports of Wiktor Daszewski in *Report of the Department of Antiquities, Cyprus* (1968), pp. 33–61, (1970), pp. 112–41, and subsequent volumes. The extent of the war damage to the mosaics of Nea Paphos and the involvement of UNESCO mosaic restoration experts is reported in Republic of Cyprus, Ministry of Communications and Works, *Annual Report of the Director of the Department of Antiquities* (1974–76).

On the walls and other municipal remains of New Paphos, see Kyriakos Nicolaou, "The Topography of Nea Paphos," in *Mélanges Offerts à Kazimierz Michalowski* (Warsaw, 1966), pp. 567–89. On the excavations at Saranda Kolones, see the summaries of Arthur H. S. Megaw in "Excavations at 'Saranda Kolones,' Paphos," *Report of the Department of Antiquities, Cyprus* (1971), pp. 117–46; "Supplementary Excavations on a Castle Site at Paphos, Cyprus, 1970–1971," *Dumbarton Oaks Papers* 26 (1972), pp. 323–43; "Saranda Kolones, 1981," *Report of the Department of Antiquities, Cyprus* (1982), pp. 210–16; and "Saranda Kolones: Ceramic Evidence for the Construction Date," *Report of the Department of Antiquities, Cyprus* (1985), pp. 333–38.

The most complete account of the discovery and interpretation of the mosaics in the House of Orpheus is Demetrios Michaelides, "A New Orpheus Mosaic in Cyprus," *Acts of the International Symposium: Cyprus Between the Orient and the Occident* (Nicosia, 1986), which includes an extensive bibliography of Orpheus mosaics found throughout the Mediterranean and the European provinces of the Roman Empire. Earlier descriptions of the progress of the excavations there can be found in the *Annual Report of the Director of the Department of Antiquities* (1982–84).

4: *Cyprus: Crusaders, Venetians, and Sugar Cane*

For a general description of the history and archaeological remains of the Temple of Aphrodite at Kouklia, see Franz Georg Maier, "The Temple of Aphrodite at Old Paphos," *Report of the Department of*

Antiquities, Cyprus (1975), pp. 69–80. For an earlier archaeological interpretation, see A. Westholm, "The Paphian Temple of Aphrodite and Its Relation to Oriental Architecture," *Acta Archaeologica* 4 (1933), pp. 210–36.

On the traditions of the foundation of the city soon after the Trojan War, see Einar Gjerstad, "The Colonization of Cyprus in Greek Legend," *Opuscula Archaeologica* 3 (1944), pp. 110–12. On the archaeological indications of Greek settlement in this period, see Franz Georg Maier, "Evidence for Mycenaean Settlement at Old Paphos," *Acts of the International Symposium: The Mycenaeans in the Eastern Mediterranean* (Nicosia, 1973), pp. 68–78. The traditional veneration of the villagers of Kouklia toward the temple ruins is reported by Maier in "Excavations at Kouklia (Paleapaphos), Fifth Preliminary Report," in *Report of the Department of Antiquities, Cyprus* (1971), p. 46.

For general historical background on Cyprus in the Crusader and Venetian periods, see, for example, G. F. Hill, *A History of Cyprus* (Cambridge, 1940), Volumes II and III; Franz Georg Maier, *Cyprus, From the Earliest Time to the Present Day* (London, 1964), chapters 5 and 6.

The archaeological discoveries from the sugar refinery at Kouklia are described in Marie-Louise von Wartburg, "The Medieval Cane Sugar Industry in Cyprus: Results of Recent Excavation," *Antiquaries Journal* 63 (1983), pp. 298–314; and in the yearly preliminary reports of the Kouklia Expedition in *Report of the Department of Antiquities, Cyprus*.

For the work of the 1888 British expedition, see *Journal of Hellenic Studies* 9 (1888), pp. 149–291. The passing reference to the medieval remains overlying the Temple of Aphrodite can be found on p. 164, note 1.

An enlightening history of the impact of sugar on Western civilization is Sidney W. Mintz, *Sweetness and Power: The Place of Sugar in Modern History* (New York, 1985). Burchard's journal was translated from Latin by Aubrey Stewart and published in the *Palestine Pilgrims' Text Society*, Vol. XII (London, 1896). On the medieval sugar industry in the Muslim world, see Andrew M. Watson, *Agricultural Innovation in the Early Islamic World: The Diffusion of Crops and Farming Techniques, 700–1100* (Cambridge, England, 1983), chapter 5; J. H. Galloway, "The Mediterranean Sugar Industry," *Geographical Review* 67 (1977), pp. 177–94; and E. Ashtor, "Levantine Sugar Industry in the Later Middle Ages—An Example of Technological Decline," *Israel Oriental Studies* 7 (1977), pp. 226–80.

For Marthono's quote, see C. D. Cobham, *Excerpta Cypria: Materials for a History of Cyprus* (Cambridge, England, 1908), p. 28

On the European trade with the eastern Mediterranean in the medieval period, see Robert S. Lopez and Raymond Irving, *Medieval Trade in the Mediterranean World* (New York, 1955). The *Pratica della Mercatura* was edited and republished by A. Evans (Cambridge, MA, 1936). For the interpretation of the names used for the various classes of sugar, see E. Ashtor, "Levantine Sugar Industry in the Later Middle Ages—An Example of Technological Decline," *Israel Oriental Studies* 7 (1977), pp. 233–35; Marie-Louise von Wartburg, "The Medieval Cane Sugar Industry in Cyprus: Results of Recent Excavations," *Antiquaries Journal* 63 (1983), pp. 310–11.

The Venetian documents chronicling the "sugar war" at Episkopi are mentioned in Marie-Louise von Wartburg, "The Medieval Cane Sugar Industry in Cyprus . . . ," p. 301; and Susan Young, "Episkopi Serayia: The Medieval Manor and the Sugar Industry of Cyprus," in *An Archaeological Guide to the Ancient Kourion Area and the Akrotiri Peninsula*, Helena W. Swiny, ed. (Nicosia, 1982), pp. 156–57. On the events leading up to the Venetian annexation of Cyprus in 1489, see most recently, John Julius Norwich, *A History of Venice* (New York, 1982), pp. 363–68.

A technical discussion of the finds at Stavros can be found in Franz Georg Maier and Marie-Louise von Wartburg, "Excavations at Kouklia (Paleapaphos), Twelfth Preliminary Report: Seasons 1981 and 1982," *Report of the Department of Antiquities, Cyprus* (1983), pp. 300–14.

For the Brazilian parallels to the sugar refinery at Kouklia, see Marie-Louise von Wartburg, "The Medieval Cane Sugar Industry in Cyprus . . . ," p. 309. The expansion of the European sugar industry is summarized by Fernand Braudel in *Civilization and Capitalism: 15th–18th Century*, Volume I: *The Structures of Everyday Life* (London, 1981), pp. 224–27, and Volume II: *The Wheels of Commerce* (London, 1982), pp. 190–94, 272–80.

For the possible discovery of a Crusader-period sugar mill at Saranda Kolones, see Arthur H. S. Megaw, "Saranda Kolones, 1981," *Report of the Department of Antiquities, Cyprus* (1982), pp. 215–16; and John Rosser, "Crusader Castles of Cyprus," *Archaeology* 39 (1986), p. 46. For a brief description of the recent finds at Episkopi, see Susan Young, "Episkopi Serayia: The Medieval Manor and the Sugar Industry of Cyprus," in *An Archaeological Guide to the Ancient Kourion Area and the Akrotiri Peninsula*, Helena W. Swiny, ed. (Nicosia, 1982), pp. 153–59.

5: Israel: The Fall of Masada

The basic source for the story of the excavations and the archaeological discoveries at Masada is Yigael Yadin, *Masada: Herod's Fortress and the Zealots' Last Stand* (New York, 1966). A preliminary report appeared in *Israel Exploration Journal* 15 (1965), pp. 1–120. An account of earlier Israeli exploration at the site can be found in M. Avi-Yonah, N. Avigad, Y. Aharoni, E. Dunayevsky, and S. Guttman, "Masada: An Archaeological Survey in 1955–1956," *Israel Exploration Journal* 7 (1957), pp. 1–60.

On the Roman siegeworks at the foot of Masada, see Christopher Hawkes, "The Roman Siege of Masada," *Antiquity* 3 (1929), pp. 195–213; and I. A. Richmond, "The Roman Siege Works of Masada, Israel," *Journal of Roman Studies* 52 (1962), pp. 142–55. Yadin's description of the excavation of the rooms in the casemate wall appears in *Masada*, p. 145. His description of the human remains found in the northern palace appears on p. 54.

An extensive bibliography of articles about Masada is provided in Louis H. Feldman, "Masada: A Critique of Recent Scholarship," *Christianity, Judaism, and Other Greco-Roman Cults: Studies for Morton Smith*, Vol. III (Leiden, 1973), pp. 218–48. See also D. J. Ladouceur, "Masada: A Consideration of the Literary Evidence," *Greek, Roman, and Byzantine Studies* 21 (1980), pp. 245–60. For a defense of the accuracy of Josephus's physical descriptions, see Magen Broshi, "The Credibility of Josephus," *Journal of Jewish Studies* 33 (1982), pp. 379–84.

On the details of Josephus's life, see Tessa Rajak, *Josephus: The Historian and His Society* (London, 1983); and Shaye J. D. Cohen, *Josephus in Galilee and Rome: His Vita and Development as a Historian* (Leiden, 1979). For Cohen's views on the Masada story, see his article "Masada: Literary Tradition, Archaeological Remains, and the Credibility of Josephus," *Journal of Jewish Studies* 33 (1982), pp. 385–405. On the checkered background of the last Jewish defenders of Masada, see Morton Smith, "Zealots and Sicarii: Their Origins and Relation," *Harvard Theological Review* 64 (1971), pp. 1–19. For a highly critical review of Yadin's version of the Masada story see M. I. Finley, "Josephus and the Bandits," *New Statesman*, December 2, 1966, pp. 832–33.

Among the other critical examinations of the public veneration of Masada are Amos Elon, *The Israelis: Fathers and Sons* (New York, 1971), pp. 286–89; Charles S. Liebman and Eliezer Don-Yehiya, *Civil Religion in Israel* (Berkeley, 1983), pp. 99–100; Baila R. Shargel, "The Evolution of the Masada Myth," *Judaism* 28 (1979), pp. 357–71; and Robert Alter, "The Masada Complex," *Commentary* 56 (July 1973), pp. 19–24.

Stewart Alsop's first article was "The Masada Complex," *Newsweek*, July 12, 1971, p. 92. His account of Golda Meir's angry response can be found in his subsequent article, "Again, the Masada Complex," *Newsweek*, March 19, 1973, p. 104.

The symbolic meaning of the Masada story has recently been interpreted from the intriguing perspective of comparative folklore. See Michael P. Carroll, "Col. Travis at Masada, Zealots at the Alamo: Reflections on Myth and History," *Cahiers de Littérature Orale* 16 (1984), pp. 105–20.

6: Israel: Fighting a Losing Battle

On the geographical and historical background of the Shephelah, see Yohanan Aharoni, *The Land of the Bible* (London, 1967), p. 23; and Efraim Orni and Elisha Efrat, *Geography of Israel* (Jerusalem, 1971). For a general history of Palestine in the Roman and Byzantine periods, see Michael Avi-Yonah, *The Jews of Palestine: A Political History from the Bar Kokhba War to the Arab Conquest* (New York, 1976).

For brief accounts of the conquest of the Shephelah in Israel's 1948 war of independence and its conquest of the southern West Bank in 1967, see, for example, Chaim Herzog, *The Arab-Israeli Wars* (London, 1982), pp. 91–97, 180–82.

On nineteenth-century demographic developments in the region of the Hebron Hills and the Shephelah, see David Grossman, "Rural Settlement in the Southern Coastal Plain and the Shephelah, 1835–1945," *Cathedra* 45 (1987), pp. 57–86 (in Hebrew); and Yehuda Karmon, "Changes in the Urban Geography of Hebron during the Nineteenth Century," in *Studies on Palestine During the Ottoman Period*, Moshe Ma'oz, ed. (Jerusalem, 1975), pp. 70–86.

On Dagan's survey discoveries, see his "Shephelah of Judah Survey,"

Excavations and Surveys in Israel 2 (1983), pp. 92–94, and "Shephelah of Judah Survey—1985," *Excavations and Surveys in Israel* 5 (1986), pp. 99–100.

For background on the history and significance of the Muslim shrines of the Shephelah and of Palestine in general, see Tewfik Canaan, *Mohammedan Saints and Sanctuaries in Palestine* (Jersusalem, n.d.), reprinted from the *Journal of the Palestine Oriental Society* 7 (1927), pp. 1–88.

7: Israel: A Modern Cult of Relics

The official opening of the Dayan Collection exhibit was held at the Israel Museum in Jerusalem on April 15, 1986. For a description of the highlighted artifacts, see the exhibit catalog written by one of the curators: Tallay Ornan, *A Man and His Land: Highlights from the Moshe Dayan Collection* (Jerusalem, 1986).

The debate over the issue of antiquities trading in Israel has been waged, for the most part, in the daily press and popular magazines. For just a few representative articles from the last several years, see Joel Brinkley, "Israel Chides State Dept. Aide for Removing Antique Coins," *New York Times*, May 21, 1988; Abraham Rabinowich, "Plundering the Past," *Jerusalem Post*, April 2, 1988; Moshe Yechtman, "Clay in Their Hands," *Monitin*, December 12, 1986, (in Hebrew); Shahar Ilan, "Kollek, Etzioni, and Hecht Against Prohibition of Antiquities Trade," *Kol Ha'Ir*, November 28, 1986 (in Hebrew).

For Dayan's own version of his long love affair with archaeology, see his *Living with the Bible* (New York, 1978). Ruth Dayan's reminiscences of early artifact-hunting expeditions appeared in Tuvi Arbel, "Living from the Bible," *Ma'ariv Magazine*, February 12, 1986, pp. 20–22. For a far less romanticized version of Dayan's archaeological preoccupations, see Dan Ben-Amotz, "Web of Lies," *Haolam Hazeh*, August 10, 1971, pp. 16–19 (in Hebrew). Dayan's response to Ben-Amotz's charges was published by Yehoshua Bitzur, in his column "At the Knesset," *Ma'ariv*, August 12, 1971 (in Hebrew).

The UNESCO resolutions regarding the sale of illegally obtained antiquities and the relevant implementing legislation in the United States were published in *Journal of Field Archaeology* 3 (1976), pp. 213–26, and 4 (1977), pp. 247–54.

On the cult of relics in Palestine in the Middle Ages, see Jonathan Sumption, *Pilgrimage: An Image of Medieval Religion* (Totowa, NJ, 1975), chapter 3; for the origin of the custom in the Byzantine period, see Michael Avi-Yonah, "The Economics of Byzantine Palestine," *Israel Exploration Journal* 8 (1958), pp. 45–46; and E. D. Hunt, *Holy Land Pilgrimage in the Later Roman Empire, AD 312–460* (Oxford, 1984), chapter 6. The miraculous regenerative power of the True Cross is described on pp. 128–29.

Jerusalem mayor Teddy Kollek's modest proposal for *increased*, official sale of antiquities was published with an interview on the issue of the antiquities trade in *Monitin*, December 12, 1986, p. 9 (in Hebrew).

8: Egypt: Strangers in the Land

On the legend of the Hyksos and the archaeological evidence, see John Van Seters, *The Hyksos: A New Investigation* (New Haven, 1965); T. Säve-Söderbergh, "The Hyksos in Egypt," *Journal of Egyptian Archaeology* 37 (1951), pp. 53–71.

For various theories and speculations on the origins, ethnic background, and technological capabilities of the Hyksos, see W.M.F. Petrie, *Hyksos and Israelite Cities* (London, 1906); E. A. Speiser, "Ethnic Movements in the Near East in the Second Millennium BC," *Annual of the American Schools of Oriental Research* 13 (1933), pp. 13–54; R. M. Engberg, "The Hyksos Reconsidered," *Studies of the Ancient Oriental Civilizations* 18 (1939); Kurt Galling, "Hyksosherrschaft und Hyksoskultur," *Zeitschrift des deutschen Palästina-Vereins* 62 (1939), pp. 89–115; Yigael Yadin, "Hyksos Fortifications and the Battering Ram," *Bulletin of the American Schools of Oriental Research* 137 (1955), pp. 23–32; and Benjamin Mazar, "The Middle Bronze Age in Palestine," *Israel Exploration Journal* 18 (1968), pp. 65–97.

On the results of Bietak's work in Nubia, see his *Eine frühdynastische Abri-Seidlung mit Felsbildern aus Sayala-Nubien* (Vienna, 1963); *Ausgraben in Sayala-Nubien 1961–1965: Denkmaler der C-Gruppe und der Pan-Graaber-Kultur* (Vienna, 1966); and *Studien zur Chronologie der Nubischen C-Gruppe* (Vienna, 1968). On his work at Tell el-Dab'a, see his "Avaris and Piramesse: Archaeological Exploration in the Eastern Nile Delta," *Proceedings of the British Academy* 45 (1979), pp. 225–89; *Avaris and Piramesse* (Oxford, 1981); "The Origin of Asiatics and the

Hyksos in the Eastern Nile Delta," *Abstracts of the IIIrd International Congress for Egyptology* (Toronto, 1982); and "Problems of Middle Bronze Age Chronology: New Evidence from Egypt," *American Journal of Archaeology* 88 (1984), pp. 471–88. For the reports of the excavations themselves, see the successive volumes of *Tell el-Dab'a* (Vienna, 1975–).

The article cited at the end of the chapter is Manfred Bietak, "Some News about Trade and Trade Warfare in the Ancient Near East," *Marhaba* 3/83 (1983), pp. 41–43.

9: Egypt: An Uneasy Inheritance

The initial projections for the future of Chicago House at Luxor are reported in James H. Breasted, *The Oriental Institute of the University of Chicago: A Beginning and a Program* (Chicago, 1922). For an account of the life and work of Professor Breasted written by his son, see Charles Breasted, *Pioneer to the Past: The Story of James Henry Breasted, Archaeologist* (New York, 1930).

Among the many general works on the history and antiquities of ancient Thebes is Charles F. Nims, *Thebes of the Pharaohs: Pattern for Every City* (London, 1965). For its rediscovery in the late eighteenth and nineteenth centuries, see Brian Fagan, *The Rape of the Nile* (New York, 1975); John David Wortham, *The Genesis of British Egyptology* (Norman, OK, 1971); and John A. Wilson, *Signs and Wonders Upon Pharaoh* (Chicago, 1964).

William Murnane's doctoral dissertation was published under the title *Ancient Egyptian Coregencies* (Chicago, 1977). In addition to his scholarly articles, Murnane has also published two guidebooks for the general public: *United With Eternity: A Concise Guide to the Monuments of Medinet Habu* (Chicago, 1980), and *The Penguin Guide to Ancient Egypt* (New York, 1983).

The Muslim attitude toward the ancient pharaohs is extensively surveyed in A. J. Wensinck and G. Vadja, "Fir'awn," *Encyclopedia of Islam* (Leiden, 1965), Volume II, pp. 917–18. For a slightly different and more positive view of the attitude of the Egyptians toward the antiquities of their country during the Middle Ages, see Ulrich Haarmann, "Regional Sentiment in Medieval Egypt," *Bulletin of the School of African and Oriental Studies* 43 (1980), pp. 55–66.

On the single most famous archaeological discovery in Egypt, see Howard Carter and A. C. Mace, *The Tomb of Tut-ankh-amen, Discovered by the Late Earl of Carnarvon and Howard Carter*, 3 volumes (London, 1923–33); Thomas Hoving, *Tutankhamun: The Untold Story* (New York, 1978); and an angry pamphlet, published "for private circulation only": Howard Carter, *The Tomb of Tut-ankh-amen. Statement with documents, as to the events which occurred in Egypt in the winter of 1923–24, leading to the ultimate break with the Egyptian government* (London, 1924).

For changing nineteenth- and twentieth-century Egyptian attitudes toward the past, see Donald M. Reid, "Indigenous Egyptology: The Decolonization of a Profession?", *Journal of the American Oriental Society* 105 (1985), pp. 233–46; Charles Wendell, *The Evolution of the Egyptian National Image: From Its Origins to Ahmad Lutfi al-Sayyid* (Berkeley, 1972); and Jack A. Crabbs, *The Writing of History in Nineteenth-Century Egypt: A Study in National Transformation* (Detroit, 1984).

On the earlier excavation and interpretation of Tomb #68, see Alan H. Gardiner and Arthur E. P. Weigall, *A Topographical Catalogue of the Private Tombs of Thebes* (London, 1913), pp. 22–23.

10: Egypt: Whose Elephantine?

The most complete account of the discovery of the papyri and the excavation of Elephantine Island is contained in Emil G. Kraeling, *The Brooklyn Museum Aramaic Papyri: New Documents of the Fifth Century BC from the Jewish Colony at Elephantine* (New Haven, 1953). See also Kraeling's article "New Light on the Elephantine Colony," *Biblical Archaeologist* 15 (1952), pp. 50–67.

Among the earliest English publications and translations of the Elephantine papyri are Archibald Sayce and Arthur Cowley, *Aramaic Papyri Discovered at Assuan* (London, 1906); Arthur Cowley, *Jewish Documents of the Time of Ezra* (London, 1919); and Arthur Cowley, *Aramaic Papyri of the Fifth Century BC* (Oxford, 1923).

For the annotated daybooks of the German excavations at Elephantine, see Wolfgang Müller, "Die Papyrusgrabung auf Elephantine 1906–1908," *Forschungen und Berichte von den Staatlichen Museen, Berlin* 20–21 (1980), pp. 75–88, and 22 (1982), pp. 7–50.

The results of the German-Swiss excavations at Elephantine have been published under the title *Elephantine: Grabung des Deutschen Archäologischen Instituts Kairo in Zusammenarbeit mit dem Schweizerischen Institut für Ägyptische Bauforschung und Altertumskunde Kairo* (Mainz, 1980–). For the Temple of Khnum, see Horst Jaritz, *Die Terrassen von den Tempeln des Chnum und der Satet: Architektur und Deutung* (Mainz, 1980).

Bezalel Porten's work on the Elephantine papyri includes his book *Archives from Elephantine: The Life of an Ancient Jewish Military Colony* (Berkeley, 1968), and, among his many articles on the subject, "The Structure and Orientation of the Jewish Temple at Elephantine—A Revised Plan of the Jewish District," *Journal of the American Oriental Society* 81 (1961), pp. 38–42.

11: South Arabia: Lost Kingdoms and Caravan Routes

For the published reports of the American Foundation for the Study of Man expedition to North Yemen, see Michael R. Toplyn, *The Wadi al-Jubah Project*, Volume 1: *Site Reconnaissance in North Yemen, 1982* (Washington, 1984); and Jeffrey A. Blakely, James A. Sauer, and Michael R. Toplyn, *The Wadi al-Jubah Project*, Volume 2: *Site Reconnaissance in North Yemen, 1983* (Washington, 1985).

On the 1950 and 1951 South Arabian expeditions of the American Foundation for the Study of Man, see Gus W. Van Beek, "Recovering the Ancient Civilization of Arabia," *Biblical Archaeologist* 15 (1952), pp. 2–18; Wendell Phillips, *Qataban and Sheba* (New York, 1955); Richard LeBaron Bowen, Jr., and Frank P. Albright, *Archaeological Discoveries in South Arabia* (Baltimore, 1958); Ray L. Cleveland, *An Ancient South Arabian Necropolis: Objects from the Second Campaign, 1951, in the Timna' Cemetery* (Baltimore, 1965); and Gus W. Van Beek, *Hajor Bin Humeid: Investigations at a Pre-Islamic Site in South Arabia* (Baltimore, 1969).

For background on the current economy and development plans of the Yemen Arab Republic, see Robert D. Burrowes, *The Yemen Arab Republic: The Politics of Development 1962–1986* (Boulder, CO, 1987); B. R. Pridham, ed., *Economy, Society, and Culture in Contemporary Yemen* (London, 1985); and J. E. Peterson, *Yemen: The Search for a Modern State* (London, 1982).

The archaeological collections of the National Museum in Sana'a are described in Paolo M. Costa, "The Pre-Islamic Antiquities at the Yemen National Museum," *Studia Archaeologica* 19 (Rome, 1978).

The best recent collection of essays on the legends and historical context of the Queen of Sheba is James Pritchard, ed., *Solomon and Sheba* (London, 1974). On the economic and political impact of the ancient South Arabian incense trade, see, for example, Gus W. Van Beek, "Frankincense and Myrrh in Ancient South Arabia," *Journal of the American Oriental Society* 68 (1958), pp. 141–52, and "Frankincense and Myrrh," *Biblical Archaeologist* 23 (1960), pp. 69–95. For the Muslim traditions of Queen Bilqis and the later history of the Sabaeans, see J. Tkatsch, "Saba'," *Encyclopedia of Islam*, Volume IV (Leiden, 1934), pp. 2–19, an article that also includes an extensive bibliography of nineteenth-century Western explorers of Yemen.

The main source of information regarding Phillips's negotiations with the imam and the subsequent adventures of his expedition to Marib is his own *Qataban and Sheba*, pp. 194–328. Phillips's brief autobiographical sketch can be found on pp. 341–50. On the finds from the "Sanctuary of Bilqis," see Frank P. Albright, "The Excavation of the Temple of the Moon at Marib, Yemen," *Bulletin of the American Schools of Oriental Research* 128 (1952), pp. 25–38; and Albert Jamme, *Sabaean Inscriptions from Mahram Bilqis (Marib)* (Baltimore, 1962).

The initial dating of the antiquities of South Arabia was established by William F. Albright in his article "The Chronology of Ancient South Arabia in the Light of the First Campaign of Excavation in Qataban," *Bulletin of the American Schools of Oriental Research* 119 (1950), pp. 5–15. The recent carbon-14 dates from Wadi al-Jubah were published for the first time in Jeffrey A. Blakely, "Wadi al-Jubah Archaeological Project," *American Schools of Oriental Research Newsletter* (Winter, 1984), p. 7.

12: Israel: Back to the Stone Age

On the excavations at Kebara Cave, see Tamara Schick and Moshe Stekelis, "Mousterian Assemblages in Kebara Cave, Mount Carmel," *Eretz-Israel* 13 (1977), pp. 97–149; Patricia Smith and Baruch Arensburg, "A Mousterian Skeleton from Kebara Cave," *Eretz-Israel* 13 (1977), pp. 164–76; and Ofer Bar-Yosef et al., "New Date on the Origin of Modern Man in the Levant," *Current Anthropology* 27 (1986), pp. 63–64. For the general archaeological background, see Ofer Bar-Yosef, "Prehistory of the Levant," *Annual Review of Anthropology* 9 (1980), pp. 101–33.

Recent studies on the philosophical and political context of human evolutionary theories include Roger Lewin, *Bones of Contention* (New York, 1987); Misia Landau, "Human Narrative as Evolution," *American Scientist* 72 (1984), pp. 262–68; Michael Hammond, "Anthropology as a Weapon of Social Combat in Late Nineteenth-Century France," *Journal of the History of the Behavioral Sciences* 16 (1980), pp. 118–32, and "The Emergence of Combat Anthropology: A Case Study in the Production and Utilization of Social Science Knowledge," in *The Political Realization of Social Science Knowledge and Research*, B. Holzner, K. Knorr, and H. Strasser, eds. (Würzburg, 1982); and Niles Eldridge and Ian Tattersall, *The Myths of Human Evolution* (New York, 1982).

On the circumstances of the discovery in the Neanderthal, see Bernard Campbell, "The Centenary of Neanderthal Man," *Man* 56 (1956), pp. 156–58, 171–73. On the ensuing controversy, see Frank Spencer, "The Neanderthals and Their Evolutionary Significance: A Brief Historical Survey," in *The Origins of Modern Humans: A World Survey of the Fossil Evidence*, Fred H. Smith and Frank Spencer, eds. (New York, 1984), pp. 1–49; Michael Hammond, "The Expulsion of the Neanderthals from Human Ancestry: Marcellin Boule and the Social Context of Scientific Research," *Social Studies of Science* 12 (1982), pp. 1–36.

The various disparaging racial theories put forth regarding the Neanderthals are described in Jacob W. Gruber, "The Neanderthal Controversy: Nineteenth Century Version," *The Scientific Monthly* (December 1948), pp. 436–39; and Loren C. Eiseley, "The Reception of the First Missing Links," *Proceedings of the American Philosophical Society* 98 (1954), pp. 453–65.

On Neanderthal research in the Middle East in general and at Mount Carmel in particular, see Erik Trinkhaus, "Western Asia," in *The Origins of Modern Humans: A World Survey of the Fossil Evidence*, Fred H. Smith and Frank Spencer, eds. (New York, 1984), pp. 251–91; Avraham Ronen, "Mount Carmel Caves—The First Excavations," in *The Transition from Lower to Middle Paleolithic and the Origin of Modern Man*, Avraham Ronen, ed., published in *British Archaeological Reports* International Series 151 (1982), pp. 7–28. The results of the Mount Carmel excavations were published by Dorothy Garrod, *The Stone Age of Mount Carmel I: The Excavations at the Wady el-Mughara* (Oxford, 1937); and T. D. McCown and Arthur Keith, *The Stone Age of Mount Carmel II: The Fossil Human Remains from the Levalloiso-Mousterian* (Oxford, 1939).

The quote by Straus and Cave on the "modern" appearance of the Neanderthals can be found in their article "Pathology and the Posture of Neanderthal Man," *Quarterly Review of Biology* 32 (1957), pp. 348–69. For examples of the reevaluation of the evolutionary position of the Neanderthals, see F. C. Howell, "The Place of Neanderthal Man in Human Evolution," *American Journal of Physical Anthropology* 9 (1951), pp. 379–416; C. L. Brace, "The Fate of the 'Classic' Neanderthals: A Consideration of Hominid Catastrophism," *Current Anthropology* 5 (1964), pp. 3–46; and W. W. Howells, "Neanderthals: Names, Hypotheses, and Scientific Method," *American Anthropologist* 76 (1974), pp. 24–38.

Among Jelinek's published work on the transition between Neanderthals and modern humans are his articles: "New Excavations at the Tabun Cave, Mount Carmel, Israel 1967–1972: A Preliminary Report," *Paléorient* 1 (1973), pp. 151–83; "The Middle Palaeolithic in the Southern Levant, with comments on the appearance of modern *Homo sapiens*," in *The Transition from Lower to Middle Palaeolithic and the Origin of Modern Man*, Avraham Ronen, ed., pp. 57–101; and "The Tabun Cave and Paleolithic Man in the Levant," *Science* 216 (1982), pp. 1369–75. The quoted passage appears on p. 1374.

For the Qafzeh excavations, see Bernard Vandermeersch, *Les hommes fossiles de Qafzeh (Israël)* (Paris, 1981); and Ofer Bar-Yosef and Bernard Vandermeersch, "Notes Concerning the Possible Age of the Mousterian Layers in Qafzeh Cave," In *Préhistoire du Levant*, P. Sanlaville and J. Cauvin, eds. (Paris, 1981). For opposing positions in the continuing controversy, see, in *Ancestors: The Hard Evidence*, Eric Delson, ed. (New York, 1985), Bernard Vandermeersch, "The Origin of the Neanderthals," pp. 306–9, and Erik Trinkhaus and Fred H. Smith, "The Fate of the Neanderthals," pp. 325–33.

13: Israel: Tobacco Pipes, Cotton Prices, and Progress

On the ruins and present state of the village of Deir Hanna, see Menachem Zaharoni, ed., *Israel Guide*, Volume 3: *Lower Galilee and Kinneret Region* (Jerusalem, 1978), pp. 57–60 (in Hebrew). On the history of Deir Hanna and the Zaydani family, see Amnon Cohen, *Palestine in the 18th Century: Patterns of Government and Administration* (Jerusalem, 1973); and Uriel Heyd, *Dahir al-Umar, Ruler of the Galilee in the 18th Century* (Jerusalem, 1942) (in Hebrew).

For surveys of the recent developments in historical archaeology and historical preservation, see Mark P. Leone and Parker B. Potter, eds., *The Recovery of Meaning: Historical Archaeology in the Eastern United States* (Washington, 1988); Robert L. Schuyler, ed., *Historical Archaeology: A Guide to Substantive and Theoretical Contributions* (Farmingdale, NY, 1978); Susan Porter Benson, Stephen Brier, and Roy Rosenzweig, *Presenting the Past: Essays on History and the Public* (Philadelphia, 1986); and Jo Blatti, ed., *Past Meets Present* (Washington, 1987).

Among the few recent excavations in Israel to include clay tobacco pipes in their reports is Tel Yoqne'am in the western Jezreel Valley. See, for example, Amnon Ben-Tor and Renate Rosenthal, "The First Season of Excavation at Tel Yoqne'am: Preliminary Report," *Israel Exploration Journal* 28 (1978), p. 70, where they were, however, initially misdated to the Mamluk period. The published reports of the recent excavations at the Jerusalem Citadel, where pipes were found in abundance, do not mention this class of artifacts and touch on the Ottoman period only briefly. Compare Hillel Geva, "Excavations in the Citadel of Jerusalem, 1979–1980: Preliminary Report," *Israel Exploration Journal* 33 (1983), pp. 55–71.

On the early archaeological use of tobacco pipes in America and England, see Ivor Noël Hume, *Martin's Hundred* (New York, 1982), pp. 119–22; J. C. Harrington, "Dating Stem Fragments of Seventeenth and Eighteenth Century Clay Tobacco Pipes," *Quarterly Bulletin of the Archaeological Society of Virginia* 9 (1954), pp. 9–13; and Lewis Binford, "A New Method of Calculating Dates from Kaolin Pipe Stem Samples," *Southeastern Archaeological Conference Newsletter* 9 (1961), pp. 19–21.

Rebecca Robinson's articles include "Tobacco Pipes of Corinth and the Athenian Agora," *Hesperia* 54 (1985), pp. 149–203, and "Clay Tobacco Pipes from the Kerameikos," *Mitteilungen des Deutschen Archäologischen Instituts*, Athenische Abteilung 98 (1983), pp. 265–85.

For the history of tobacco and its spread, see, for example, Count Corti, *A History of Smoking* (London, 1931); Alfred Dunhill, *The Pipe Book* (London, 1924); B. Laufer, "The Introduction of Tobacco into Europe," *Field Museum Anthropology Leaflets* 19 (1924) and 29

(1930); and Fernand Braudel, *Civilization and Capitalism: 15th–18th Century*, Volume I: *The Structures of Everyday Life* (London, 1981), pp. 260–65.

The significance of pipe forms in tracing their origins and diffusion was first noted in Thurstan Shaw, "Early Smoking Pipes: in Africa, Europe, and America," *Journal of the Royal Anthropological Institute* 90 (1960), pp. 272–305. Among the recent important studies of tobacco pipes in the Ottoman Empire is John Hayes, "Turkish Clay Pipes: A Provisional Typology," *The Archaeology of the Clay Pipe, IV*, published in *British Archaeological Reports* International Series 92 (1980), pp. 3–10.

On the documentary sources for the history of early Ottoman Palestine, see Uriel Heyd, *Ottoman Documents on Palestine, 1552–1615* (Oxford, 1960); Amnon Cohen, "Some Notes on the Marseilles Archives as a Source for the History of Palestine," in *Studies on Palestine During the Ottoman Period*, Moshe Ma'oz, ed. (Jerusalem, 1975), pp. 578–82; Wolf Hütteroth and Kamal Abdulfattah, *Historical Geography of Palestine, Transjordan, and Southern Syria in the Late 16th Century* (Erlangen, 1977); and Amnon Cohen and Bernard Lewis, *Population and Revenue in the Towns of Palestine in the 16th Century* (Princeton, 1978).

For the rise and fall of the cotton economy of the Galilee, see Uriel Heyd, *Dahir al-Umar, Ruler of the Galilee in the 18th Century* (Jerusalem, 1942) (in Hebrew); Amnon Cohen, *Palestine in the 18th Century: Patterns of Government and Adminstration* (Jerusalem, 1973), and his article "Ottoman Rule and the Re-emergence of the Coast of Palestine," *Cathedra* 34 (1985), pp. 55–74; and Shmuel Avitsur, "Cotton Growing in Israel," *Nofim* 3 (1976), pp. 7–35 (in Hebrew). The statistics for the dramatic drop in the export of Galilean cotton are quoted in Avitsur, pp. 16–18.

Among the many recent studies of the complex technological, economic, and demographic transformation of Palestine in the late nineteenth century, see Fred M. Gottheil, "Money and Product Flows in Mid-19th Century Palestine: The Physiocratic Model Applied," in *Palestine in the Late Ottoman Period*, David Kushner, ed. (Jerusalem, 1986), pp. 211–30; Shmuel Avitsur, "The Influence of Western Technology on the Economy of Palestine During the Nineteenth Century," and Gabriel Baer, "The Impact of Economic Change on Traditional Society in Nineteenth Century Palestine," in *Studies on Palestine Dur-*

ing the Ottoman Period, Moshe Ma'oz, ed. (Jerusalem, 1975), pp. 485–94, 495–98; Iris Agmon, "Foreign Trade as a Catalyst of Change in the Arab Economy in Palestine," *Cathedra* 41 (1986), pp. 107–32 (in Hebrew); and Simon Schama, *Two Rothschilds and the Land of Israel* (New York, 1978).

Epilogue: Looking Ahead

For the early history of the American School in Jerusalem, see Philip King, *American Archaeology in the Mideast: A History of the American Schools of Oriental Research* (Philadelphia, 1983); and Leona Glidden Running and David Noel Freedman, *William Foxwell Albright, A Twentieth Century Genius* (New York, 1975).

Index

About the Author

NEIL ASHER SILBERMAN, an archaeologist and author, has excavation experience in the Middle East. He has worked for the Israel Department of Antiquities and was a Fellow of the Institute of Current World Affairs. He lives in Conneticut with his wife and daughter and is the author of *Digging for God and Country: Exploration in the Holy Land, 1799–1917*.